Men of the Code

Men of the Code

Bohdi Sanders, Ph.D.

Library of Congress Cataloging-in-Publication Data
Bohdi Sanders, 1962-

Men of the Code

ISBN – 978-1-937884-14-7

1. Men. 2. Self-Help. 3. Philosophy. 4. Title

Kaizen Quest Publishing

Endorsements for *Men of the Code*

Every single page of this book is filled with motivating, inspirational, and relevant information for men in today's world. Dr. Sanders brings to light many issues and struggles for men in today's society.

The real life applications, and character building teachings in this text will surely benefit you time and time again. This is a book that every young man needs to read to start his life off on the right foot and that every grown man should read in order to either continue to live a life of character or to start living a life of character and honor.

This is a must read, five star book for anyone who is a warrior in life, dealing with character development, integrity building, loyalty, and honor. I highly recommend *Men of the Code* to everyone. This book is eye-opening and will motivate you to live a better life. I highly recommend it!

Grandmaster Al Dacascos

Grandmaster Al Dacascos was inducted into the Black Belt Hall of Fame in 1977. He has been on the cover of over 185 National and International Martial Arts magazines and has won over 200 martial arts championships. He is a three time North American Grand Champion in martial arts, the first American Kung Fu artist to reach the top ten in fighting competition, having fought against the greats such as Chuck Norris, Bill Wallace, and Joe Lewis. Al is also the founder of the unique fighting art, Wun Hop Kuen Do, a system that incorporates Chinese and Filipino martial arts into the traditional KAJUKENBO system.

Grandmaster Dacascos has trained many celebrities including Eric Lee, Karen Shepard, and his son, Mark Dacascos who is currently the Chairman on Iron Chef America. Grandmaster Al Dacascos has been working on the book, *LEGACY: Through the Eyes of the Warrior*, which is the story of his life in the martial arts. LEGACY will be released in 2016.

Endorsements for *Men of the Code*

To describe my feelings after reading *Men of the Code* by Dr. Bohdi Sanders, I would humbly admit that it is perhaps the single most interesting book I have read in my life. It is jam packed with the tools and tips of becoming manly in this gender neutral world that we live in today. If I had an opportunity to layout step by step the information needed to live life as an honorable man it would ideally be exactly what is in this book. This is the ultimate handbook for any man who wants to live a better and longer life.

Neatly laid out in the pages of this book are thousands of useful tips and action items to upgrade your self-esteem, self-confidence, health, relationships and in general – life in whole. This book will help us older men to be reminded of the way men are supposed to be, like the heroes that we had growing up. It will give younger men the guidance and advice that a good father would teach if he had the time.

The title can be a bit misleading. *Men of the Code* is not a book specifically for men. Mothers will find the information incredibly helpful in raising sons and understanding males better in general. Anyone who reads this book and follows its advice is sure to experience success in personal relationships, career success and become a great leader and role model for the members of his family.

There are so many character lessons built into the pages of this book but what interested me the most was the information on Roles, Relationships and Duties of a man. Every parent will find the information about raising men instead of boys particularly helpful. I highly recommend this book to anyone who wants to know what nature intended men to be and not what our modern media portrays them as. I suggest that you try to get an autographed copy. This is sure to become a best seller.

Grandmaster Richard Hackworth

Richard Hackworth is 8th Dan Taekwondo, 8th Dan Hapkido, 8th Dan YuSool, 6th Dan TangSooDo, and is the C.E.O. of World Martial Arts Media, Inc. He is also the publisher of World Martial Arts Magazine. GM Hackworth is the President of the U.S. National Taekwondo Association and the first non-Korean to attend and graduate the Hapkido Masters Course in Seoul, Korea. Under the guidance and approval of the World Headquarters in Korea, he founded the Korean Hapkido Federation Haemukwan, an organization for traditional authentic Hapkido.

Endorsements for *Men of the Code*

I am not a person easily impressed, but Bohdi Sanders' book, *Men of the Code*, is everything that I embrace and live my life by. The teachings in *Men of the Code* are exactly what I teach my students to live by and how I hope that they teach other men to live.

The information in *Men of the Code* is critical information for today's man. During times past, men used to gather together to discuss and share this kind of information. They taught these principles to their sons, who in turn, taught it to their sons and these principles of character, honor and integrity were passed down, and the tradition was kept alive.

But in our modern world, our society is scattered. Family members and friends live far apart from each other and we have lost this tradition of true male bonding. Men no longer gather around the fire and share tales of courage and honor. We have lost the tradition of passing the manly arts from one generation to the next.

This is where Dr. Sanders' book excels and fills a large void. Dr. Sanders has compiled the teachings, the wisdom and the traits that every man should center their life around. I love this book. It gets right down to the core of what it means to be a man.

I highly recommend *Men of the Code* to every man. It is very well put together and Dr. Sanders obviously put a lot of thought into it, both in his teachings and in the great quotes that he has included at the end of each chapter and throughout the book. The wisdom and teachings in this book are invaluable and something that seems to have been lost in our modern day culture. I can't recommend this book highly enough!

Frank Dux

Hanshi Frank Dux is immortalized by the motion picture based upon his life – *Bloodsport*. Jean-Claude Van Damme played the role of Frank Dux in this amazing tale of Hanshi Dux's life. From the years 1975 through 1980 he was the World Full Contact Kumite (no-holds-barred) Champion. He holds 16 world records which have been standing for little over a quarter of a century and has been inducted into five martial arts Hall of Fames as a *"Living Legend."* Frank is also the author of *The Secret Man* and *The Martial Arts Bible*.

Endorsements for *Men of the Code*

Dr. Bohdi Sanders has nailed it. *Men of the Code* is one of the best books that I have read for helping men to realize and to develop their true potential and is one of those rare books destined to be an instant classic.

This book is easy to read and to understand, and is one of those timeless books that will be reread time and time again, as the readers embarks on a journey that will both enlighten and transform him. The chapters are easily laid out so that the reader can reference any chapter to find the information he is looking for.

This book is essential to the library of every man and any martial artist who is a serious practitioner of his art. *Men of the Code* will not only benefit men, but everyone who reads it will come away with the knowledge that can be a life changer.

Men of the Code is one of those books that is hard to put down, once one starts to read it, because it is entertaining, informative, and takes the reader on a refreshing journey on understanding oneself on a deeper level.

Michael McGann, Hanshi

Michael McGann, Hanshi, Judan, has studied martial arts for 52 years. He has been the Deputy Director of Police Tactics Instructors of America. Hanshi McGann has served as the liaison and scout for the United States Martial Arts Team and has been both a competitor and judge at the United States Open ISKA World Martial Arts Championship. Also, Hanshi McGann served as the President for Suncoast Bonsai Society.

Endorsements for *Men of the Code*

The book, *Men of the Code*, written by Dr. Bohdi Sanders, is a real insight into our inner thoughts and desires. This book focuses on right and wrong, based upon honor, integrity and courage. It is the actions that define these qualities that make each man a man, and not the artificial application of each character.

Dr. Sanders brings to our attention these basic ideals and how they relate to each of us and those whose lives we touch in one way or another. Many of the words in this book have crossed our minds at one time or another, but most of us lack the ability to put into the written word how we think or feel. I like to believe that I live my life with the qualities that I read about in this book. Of course, to even make such a statement would mean narcissism has infiltrated the mind and has overthrown all that is right for this descriptive personality trait.

I am amazed at how the words in this book have become an affirmation of thoughts that I, and so many others, have had over the years. It's as if someone else has been interviewing my thoughts of life and how to live it. There are so many types of men in our world and yet there are so few types, all at the same time. Identifying with the entire process of man and his coming into the world, either one way or another, is so insightful and obvious after reading this book.

It is with a great amount of humility and honor that I highly recommend this book for everyone - man, woman or young adult to help in the direction of either the development, or turning point, of each man from a real and honest desire to be a member of "Men of the Code."

Dan Tosh, PhD, JD

Grandmaster Dan Tosh has been training in Shorin-ryu Karate since 1958 and now holds the rank of 10th degree black belt. Dr. Tosh has a Ph.D. in economics, as well as a law degree, and has served as an adjunct professor for Novus Law School. Grandmaster Tosh has been involved in choreography, movie production, stunt work, workshops and tournament competition for many years.

Endorsements for *Men of the Code*

A great deal of my life has been spent in search of the high road. Traveling along the highways of life, I tried to live by a certain set of ethics, morals and rules, which I hope kept me safe and sound during my twenties through forties. These rules also provided a strong foundation and guideline to live my life by. Wherever I visited during my treks, these basic things were always brought to mind as I viewed other cultures. We are more alike than one would think.

Over the past few decades, the code we all strive to live by has increasingly become ambiguous. It is difficult to explain, challenging to teach, and even harder to understand. That is, until Dr. Bohdi Sanders wrote his very captivating book called, *Men of the Code.* Dr. Sanders has laid it out in black and white. As I read the chapters, I occasionally reminisced about the "superior men" who had offered me advice and insight on successes and failures.

Men of the Code offers the reader perceptive ways to develop a sound foundation to live by in today's society. The more society changes, stronger men who follow the code will persevere. I believe *Men of the Code* is a must read and a "go to" book that can be perused over and over. This book offers an excellent written guideline for how to live as a man of honor. I have taken it upon myself to share this book with my adult children to help guide them in their future.

Dana Gregory Abbott, Shihan

Dana Gregory Abbott, Shihan is an internationally recognized expert of Japanese swordsmanship who has been influential in advancing and spreading the martial arts. He holds a 7th Degree Black Belt, is an inductee into the prestigious Black Belt Hall of Fame and has practiced for 38 years throughout the world, including 14 years in Yokohama, Japan. In addition to teaching and advancing the arts, he is published, and is the inventor and patent holder of the ActionFlex product line by Century Martial Arts.

Endorsements for *Men of the Code*

If you have read Dr. Bohdi Sanders' books on warrior wisdom, and you expect this to be the same, or similar, then you are about to be stunned. The style is similar, and this book contains the same great wisdom from the masters of the ages, but that is where the similarity ends. This book is captivating and provocative in a whole new way.

Dr. Sanders breaks the mold with this book. He challenges us, and our society, in ways that will motivate you, anger you, and build confidence in you.

Men of the Code covers the usual warrior wisdom tenets of being a better person, but that is just the tip of the iceberg. It covers courage, honor, and commitment, overcoming fear, spirituality, manners, culture and so much more. This book is epic!

Let me just say that if I wanted my son to know exactly what I stood for and what I want to be remembered by, if there was a way to sum up all of my 60 plus years of studying the philosophies of the martial arts masters so that he could aspire to be a better man, then I would give him a copy of this book...and I will.

This book will take an honored place beside *The Dao of Jeet Kune Do*, by Bruce Lee, in my collection. I can think of no higher recommendation.

Renshi Bill Holman

Bill Holman has been a consistent student of martial arts for almost 45 years. During that time he has studied Jeet Kune Do, Vovenam, Kyokushin Karate, and Taekwondo. The last 28 years he has focused on Kempo Karate, Jeet Kune Do and Akijitsu with Self Defense Systems, Intl. In addition to earning a 5th Dan in Bushido Kempo at 62 years of age, he has earned and been awarded the title "Renshi" which literally means "Polished Master," for dedication, perseverance, and loyalty to the system.

Endorsements for *Men of the Code*

Dr. Sanders has hit a grand slam with his new book, *Men of the Code*! This book really hits home concerning a subject that most seem content to either ignore or to overlook in today's world. I remember a time when, if a man made a promise and shook on it, you could consider it done. For the most part, those times are long gone. Those of us who want to raise our boys with honor are facing an uphill battle in today's social climate.

Men of the Code addresses this issue and many more. This book is packed with hard-hitting wisdom and sage advice for men. I have read other books for men, on the subject of being manly or living like a man, and they all focus on how to dress, how to shave, and mostly materialistic subjects. But *Men of the Code* goes much deeper and really gets to the core of what it means to truly be a man. All of the grooming tips, dressing tips, etc., that other books spend time on, are meaningless and trivial compared to what is really inside the man. This is where *Men of the Code* excels.

Dr. Sanders gets to the center of what being a man is all about. It is not about materialistic things or external looks; it is about what is inside a man, his character, his honor and his integrity. Dr. Sanders covers all of this and more in great detail, but in a way that is easy to read and easy to understand.

I have read Dr. Sanders' #1 bestseller, *Modern Bushido: Living a Life of Excellence*, and I can tell you that *Men of the Code* expands on *Modern Bushido*, going into even more detail and into more topics which are of vital importance to every man. I consider this book, not only timely, but extremely important. *Men of the Code* is sure to become a classic. I highly recommend this book. Every man should read it and every parent should use it to teach their sons how to become men.

Billy Matheny

Billy Matheny is currently in his tenth year as an instructor for the U.S. Air Force Security Forces. He served 20 years in the Air Force and 10 years as a law enforcement officer. He is also the owner and coach of one of the most successful MMA gyms in the country. Billy is also the author of the new book, *The MMA Art of War*.

Endorsements for *Men of the Code*

Dr. Bohdi Sanders defines what manhood is about, and what today's men should strive to be. In an automated world that desensitizes and emasculates men, it is important that someone stand up and let it be known what masculinity truly is. Men are the hunter/gatherers, and despite what many proclaim manliness to be (human, without gender, minus that very chromosome that makes us what we are), Dr. Sanders spells out how boys should develop into men, and what their respective role is in society and interpersonal relationships with women.

Dr. Sanders made a name for himself in the literary world by writing and detailing the "warrior code" for those pursuing rank and credentials in the martial arts. His notoriety is such that many have flocked to his wonderful books that help the mindful warrior along his path. This book, however, is not one for the warrior, but for the boy who would become a man.

From birth to death, Bohdi defines a man's journey in *Men of the Code* and how it should be lived. Living life not as an alpha-male, but simply as a man, should be every male's goal. This book should not rest on your bookshelf; rather, it should be a reference model for you, your male children, and your grandchildren.

Howard Upton

Howard Upton is the author of the critically acclaimed novel *Of Blood and Stone: A Bill Evers Novel*, as well as the second in the series, *Occam's Razor*. A lifelong student of the martial arts, a former collegiate football player, and national champion power lifter, Howard continues to pursue those things that excite and interest him.

Men of the Code hits upon the core values that all men, especially warriors, know to be true in their hearts. This book spells out exactly what it takes, a blueprint if you will, for living your life with honor as a man of the code. It is a must read. It is a great book!

Thomas J. Mota

Thomas J. Mota is a Fugitive Recovery Agent in Cleveland, Ohio. He is also a team member on the Perry Nuclear Power Plant, Tactical Response Team. In addition, he is Sergeant in the United States Air Force, Emergency Service Team.

Table of Contents

Forward: Colonel Phil Torres... xi
Introduction... xv

Chapter 1:   What is a Man of the Code?   1
Chapter 2:   How Men are Portrayed in Today's World...............   9
Chapter 3:   The Superior Man and the Inferior Man................ 21
Chapter 4:   The Characteristics of a Real Man.................... 33
Chapter 5:   Character and Excellence............................. 43
Chapter 6:   Honor.. 51
Chapter 7:   Integrity.. 57
Chapter 8:   Courage.. 63
Chapter 9:   Endurance and Fortitude.............................. 69
Chapter 10: Actions.. 77
Chapter 11: Respect and Courtesy................................. 87
Chapter 12: Truth and Honesty.................................... 95
Chapter 13: Justice.. 103
Chapter 14: Dignity and Sincerity................................ 109
Chapter 15: Discipline... 115
Chapter 16: Self-Reliance.. 119
Chapter 17: Self-Confidence to do What's Right................... 123
Chapter 18: Roles, Responsibilities, and Duties.................. 127
Chapter 19: Relationships.. 143
Chapter 20: Wisdom and Knowledge................................. 165
Chapter 21: Mental and Spiritual Strength........................ 171
Chapter 22: The Power of Your Words.............................. 181
Chapter 23: Learning from Your Mistakes.......................... 191
Chapter 24: Helping Others....................................... 199
Chapter 25: The Code and the Law................................. 207
Chapter 26: Raising Men Instead of Boys.......................... 215
Chapter 27: Facing Death Like a Man.............................. 227
Chapter 28: Conclusion... 235

Appendix A.. 239
Appendix B.. 248
Index... 249
About the Author.. 256
Other Titles.. 257

Foreword

We live in trying times, but we can probably make that statement about most eras in history. Only the challenges change. We do, however, live in a constantly changing, technologically-driven, culturally-blended, sexually-normed society where roles, at times, seem blurred, and acts once considered welcomed from gentlemen, are no longer in vogue and may at times be considered offensive to some.

In our all-consuming, politically correct world, it is a challenge for many men to maintain a set of principles to live by, regardless of circumstances, but some men choose to live a principled life. These are men of honor - men of the code. Some men live by a code immune from, or impacted little by, societal influences. These men live their lives by what they know in their hearts to be right. They live as they have been taught from early childhood. To these men, chivalry is not dead. Their word is their bond. They deliver on their promises. They do not hesitate to act. It isn't that they are not fearful, but rather that they act in spite of their fears. What is right is more important than their comfort.

Dr. Bohdi Sanders captures what sets these men apart from other men and provides a template for achieving a principled life. Principled men live by what Dr. Stephen Covey called a "Constitution," a set of guiding principles that allow them to live life as it should be lived and interact with, and significantly contribute to, our society in a positive manner. They don't say or do what is expedient or nice sounding because of political correctness; they do what is right regardless of circumstances.

We live in a fast-paced pressure-cooker society where many parents, for a variety of reasons, have acquiesced their parenting roles to the schools, the neighborhood, and technology. These entities, who have assumed the parenting role, do not necessarily act in the best interest of the children. These children, therefore, do not receive the foundational, character building blocks necessary for success in life. I believe that a parent's first duty is to raise children to become responsible adults. Many of today's parents compete with social media and other outside influences for the instilling of values to their children and come out on the losing end.

The book, *Men of the Code*, is not about men being superior to women, or about being sexist, although there are those in our society who look at life through rose-colored lenses and may opine so. It is a book about how to be a man of honor in today's society.

Perfection is a target or goal. There is no perfect, only continuous striving; toward perfection. None of us are perfect, but to truly live a life of honor, one must continually strive toward the goal of personal improvement. Only then can we have the impact in our lives and the lives of others that we truly seek. No one likes dealing with an unprincipled person. An unprincipled person can never truly be trusted

We have organizations, like the military and other institutions, that do a wonderful job of instilling the desired virtues we want in our young people so that they succeed and contribute to society. Most of our young people, however, are never significantly exposed to such organizations.

Excellence in life should not be about a catchy sounding word, phrase, or quote. It should be a way of life, a blueprint for thinking and living a quality life. It should be an internal filter through which thoughts and actions must pass. It should be a set of formed habits when dealing with yourself and others. Excellence must be an active way of thought that always seeks the best in everything one does regardless of energy expenditure.

It is well to remember that character building for men starts with building a solid foundation and the following quote by, Frank Outlaw, captures the essence of the building blocks,

> "Watch your thoughts, they become words;
> watch your words, they become actions;
> watch your actions, they become habits;
> watch your habits, they become character;
> watch your character, for it becomes your destiny."

Many of today's academic institutions do not necessarily build character and how to successfully navigate life. Certain aspects of academic institutions may help develop character through team sports and related activities, but that is not their charter. I would dare say that some institutions teach little and indoctrinate a lot.

I was a guest speaker recently at a major martial arts event, and part of my speech involved making a connection between the rigors of martial arts training early on and success in general in life. Most in the martial arts start at a young age and create a solid structured framework or foundation of discipline, ability to focus, perseverance, respect for others, teamwork, sacrifice, overcoming handicaps (physical and mental), tolerance to discomfort, to get back up when knocked down, and developed "heart."

Many of our young people today are socialized to admire, idolize, copy, follow, and/or worship athletes and actors with checkered lives and, who, outside of providing us with the entertainment in our lives, provide little in the way of positive role modeling, mentoring, or example setting.

We live in a world of self-generating beliefs which remain largely untested. We adopt those beliefs because they are based on conclusions, which are inferred from what we observe, plus our past experience. Our ability to achieve the results we truly desire is eroded by our feelings that:

- Our beliefs are the truth.
- The truth is obvious.
- Our beliefs are based on real data.
- The data we select are the real data.

Character building in men, and success in life as we interact with one another, involve EQ (Emotional Quotient) as well as IQ (Intelligence Quotient) and some would say that EQ is more critical - especially when dealing with people. Daniel Goldberg, in his book, "Emotional Intelligence," breaks the domains of EQ into the following four domains of personal competence:

- Self-awareness
  1) Emotional self-awareness: Reading one's own emotions and recognizing their impact; using "gut sense" to guide decisions.
  2) Accurate self-assessment: Knowing one's strength and limits.
  3) Self-confidence: A sound sense of one's self-worth and capabilities.

- Self-management
  1) Emotional self-control: Keeping disruptive emotions and impulses under control
  2) Transparency: Displaying honesty and integrity; trustworthiness.
  3) Adaptability: Flexibility in adapting to changing situations or overcoming obstacles
  4) Achievement: The drive to improve performance to meet inner standards of excellence

- Social awareness
  1) Empathy: Sensing other's emotions, understanding their perspective, and taking active interest in their concerns
  2) Organizational awareness: Reading the currents, decision networks, and politics at the organizational level
  3) Service: Recognizing and meeting follower, client, or customer needs

- Relationship management
  1) Inspirational leadership: Guiding and motivating with a compelling vision
  2) Influence: Wielding a range of tactics for persuasion
  3) Developing others: Bolstering other's abilities through feedback and guidance
  4) Change catalyst: Initiating, managing, and leading in a new direction
  5) Conflict management: Resolving disagreements
  6) Building bonds: Cultivating and maintaining

Men of the Code is a timely book in a somewhat chaotic time, a time when almost everything men do is questioned and makes some men pause. It is a time of political correctness run amok. This book provides a blueprint, a compass for men in these turbulent times. Like Dr Bohdi Sanders' previous award winning works, I thoroughly enjoyed this book. I believe it will make a difference in the lives of those who read it and heed its advice.

Colonel Phil Torres

Phil Torres rose from Private to Colonel in the U. S. Marine Corps and retired after an illustrious career lasting more than 34 years of active duty. Highlights among his responsibilities included Chief of Nuclear Security Policy and Chief of Command Security for the U. S. Strategic Command, Offutt Air Force Base, Nebraska; Commander of the Marine Corps Security Force, Naval Submarine Base, Kings Bay, Georgia - responsible for one of the nation's largest strategic nuclear weapons site in the U.S.; Advisor to the Commandant of the Marine Corps on human climate issues, Headquarters Marine Corps, Washington DC; and Inspector (Inspector General) for Marine Corps Bases Japan. He served in Vietnam, to include the battle for Khe Sanh during the 1968 Tet Offensive, and was awarded the nation's third highest combat decoration, the Silver Star Medal, for actions as a Platoon Sergeant.

He entered the Marines with a ninth grade education and retired pursuing a doctorate degree. Since retirement, he has been a Leadership and Management Consultant, a Security Management Consultant, a Team Building Facilitator, an Advisor to the Secretary of Defense on readiness issues, and is currently an Advisor to the Secretary of Veterans Affairs on veteran's issues. He is a lifelong martial artist with over 53 years in the martial arts. He currently holds the title of Kyoshi (Master) in Okinawan Shorin Ryu Kenshinkan Karate, the title of Hanshi (Grandmaster), and has practiced several styles of the martial. Phil is also a competitive shooter in the action shooting sports. He competes and officiates in major competitions across the country throughout the year. Phil resides in San Antonio, Texas.

Introduction

Over the centuries, men of character have lived by a set of principles and standards that have guided their lives. These were men of honor and esteem. They took their honor and their principles seriously and lived life as men, not merely adult males, but true men – men of character, integrity and honor.

But, in today's modern society, it seems that the vast majority of men have forgotten how to live by these principles. They have forgotten what it means to truly be real men. They have forgotten the ways of honor.

Gone are the days where boys and young men could find good role models in movies, on television, or elsewhere in their lives. The majority of young men today have no manly role models. Oh, there are those role models in movies, but they aren't really the role models that you want for your sons.

They teach them to either act brutish and crude, or feminine and wimpish. Where are the role models like John Wayne or Jimmy Stewart? Where do boys and young men learn to be men of honor in today's world? What has happened to the men in our world, that they no longer have pride in being men of respect, men of courage, and men of honor?

What happened to the days when a man's word meant something, when a handshake was as good as a contract? What happened to respect, honor, and chivalry? Do you think that our modern society is producing any more men like Thomas Jefferson or George Washington? What has happened to men of courage, men who were willing to stand against wrong wherever they might find it?

These are not simply rhetorical questions; there is a very real risk of losing an entire generation to political correctness, to the unbridled influence of Hollywood, and to selfish neglect. We need men of honor, men of the code, to step up and take responsibility for both living life as they should, and for teaching the next generation of young men how to be men of character and honor. We need to stand against the wave of neglected standards in this world.

Men use to live by principles like courage, respect, honor, and integrity, but these traits don't seem to get a second thought in today's world. There is very little self-respect left today; self-respect has been replaced with a counterfeit replacement. Today, men dress and act like boys; they seem to not want to grow up and become men. Thus, boys and young men have no role models to look up to; so they turn to celebrities, sports figures, and musicians as their role models.

This decline in values and principles can be seen across the board. It is evident in the music lyrics, the foul language which has now become common place, pants that hang below the butt, and an overall attitude of disrespect that permeates throughout our culture. F-bombs are now as common as saying hello, and are heard in music, on movies, on television, in mixed company, and just as often by women as much as men.

Respect and honor have fallen by the wayside. Standards have been lowered to the lowest common denominator. The good news is that not everyone has lowered their standards, not everyone has accepted this decline in our culture. There are still men out there who know what it really means to be real men.

It is high time for men to get back to being men of honor. *Men of the Code* is a guide to living life as a superior man, a man of honor. In *Men of the Code*, you will learn what has happened to our culture that has led to this erosion of morals and honor among both men and women. I delve into how our entertainment, schools, and government have played a major role in the lowering of the standards of our modern culture, and how we are losing an entire generation of young men to these "new standards," or more fittingly, the new lack of standards.

I also take the reader on a journey through the character traits that all men should integrate into their lives. These character traits are universal. Men throughout the world recognize the value of being honorable, of being honest, courageous, and having integrity. The traits that are covered in *Men of the Code*, are traits which everyone should live by, but unfortunately, very few actually do.

Everyone should know what they stand for and what they won't stand for in life, but most people in today's society never slow down enough to even consider what they truly stand for. *Men of the Code* takes the reader step by step into the world of the real man – the man who lives life with gusto, courage, honor, character, and integrity. It guides the reader through the character traits, roles and duties of men who live a life of honor and character.

Men of the Code should be read more like a guide book for the man who wants to live by the old ways of honor, in a modern world that has largely forgotten what honor truly means. Not everyone has accepted the lower standards that have gradually slithered into acceptance in today's world. There are still men in this world who live by a code of honor.

What each man has to decide is how he wants to live his life. This is a vital question for you, and every man, to answer. Do you want to simply go along to get along, or do you want to go you own way in a society of sheep? Do you want to be an average man or do you have the courage to step up and be a superior man – a man of honor and courage? I hope that you decide to be a superior man.

I use the symbol of a man holding a samurai sword on the cover because the sword symbolizes power, protection, authority, strength, courage, and is the symbol of knighthood and chivalry. It also symbolizes discrimination and the power of manly intellect. These are all traits of men of the code, and traits which have all but vanished in our modern culture.

It is my goal to give men a guide for living a life of honor, for living by a code. *Men of the Code* is a guide for doing just this. By the time you finish reading this book, you will not only be able to discern what has been missing in your life, but you will also be prepared to change your life in a positive way. You will have all of the information that you need to develop your own code of ethics that will guide all of your actions and decisions throughout your life.

My hope is that *Men of the Code* will awaken men to the deception that has slowly caused them to lower their standards and that it will lead to revival of men who take honor and character seriously. I hope that it will help stop the regression of our standards and principles, and that it will cause men to awaken and to once again find the desire to become MEN of the CODE.

Bohdi Sanders

Men of the Code

Bohdi Sanders, Ph.D.

Chapter 1

What is a Man of the Code?

*Show me the man you honor, and I will know what kind
of man you are, for it shows me what your ideal of
manhood is and what kind of man you long to be.*
Thomas Carlyle

What is your target?

*Without goals, and plans to reach them,
you are like a ship that has set sail with no destination.*
Fitzhugh Dodson

What kind of man do you long to be? Most men never stop to consider this question, but it is one that must be asked and answered by every man who wants to be a man of the code. Becoming a man of character doesn't simply happen by chance. You first have to decide that you *want* to be a man of character, a man of honor, courage, and integrity.

Deciding what kind of man you want to be is the first step to becoming that kind of man. If you put this question out of your mind, with the hopes that you will eventually become the man that you want to be naturally, you will most likely never become the kind of man that you desire to become.

That is like wanting to drive to a specific lake in the mountains, but refusing to slow down and take a look at a road map in order to plan your route. You just jump in your car and take off, assuming that you will eventually end up where you want to go. Your chances of getting to your desired destination with this strategy are slim to none, unless of course someone has already shown you the way.

Life works in much the same way. You can't just assume that you will become the man that you want to become simply because that is what you want. You have to take action to design your life the way you want it to be. You have to plan how you will get to the place that you want to go. It doesn't just happen on its own. No successful man ever achieved lofty goals by accident. That is not the way life works. If you truly want something in this life, you must have a plan to follow. Without a plan, you are simply blowing in the wind.

Before you can achieve your objectives in life, you must first understand what your objectives are and why you want to achieve them. This knowledge is vital in order for you to stay motivated over the long run. If you want to become a man of the code, you first need to know what a man of the code is and why you actually want to become one. You must understand the benefits and why it is important to you.

What is a man of the code?

You become a man not when you reach a certain age,
but when you reach a certain state of mind.
Habeeb Akande

A man of the code is a man who has decided to live his life by a certain code of honor, a specific set of standards or principles which guide his life. Most men simply go through life on auto-pilot, doing whatever they are in the mood for or whatever is best for them personally. They don't base their decisions on a set of principles, but rather on emotions or what they feel at the time.

The man of the code, on the other hand, takes the time to reflect on the values and principles that are important to him in his life, and bases everything in his life on those principles. He takes life a little more seriously than other men, but at the same time is not rigid or sanctimonious. He simply understands what principles are important to him and he lives by those principles.

To be a man of the code, you must live by the principles of your code. They must be real for you. The decisions in your life must be based on the principles that make up your code.

The man of the code lives his life by these principles every day. His principles do not change according to the situation, but are firm and command his attention to detail. They are an integral part of his life. Every decision, whether small and insignificant or of the utmost importance, are based on his principles.

This does not mean that men of the code are inflexible and rigid. They aren't. Living your life by your own standards does not mean that you are locked into any specific ways of doing things. It merely means that your deeply held beliefs and values guide your actions, whatever they may be.

Although the specific actions of men who live by the code will differ, their inner intentions will remain the same – to do what is right. Doing what is right is the basis of living by a code of honor. But, what is right is not always set in stone; honor is not black and white. What is right in one situation may be completely wrong in another.

Please don't get this confused with situational ethics. While it might seem the same, there is a very distinct difference.

Situational ethics is a philosophy pioneered by Joseph Fletcher. According to Fletcher's model, the decision-making process should be based upon the circumstances of a particular situation, and not upon any fixed morals. The only absolute in this philosophy is love. Love should be the motive behind every decision. As long as your intentions are based on love, the end justifies the means.

At first, this sounds pretty good, but if you look deeper, this philosophy is flawed. Most any action can be justified by using the argument, "Love was my intention." If love is the only absolute in your decision making process, that leaves the door wide open for anyone to justify almost any action.

For example, Hitler could have justified his actions of killing six million Jews, by stating that his actions were based solely on his *love* for the Aryan race. The bank robber could justify his actions by stating that his intentions were to better provide for his family because of his overwhelming *love* for them. Basing your actions solely on love is simply not good enough.

The man of the code does not base all of his decisions on love, but rather on what is right. His actions do differ according to the requirements of each specific situation, not simply according to the situation or based on love, but according to what is right in that particular situation.

His philosophy is not based on actions which are always right or always wrong. That is to say, his actions are not necessarily set in stone. What is right in one situation may not be what is right in another situation. While his principles do not change, his application of those principles will be different in different circumstances.

For example, part of your code may be that you are dedicated to the truth and that your word is your honor. Simply put, you say what you mean and mean what you say; you are not a liar. This is a fairly standard trait for men of the code. But this doesn't mean that lying is always wrong.

Say for instance, you are the victim of a home invasion and you have hidden your children for their safety. If the criminal, who has just broken into your home to do you harm, asks you if there are any other people in the house, would it be wrong to lie to him and tell him no, or would it be wrong to be completely honest and put your children at risk?

Of course, you could argue that this is a perfect example of situational ethics, and indeed it is an example of situational ethics. That action was based on love. But even though this example was based on love, the underlying principle behind this action was based on what was right. There are many examples that are not based on love, but rather merely on what is right. Men of the code do not live by rigid moral restraints; they live by what is right.

A man of the code must be able to look at himself in the mirror and feel no shame; he must be proud of the man that he sees. This can only be achieved by knowing that, in every situation, you have done what is right, to the best of your abilities. A clear conscience and deep sense of personal satisfaction is the reward for being a man of the code and for knowing deep within your spirit that you are a man of honor.

That brings us to the answer of the question, "What is a man of the code?" A man of the code is a man who lives his life, and bases his decisions, according to what is right, based on the principles of his personal code. Of course, in order for his code to be right, it must be based on certain overriding principles which are based on honor, integrity, and character.

The man of the code is a real man. (I will discuss the difference between a real man and the average male in a later chapter.) He lives his life with a deep sense of honor and integrity. He is courageous and takes pains to ensure that his actions are just and right.

Respect and courtesy are important to him and he integrates them into his life, in spite of how other people live. He values truth in all things and does his best to see things as they are, not as others say they are, or as he may wish they were.

Men cut from this cloth live their lives with dignity, no matter what they are doing. They are sincere in their beliefs and sincerely do their best to live their lives by.

Being a man of the code takes great discipline. In fact, men of the code enact discipline throughout every part of their lives. Without discipline, they could not possibly live up to their high standards. They do not depend on others, but instead do their best to be self-reliant and independent. These men do not follow the crowd, but rather they make their own way and think for themselves.

Their dedication to what is right has no limits. In fact, what is right is their compass in all of their ways. The man of the code has taken the time to know and understand exactly what he believes and why he believes it, and from this knowledge, his self-confidence is built. He has no doubts about the lifestyle he has chosen to live; it is the core of his existence.

The man of the code is a warrior and a hero to those that he loves and those who need his help. He is the protector of his family, his friends, the young, the elderly, and the weak. He understands his personal duties and takes his responsibilities seriously.

He values his relationships and treats others with respect and courtesy. He takes his responsibility as a husband and a father seriously and fulfills his duty as the leader of his family by guiding and teaching his children, working in unison with his wife, and providing for them the best that he possibly can. He and his wife are partners in life.

These rare men understand the importance of wisdom and knowledge. They seek it out everywhere they go and spend time meditating on what they have learned in order to improve themselves and their lives.

Men of the code understand that they must balance all of the parts of their lives – spiritually, mentally, and physically. They are men of their word. Their word is their bond and if they say something, they mean it.

When the man of the code makes a mistake, he is quick to admit it and make amends. He also knows the importance of learning from his mistakes and tries his best to take away something positive from every mistake. Once he has learned what he can, he moves on. He knows nothing constructive comes from wasting time on regrets.

He does what he can to help those around him, understanding that helping others is one of his purposes on this earth. He is quick with a kind word, but only gives advice to those outside of his family when asked. And then, he offers the advice, but doesn't insist that it is taken. He gives criticism in private and from a sincere desire to help.

Since he values what is right above all other virtues, he is not afraid to break the law in order to ensure that the right thing is done. He understands the difference between being right and being legal, and has the courage to do what's right, in spite of any possible consequences.

Death and fear no longer control his mind. He is secure with his beliefs and knows that everyone must die; it is simply a part of the human experience. Therefore, he doesn't fear death, but at the same time, he doesn't seek it out either. Although he is in no rush to die, he has spent time in meditation on his own death, and is prepared for death when his time comes. He is prepared for whatever may come.

Being a man of the code is not easy; if it were, every man would live his life in this way. But it takes time and discipline. It takes living life with purpose instead of merely walking through life in a fog, keeping yourself sufficiently entertained until you kick the bucket.

All of these things, and more, compose his code, his way of living life to the fullest. His code is his roadmap to living a life of character, honor, and integrity. It is the ideal for what he holds sacred in this life. He takes his code as seriously as the most devout religious practitioner takes his religion. Now you may be asking yourself, "What is this code?"

What is the Code?

A man's *got to have a* code, *a creed to live by.*
John Wayne

The code is a specific set of principles by which you have resolved to live your life. Just as it is important to write down your personal goals in life, in order to achieve them in a more proficient manner, it is important for you to put your code in writing.

Your code will list the important principles that you want to make an integral part of your life. These will become the basis of how you make all your decisions, both large and small.

Each man's code will be slightly different, as we are each distinctly unique individuals, but each code will be based on the same underlying principles. The cornerstone for each man's personal code will be based on what is right, not on cut and dried moral absolutes.

While each man's code may vary a little, the basis stays the same. No two codes will ever be exactly the same. If they are, then someone has tried to take a shortcut, instead of actually taking the time to meditate and reflect on what is truly important to him in his life. Don't shortchange yourself by just using someone else's personal code; take the time to make your code distinctly yours. This may sound a bit confusing to you, but it will become clear and make perfect sense by the end of this book.

Bruce Lee stated, "I'm not in this world to live up to your expectations and you're not in this world to live up to mine." Each man's code is distinctly personal. There may be certain things in my code that are not important to you, and there may be things in your code that I don't feel are important to me.

What's important is that your code is based on both what is right and the universal virtues that all men of honor hold dear. As I stated, the specifics may differ, but the underlying principles will be the same. It is these underlying principles that bind all men of the code together. They may disagree on the specific details, but they will always agree on the fundamental principles.

Although the code is based on universal virtues that are held in high esteem around the world, this doesn't mean that every culture holds all of these virtues to be sacred; they don't. But real men of honor do. Specific customs and morals differ from culture to culture, but there are some virtues in which all men of honor admire and hold as universally right.

I will cover these virtues one at a time and by the end of this book you will have everything you need to develop your own personal code. As Lao Tzu stated, "A journey of a thousand miles begins with a single step."

I want to address one thing before I continue. It is never too late to be the man that you want to be. The past is the past; it is over and done with. While you may have done things in the past that you are not proud of, every day is a chance to begin anew and to become the man that you are meant to be.

Think about it. What are your choices? You can continue to live life as you have been or you can make a decision to become a man of the code, a man of honor, character, and integrity. Being a man of the code is not some club that you gain admission to; it is a personal decision that you make for yourself.

You have to decide if you want to become a man of honor, a man who lives his life by a higher standard than average guys, a man who lives with honor and integrity, who can look at himself in the mirror with no regrets, or if you want to be mediocre, common and live with no real guiding principles or standards.

A man should have a purpose in life. He should know what he stands for and what he won't stand for. Most men have never taken the time to even think about what they really believe in or the principles that they truly hold dear. They simply make snap decisions on the spot, and usually those decisions are made according to what is best for them, not according to what is right.

That is not the way a man of honor lives his life. It is time for you to make a decision about the kind of man that you truly want to be. It is my hope that you choose to be a man of principle, a man of honor and character – a man of the code.

Reflections for the Superior Man

I'm not in this world to live up to your expectations
and you are not in this world to live up to mine.
Bruce Lee

Masculinity is not something given you, but something you gain.
And you gain it by winning small battles with honor.
Norman Mailer

The things a man has to have are hope and confidence in himself
against the odds...He's got to have some inner standards worth
fighting for...And he must be ready to choose death before
dishonor without making too much song and dance about it.
Clark Gable

This is the test of manhood:
How much is there left in you after
you have lost everything outside of yourself?
Orison Swett Marden

A man does what he must – in spite of personal consequences,
in spite of obstacles and dangers and pressures – and
that is the basis of all human morality.
Winston Churchill

It's never too late to be who you might have been.
George Eliot

It is the first principle that in order to improve yourself,
you must first know yourself.
Baltasar Gracian

Do not go where the path may lead,
go instead where there is no path and leave a trail.
Ralph Waldo Emerson

The real man smiles in trouble, gathers strength from distress,
and grows brave by reflection.
Thomas Paine

The important thing is that men
should have a purpose in life.
The Dalai Lama

Chapter 2

How Men are Portrayed in Today's World

*Because there is very little honor left in American life, there
is a certain tendency to destroy masculinity in American men.*
Norman Mailer

You are Being Sold a False Image

*We (modern society) make men without chests and expect of
them virtue and enterprise. We laugh at honor and are shocked to
find traitors in our midst. We castrate and bid the geldings be fruitful.*
C. S. Lewis

In this chapter, I want to examine how men are being depicted by
Hollywood, on television and in commercials. You may ask yourself why
this matters, and that would be an appropriate question. The answer is that
young men and boys are influenced by what they see on television, in
movies, and the lyrics that they listen to on CD's and music videos. All of the
above have been influencing children and young adults for years now, and
we are starting to see the effect that it is having on men and boys throughout
the world.

Before I really get into this topic, I want to emphasize that I am not in
favor of censorship. Freedom is of the utmost importance to me. Everyone
has a choice when it comes to what he watches or what he listens to. It
shouldn't be the government's job to censor what children see on television
or what kind of music they listen to; that's the parents' job.

The problem is that parents have not been doing their job. Too many of
them simply don't care what their kids watch or listen to, as long as they are
not getting in trouble or causing them problems. This is not good parenting,
not even close, but I will address being a father in a later chapter. Right now
I want to delve into the issue of how our modern society is depicting men.

Today's society portrays men on television sit-coms, commercials,
television shows, music videos, etcetera, typically as one of these
stereotypes: an overgrown boy, a mindless brute, a spineless wimp, or a
spoiled, egotistical jerk. We rarely see men who are portrayed as a well-
balanced warrior, who lives a life of honor, character and integrity, who is a
great father and husband, a good provider, or a man of wisdom and

knowledge, with a sense of duty and adventure. More often, we see men portrayed as one of these four stereotypes.

This is important because, as I stated, media influences young men and boys, and even grown men who are not secure in their role as a man. This is especially true when they do not have a strong role model in their life to counteract what they see on television and the movies. While it is true that it is not Hollywood's job to make sure that they give young men good role models, it is also true that they are depicting men in a certain way because they have an agenda.

For years now, there has been a movement to make boys less masculine. This may seem like a radical statement, but it is blatantly true to anyone who pays attention to how men are represented by the entertainment industry. If you don't believe me, pay attention to the television commercials, sit-coms, and movies that you see for the next week. Look for the things that I will be discussing in this chapter and find out for yourself.

Men are often portrayed as mindless, shallow, overgrown boys preoccupied with sex, their ego, toys, power, etc. They are shown as wimps, scared of bugs, mice, women, and responsibility. This is being done purposely to tame men, to make them less manly and more *civilized* and refined. Any hint of being too assertive, or being willing to fight, is portrayed as someone with anger issues who needs counseling. Of course, it is not this way in every television show or movie, but it is in the vast majority of them.

I will give specific examples to back up this claim, as I cover each of the four stereotypes. These examples will be straight from what is being shown on television today. No doubt, you will be able to come up with many more examples and you too will start to see the pattern that I am referring to in each category. Let's start with the overgrown boy.

The Overgrown Boy

This portrayal of men is seen throughout television shows, movies, and commercials. How many times have you seen a commercial where the couple goes shopping and the man acts like a two year old in a candy store? He wants the new car, the new boat, the new lawnmower, etcetera, without giving any thought to whether or not he can afford it. He looks like a giddy kid getting a new toy.

Fortunately, he has his wise, level-headed wife there with him to keep him from destroying the family's finances or to ask the wise questions that the immature man is not intelligent enough to ask. He is more like the lady's son than her husband, being told whether or not he can have his new toy. In essence, he is just like another kid for the wife to take care of, as if she is a single mom with all the responsibilities on her shoulders.

Many commercials and television shows depict men in this way. Men are shown as nothing more than big kids. They are irresponsible, constantly lying around watching sports, drinking beer, playing golf, or hanging out with his buddies, while his wife takes care of all of the important stuff because she can't depend on him to be a man.

Men are portrayed as taking almost no responsibility outside of keeping their job. They are shown as being over-powered by strong women, irresponsible, gullible, easily manipulated, and having to be constantly watched or kept in line.

A perfect example would be the sitcom, *Everybody Loves Raymond*. Look at the difference between how Raymond is portrayed and how his wife is portrayed. Raymond is like a big kid. When he is not at work, which by the way, is totally focused on sports, he is only interested in watching sports on television, playing golf, or sex. His wife, Debra, on the other hand, is the responsible one who pays the bill, does all of the work around the house, is in charge of the children, and has to keep Raymond in line.

Don't get me wrong, I think the show is very well done and extremely funny, but it is a great example of what I am talking about. The other male characters on the show are no prizes either. Frank, Raymond's dad, is rude, crude, thoughtless, and only cares about eating and watching sports. Raymond's brother, Robert, is also portrayed as a loser. This portrayal of men is very evident on television shows and commercials.

On the other hand, their wives are shown as being responsible and doing almost all of the work at home, and having to hound the man to do what little he does. They are portrayed as the sensible and logical ones in the relationship, being the boss or the head of the household, being in charge of the money and bills, all while the husband is just the other child in the family.

Now, I am not saying that there aren't many households like this. There are. And that is because men have not been taught how to be real men. If a boy is not taught how to conduct himself like a man, when he becomes a father, he will not know how to teach his sons either, and the whole cycle continues. This has been going on for far too long. It is high time that men start acting like men, real men, not overgrown boys.

Men are also portrayed as overgrown boys in another way – as the single party animal who cares about nothing but partying with his buddies, playing or watching sports, and of course, women. This depiction shows young men, and sometimes older men, as merely party boys, drinking to excess and being as irresponsible as possible. It is an anything goes, raunch-fest, and the thought of being honorable or acting with any type of integrity never crosses their minds.

In all fairness, a lot of young women are being portrayed in this manner as well. And, this is having a huge affect on our young men and women. If you have any doubts about this, check out some videos of the spring break parties. In fact, at the time that I am writing this, there were just three college boys arrested for gang rape on a popular Panama City beach in Florida. The girl had passed out from drinking, and three college boys had their way with her.

And, to make this even worse, this happened in broad daylight, with hundreds of college kids, boys and girls, just standing around and watching it. And the kicker is, not one single person lifted a finger to stop it. Not one person objected and stepped up to help this girl, who had unwisely put herself into a very bad situation.

How could this be? How could there not be even one true man in that crowd that would step up, be a hero, and stop this horrid act? The answer is that we are not teaching our young men to be heroes. Society is teaching them that there is never a good reason to fight, that violence is always wrong, only the weak and uneducated have to resort to violence. This is total garbage, but it is exactly what is being taught to our young men.

Moreover, television and movies teach our young men that they are supposed to go on spring break, get totally wasted, and act like fools. It is their right; after all, they have been "working" so hard by going to college all year. They deserve to go blow off some steam and act like morons. Right?

We now live in a culture where young men are expected to be overgrown kids, irresponsible, reckless, and childish; and they aren't letting us down. Parents enable their sons to act like this, and in fact, many simply expect this and consider it a part of the "college experience."

When did this become the college experience? When did college become about partying until you puke or girls getting wasted and dancing like strippers on the beach? There was a time when college boys were expected to have character, honor and integrity. Where men were expected to be the head of the household and protect and provide for their family. It seems that today's society has lowered its standards to the point that not much is expected from men, and in return, many *men* have now become overgrown boys instead of real men.

The Mindless Brute

On the other end of the spectrum, we see men depicted as mindless brutes. This is how Hollywood wants to portray men who are willing to stand up and fight, even if they are in the right and are doing the right thing. They are shown as men who always try to solve their problems with violence and never think about their actions.

This is also the way boys are depicted if they get in a fight for any reason at all. In the movies, you will see a boy fighting to protect his girlfriend, and the girlfriend, who is always the intelligent, level-headed one, gets furious with her boyfriend for resorting to violence. This is a pretty common scene in many television shows and movies. Is it any wonder why we rarely see boys do what's right and man up when is it appropriate to do so?

This ridiculous attitude can also be seen in our public schools. If there is a fight of any kind, it doesn't matter who started it. It doesn't matter if the boy was doing nothing more than defending himself, which, by the way, is his legal right, not to mention the right thing to do; *both* boys get suspended for fighting. What is this teaching our young men? Is it teaching them to be heroes and stand up for what's right? Of course not!

Young men are being taught through television, movies, and in school, that they should never fight, not even if they are just in doing so. They are being taught that violence is always wrong, that if you fight, you are nothing more than a mindless brute. They are being force-fed a utopian, pacifist doctrine that stops boys from becoming men of honor.

They are being taught to be victims and let the authorities take care of them. This warped philosophy is teaching young men that there is never a reason for violence and subsequently, turning them into good little sheep, always depending on the shepherd to protect them.

When I was in school, boys got into fights and were friends again the next day. Yes, we were punished for fighting, but the punishment fit the crime. The principal was not too lazy to get to the truth and enact justice. If you were simply defending yourself, you were in the right and were not punished. If it was a case of "boys being boys," both boys were punished, made to shake hands, and sent back to class, not both suspended. The principal was intelligent enough to use the whole situation as a teaching opportunity.

Today, principals are too lazy to take the time to find out if one of the boys was just defending himself. It is just much easier to impose their *no tolerance policy*, which would be more accurately called their "no justice policy." What these indolent administrators are really teaching our young men is that, even if you are in the right, you can't trust the authorities to support you or to care enough to do the right thing. They learn not to trust those in authority. They learn that right and wrong do not matter as much as the all important rules. Our institutions of education are training sheep, not men of character.

What they should be taught is that they should never fight when they can avoid it, but that there are times when a man must fight for what is right. If the situation calls for it, they should have both the courage and the nobility to fight for what's right, no matter what others may think about it. It is not fighting that makes you a brute; it is fighting over trivial things or bullying people. Real men should always have the courage to fight for what is right and to prevent injustice.

And the schools aren't alone. Many workplaces today have adopted the same asinine no tolerance policies, where even if you are attacked and you defend yourself, you will be fired for workplace violence. I am not sure how this politically correct policy, which takes away your right to defend yourself, will stand up in court, but many places of business have it in place nonetheless.

In addition, many businesses take this unjust policy to an even more ridiculous level. Employees, who have been courageous enough to stop thieves or even armed assailants, have been fired because they were told to never intervene in such circumstances.

An employee of a national department store, I won't state which one, was fired for stopping an assault on a woman in the parking lot during his lunch break. He was eating outside in his car, when he heard a woman screaming for help. He heroically ran over to where he heard the screams, to find a man pushing a woman up against her vehicle.

The man asked her if she needed help, and the attacker abruptly turned and attacked the employee, hitting him several times in the head and screaming, "I'm going to kill you!"

Fighting back, the employee was able to get the upper hand and was holding the attacker down, when two other men attacked him. At that time, the sheriff deputies arrived on the scene and stopped the attack. The next day, the employee was terminated for "violating company policy on his lunch break."

Another example is the employee of a fast food chain, whose quick thinking and bravery actually saved countless lives. An armed gunman came into the store, robbed it, and looked as if he was about to shoot both employees and customers. A young man working in the restaurant made a courageous decision to try to stop the gunman, attacked him, putting his own life at risk to save the lives of his co-workers and the customers, and was able to stop the armed criminal from hurting anyone.

Two days later, after being heralded as a hero in the news, the man was fired for not following the store policy concerning robberies. And we wonder why young men are not willing to stand up, be heroic and do the right thing when they see an injustice!

There are many other examples like these, where a guy with the courage to put his life on the line to do the right thing and help those in need, is fired by a politically correct company, run by a spineless CEO, which puts its own policy ahead of people's lives. Companies like these are promoting the same policies that our public schools are enforcing and it's disgraceful.

Under pressure to conform, men are losing their confidence in standing up for what is right and doing the right thing. They are becoming afraid of getting involved because they may be looked at as violent, brutish or even lose their livelihood and go to prison.

The images portrayed by Hollywood, and the unjust policies enacted by our public schools and many companies, are feverishly destroying the heroic spirit in our young men. Furthermore, in doing so, they are creating a nation of spineless wimps who are too afraid of being kicked out of school or fired from their job, to do what's right. And this brings me to the next category – the spineless wimp.

The Spineless Wimp

We see this image of men consistently in commercials, sit-coms, television shows, and movies as well. This is the man who has been completely tamed by the politically correct policies of our schools, businesses, and governments. He refuses to defend himself. In fact, when faced with someone who looks bigger or tougher, he trembles at the possibility of having to confront such a man.

At the same time, this wimpish excuse for a man is praised as a civilized man, while the muscle bound, rough looking guy is looked at as a dangerous brute. Why is it that our modern culture wants to elevate the soft, cowardly man, and demonize manly men? Why does our society want to raise a generation of men who quake in their shoes at the first sign of trouble, instead of raising real men who live by the ideals of honor and courage, and can handle whatever situation he may find himself in at any given time? Why are we championing weakness and denouncing strength?

It would seem absolutely ridiculous if it weren't true. While not every man is born with the spirit of a courageous warrior, it is ludicrous to try to sell the image of the trembling wimp as being the average man. This is not the ideal for our young men to strive toward.

We can see this image, not only in commercials and on the television, but in advertising for clothes, watches, jewelry, and cologne. Gone are the days of advertising spreads with the Marlboro man or the hero archetype. Now we see advertising spreads with the metrosexual guy with no muscles, pink pants, and a baby blue bow tie, looking proudly confident in the fact that he is meticulous about his grooming and appearance, and spends at least as much time and money shopping for clothes as the woman who has him on a leash.

Can you imagine John Wayne, Charles Bronson, or Clint Eastwood wearing the clothes that we now see advertised in many men's magazines? Banish the thought!

The image of the fragile, wimpish man is also becoming much more popular on television. We see this type of "man" getting into hot water on sit-coms, and his beautiful wife rising to defend him, while he sits nervously on the sidelines.

Is this really the image that we want to constantly push on our young men? Do we want to raise an entire generation of men who can't, or won't, defend themselves? Do we want to raise boys who need a strong woman to stand up for them because they are too weak to stand up for themselves? I don't know about you, but that certainly isn't my dreams for my sons.

Hollywood wants to impress on us that men should use their mind, instead of their brawn, to settle disputes. And to be honest, that is true, but not always possible. Men should also be able to handle themselves physically, as well as be intellectually adept.

There is no honor in being a wimp. Please don't get me wrong, I am not saying that every real man must be a tough guy or Chuck Norris. Not everyone is going to be a warrior, and that is perfectly alright. We all have to do the best that we can with the genes that we are given.

What I am saying is that we shouldn't glorify wimpish behavior. Being like one of David Spade's characters and having a smart mouth and no muscles is not cool, no matter how much Hollywood would like to convince us otherwise. You don't have to be muscular to act with courage and stand up for yourself. Being a wimp is more about your mental attitude than your physical body. Don't be a wimp, but don't be a jerk either.

The Egotistical Jerk

The last category that I want to address is the depiction of men as being spoiled, egotistical jerks. Television and movies portray this kind of man as usually being good looking, but once the girl gets to know him, she finds out that he is a spoiled jerk with an ego the size of Texas. This is another fairly common stereotype.

These men are shown as being spoiled or having a lot of money, which adds to their overblown self-image. They are usually depicted as being selfish and only caring about their own wants and needs. Fun is their top priority, much like the overgrown boy. At the same time, much of their fun comes at the expense of others who they have no problem treating like garbage.

Today's parents want to give their kids the best, just like most parents always have. What they don't seem to think about is the fact that they are spoiling their kids and turning them into these spoiled, egotistical little jerks, who then become rich, snobby men who only think about themselves and consider themselves better than everyone around them.

It would appear that this image appeals to many parents, as it seems that there are more parents than ever who are spoiling their children rotten and actually teaching them to look down on those who do not have as much as they do.

Whether this is done on purpose or is just a side effect of spoiling your son without also teaching him values, it is not producing quality men. A spoiled rotten boy rarely turns into a well-rounded man.

Again, this is not the kind of men that we want our sons to grow up to be, but this kind of man is often glorified in the movies and on television. The focus is placed on being rich, but no attention is given to how to be rich *and* respectful, or how to be well off *and* use your resources for good instead of simply for selfishness. No attention is given to how to be responsible with your money or how they should treat other people.

What we usually see with this stereotype is that it is cool to waste as much money on yourself as possible, all in the name of fun. When young men see this image of rich guys rolling in money, with girls throwing themselves at them, all the best clothes, cars, etcetera, that a young man could want, of course this lifestyle looks good to them and they try to imitate their actions.

I have nothing against being rich. In fact, I would love to be rich myself. There is nothing wrong with money. What is wrong with this image of men is that it portrays all men with money as egotistical jerks and influences them to act the same way.

This image of the young man who gets everything he wants without having to work for it, is producing a generation of people who feel entitled to whatever they want in life, but who don't want to work for it. It has produced an entitlement culture. After all, why should one person get to enjoy life in this way, and others have to work for it, right? Wrong!

Young men should be taught to stand on their own feet, to earn things for themselves. They should be taught that nobody owes them anything in this world. If you want something, get off your butt and work for it.

But young men today do feel entitled. They feel that their parents should buy them a car, that their parents should pay for their college, for their vacations, for the best clothes, basically, for whatever they want. This entitlement culture is not building men of character.

And this is not just coming from television and movies. Our government is doing its part to make young people feel entitled as well. Look at all of the entitlements that the government gives out using your tax money. Whatever happened to the idea of being self-reliant and independent? What happened to having pride in yourself and your ability to take care of your own needs?

We need to teach young men to work for what they want in life. We need to teach them that hard work is worth it, not only because of the paycheck, but because it gives them a sense of accomplishment and self-worth. We need to teach them that there is no honor in being rich and wasteful. That if they are blessed enough to have abundant riches in their life, that they should find a way to use them to help others, as well as enjoy themselves. We need to teach them the way of the superior man – the way of honor.

Summary

There are very few role models on television, in movies, in commercials, or in the music world that will help young men and boys grow into men of the code. As I have shown, the images of men that we frequently see portrayed for our sons, do not foster pride in being a man of honor, but instead teach them the exact opposite. We have gone from admiring those who work hard and succeed, to admiration for those who do nothing, from honoring real heroes to the deification of celebrities and politicians.

Young men are taught not to stand up for what is right, that there is never an excuse for any kind of violence. They are taught to back down and expect the authorities, their parents, or the government to take care of their problems. Young men are taught to stay a boy for as long as possible, instead of being taught to grow up and become responsible and self-reliant as soon as possible. They are taught to be soft, whiney, and bored.

Our culture, our government, Hollywood, and television are actively trying to destroy masculinity in American men, as Norman Mailer stated, and they are being successful. Our boys are having their masculinity subdued from the earliest age in our misguided schools. In fact, boys are hardly able to be boys in school at all. There is no longer any quest for adventure, no rough-housing at recess, no learning to really be boys.

If they defend themselves against a bully in school, they are punished for it. In many schools today, boys are not allowed to play football, tag, or any type of activity where they may get too rough or aggressive. Boys are taught to be docile and stationary, to see the counselor for their problems instead of learning how to take care of their own problems and be independent.

This situation leaves only one option for parents to ensure that their sons and daughters grow up to become men and women of character – take an active role in the development of your children. Teach your son's to be men of the code and teach your daughters not to settle for anything less than a real man.

You must fight against the images that are now sold as the way men should be. Don't buy into the portrayal of the new, more enlightened man. The truly enlightened man is the man of the code. It is the difference between being a superior man and an inferior man. Choose to be a superior man and to teach your sons to be superior men as well.

Reflections for the Superior Man

We laugh at honor and are shocked to find traitors in our midst.
We castrate and then bid the geldings be fruitful.
C. S. Lewis

Far better it is to dare mighty things, to win glorious triumphs,
even though checkered by failure, than to take rank with those
poor spirits who neither enjoy nor suffer too much, because
they live in the gray twilight that knows not victory nor defeat.
Theodore Roosevelt

I think that the sense of adventure gets tamed out of us. We also get
frightened. Somewhere along the way, a man loses that confidence,
that reckless or fearlessness he had as a boy. Somewhere along
the story of his life, doubt comes in. And a doubt goes like this:
"No you don't. You don't have what it takes. You can't come through.
You can't pull this off. So just put your nose to the horse in front of
you and get in line and just become a gelding. Tie your reins up
there at the corporate corral and give up any sense of risk.
John Eldredge

You have to be a man before you can be a gentleman.
John Wayne

No man is more unhappy than he who never faces adversity.
For he is not permitted to prove himself.
Seneca

We do not admire the man of timid peace.
We admire the man who embodies victorious effort;
the man who never wrongs his neighbor, who is prompt
to help a friend, but who has those virile qualities
necessary to win in the stern strife of actual life.
Theodore Roosevelt

Private and public life are subject to the same rules - truth and
manliness are two qualities that will carry you through this world
much better than policy or tact of expediency or other words
that were devised to conceal a deviation from a straight line.
Robert E. Lee

A man must stand erect, not be kept erect by others.
Marcus Aurelius

Chapter 3

The Superior Man and the Inferior Man

The ultimate measure of a man is not where he stands
in moments of comfort and convenience, but where
he stands at times of challenge and controversy.
Martin Luther King, Jr.

The Superior Man and the Inferior Man

The superior man is aware of righteousness,
the inferior man is aware of advantage.
Confucius

Confucius spoke a lot about the superior man and inferior man in his teachings. He used the terms to refer to men who did and did not live life according to a certain set of principles. The main idea behind the concept of the superior man and the inferior man is that all men should strive to become a superior man, men who live life with character, honor, and integrity, but Confucius also added that very few men actually reach this lofty goal.

Confucius, his followers, and Mencius, the most famous Confucian philosopher, with the exception of Confucius himself, all taught about specific attributes of the superior man, with the inferior man basically having the opposite characteristics.

Character traits assigned to the superior man are: purpose, poise, self-sufficiency, sincerity, thoroughness, truthfulness, purity of thought and action, love of truth, courtesy, integrity, prudence, composure, fearlessness, dignity, firmness, personal growth, competence, benevolence, open-mindedness, charity, moderation, reciprocity, and power. While this is not an exhaustive list of the character traits of the superior man, it is more than enough for you to get the picture of how Confucius thought men should live.

The terms superior man and inferior man were not meant as some snobbish way of judging people, but more of a way of distinguishing men who do their best to live their lives by high standards, versus the ordinary man who really doesn't give such things much thought. Confucius summed this up by teaching, "The progress of the superior man is upward; the progress of the ordinary man is downward." There is no such thing as standing still; you either move forward or regress.

Basically, superior men continue to evolve and improve their lives, doing their best to strive for perfection, while inferior men, or average men, merely go through life without giving such things much thought, thus their progress is downward or backwards.

Another way to look at this would be to imagine a man paddling a boat up a river with a fairly strong current. The man has to continually work and paddle to move his boat up the river. If he stops paddling and simply rest on his laurels, the natural current of the river would take him back down stream.

He is either working to maintain his position in the river or working to make progress by paddling his boat up stream, but there is no such thing as simply resting, doing nothing, and staying in the same place in the river. If he stops progressing upstream, his boat will start to drift back downstream. He is either moving forward or backwards; there is no point where he is just staying in one spot.

The superior man is constantly working to improve himself, so his progress is continually upstream or forward. The inferior man, or the average man, rests on his laurels, thinking that he has done enough and he is satisfied with where he is in life, not understanding that there is no such thing as getting to one spot in the river of life and then staying there from now on without constant effort. Thus, his progress is backwards or downward as Confucius put it.

As the superior man continues to work and strive to move further up the river, and the inferior man foolishly believes that he can stop endeavoring to move upstream and just enjoy his current place in life, thus the two get further and further apart. The superior man keeps progressing, improving, and moving closer to excellence, while the natural progression of life gradually takes the inferior man backwards or further away from excellence.

All of the detailed differences in personal traits between the superior man and the inferior man can be summed up by the fact that the superior man is driven to be the best that he can be, in every area of his life. Whereas, the inferior man is merely content to be average. He doesn't continually strive to improve himself.

While he may envy the superior man for his character traits and the way he lives his life, he doesn't have the drive or the discipline to work to develop those same character traits in his own life. Average, or below, is good enough for the inferior man, but not for the superior man.

The superior man understands the way of the world; he knows that there is no such thing as reaching a point of success where he no longer has to strive to be a better man than he was the day before. In life, you are either moving forward, closer to perfection than you were the day before, or you are moving backwards, further away from perfection than you were the day before. There is no neutral ground in the quest for the perfection of your character.

The superior man will always strive to improve himself. He will remain true to his standards, even when those around him do not. He refuses to compromise and lower his standards. Peer pressure is a phrase which has no meaning to him, as he is independent of the thoughts and opinions of others, especially where his actions are concerned. While he walks among other men, his loyalty to his own principles is not dependent on them. He is among them, but not of them.

Chung Yung stated that, "The superior man is watchful over himself even when he is alone." The superior man does not strive for excellence, or the perfection of character, in order to impress other men. His actions are totally independent of others. He lives his life, his way, by his principles, and he does so consistently, whether he is alone or in the presence of kings, thugs, or bums. His concern is only with his own duty and constantly striving for self-improvement in every area of his life. The actions of others do not concern him.

He strives to always remain himself in all of life's situations. The superior man sees the actions of others, and the consequences of their actions, and learns from them, but is not moved by them. He is so devoted to living his life by his own principles, or the code that he has sworn to live by, that nothing can move him to lower his standards.

This cannot be said of the inferior man. The inferior man is not loyal to any code or any set of principles; he merely does what seems best for him in each situation. While this may sound like the same thing that the superior man does, it is distinctly different.

The inferior man does not make his decisions according to certain principles or a code. He decides on the spot, what is best for him, and that is what he does. If the best thing for him is to lie in order to avoid an unpleasant situation, he lies. If the best thing for him is to cheat someone in a business deal, in order to put more money in his pocket, he cheats.

His guiding principle is whatever he perceives is best for him, not what is right. Doing the right thing only crosses his mind when the right thing won't cost him in any way. If he feels that doing what's right will be hard on him, he is completely open to other options. He has no devotion to doing what is right; only to what he believes is right for him personally.

I will continue to discuss the differences between the superior man and the inferior man, but will do so by discussing some of the character traits, which Confucius associated to the superior man, individually, starting with the trait of having a purpose in life.

The Superior Man has a Purpose in Life

The superior man learns in order to
attain to the utmost of his principles.
Confucius

Superior men have a purpose in life. They do not wander aimlessly through life, doing whatever they are on in the mood for at the moment, or wasting their precious time by lazily doing nothing at all. These men are driven; they have goals for their life. And all of their goals fall under one single purpose – to be the best that they can be in every area of their life.

Perfection of character is the common thread, the underlying purpose, which runs through all of their actions. This is not some goal that the superior man obtains and checks off of his list. Instead, this is an ongoing objective that he never quite reaches, but continually strives for until his dying day.

And, this is not a goal which is conspicuously separate from the rest of his life, but rather it permeates every part of his life. All of his thoughts, all of his words, and all of his actions, either bring him closer to the perfection that he seeks, or further away from it. Everything in his life is guided by his quest to perfect his character and live according to his code.

The inferior man, on the other hand, lives life without a true, overriding purpose. While he may have personal goals, these goals are more about the things which make him happy in life, not about character. His goals are more trivial and material, whereas the superior man's goals all adhere to his overall purpose for his life.

Both the inferior man and the superior man may have some goals in common, but those goals will be approached in a distinctly different way. The superior man's goals will always be accomplished in the right way, with the right intention. He will not set his principles aside in order to accomplish one of his goals, because all of his goals fall under the same overriding purpose – to be the best that he can be.

Inferior men are not restrained by such things as honor or integrity. They look at the accomplishment of their goals in the terms of "the ends justify the means," where the superior man sees it as the means must comply with his principles for the ends to truly be meaningful. The goal is only truly accomplished, in a meaningful way, if it is done with honor and integrity. He doesn't see winning by cheating, as truly winning at all. Only an honorable victory is a true victory.

You could look at it like the Super Bowl. The goal for a football team is to win the Super Bowl. If they look at winning the Super Bowl in terms of the ends justify the means, they would be free to cheat, to take cheap shots, and to basically do whatever it takes, no matter what, to win the game. The only thing that would matter to a team with this philosophy is that they get the win at the end of the game. This would be how the inferior man looks at his goals.

The superior man on the other hand, wants to win the Super Bowl just as much as the inferior man, but he puts his principles first. Honor and integrity are his main purposes in life. He is not willing to take the cheap shots or to cheat in order to win, but rather wins by working harder, being better prepared, and playing smarter. He would never lower himself to win by cheating, as in his eyes, that is not really winning at all. There is no pride in achieving a goal by underhanded means.

While both the inferior man and the superior man may both want to win the Super Bowl, they have totally different ways of looking at their goal, and completely different mental attitudes about achieving their objectives. One has a true purpose in life, the other merely has vain goals, and the difference is shown by their thoughts and their actions.

Most average guys do not truly have a clear direction for their life or clear cut goals that guide them in a precise way. Superior men have goals; they have a purpose. They are able to clearly define what they want from life and what kind of man they are committed to becoming. This clarity keeps them focused on their target.

They know why they do what they do. The superior man does not simply go from one crisis to the next, but rather he has a laser-like focus on who and what he wants to be. His intention is to move closer to his ultimate objective daily. The superior man keeps his purpose fresh in his mind for exactly this reason.

To achieve any objective, one has to work towards fulfilling it every day, keeping his intentions focused on what it is that he truly wants to accomplish. It is like this with any goal. Being clear about what you want and why you want it, keeps you motivated and moving forward. No one makes sacrifices to achieve his goals if he isn't clear about what he wants, why he wants it, and why it is important to him. Clarifying your purpose helps keep you motivated and excited.

The superior man lives his life with a solid purpose that underlies all of his other actions. It guides all of his decisions and his choices. He knows why he does what he does. His purpose keeps him driven, motivated, and focused. And because of this, he continually makes strides towards his ultimate goal. This underlying purpose gradually leads him to purity in both his thoughts and actions.

Purity of Thought and Action

We are the masters of our fate, the captains of our souls,
because we have the power to control our thoughts.
Napoleon Hill

Although I will cover the topics of your thoughts and your actions in more detail in later chapters, I do want to touch on these topics now with an emphasis on the differences between the superior man and the inferior man.

Confucius spoke about the need for purity of thought and action, and for good reason. Your thoughts lead to your actions. If your thoughts are not right, your actions won't be right. Things have to be right on the inside in order for them to truly be right on the outside. Since doing the right thing is at the core of the superior man's actions, he must work to purify both his thoughts and his actions.

The superior man takes his thoughts and actions seriously. He monitors both daily to ensure that he is living according to his high standards. Where he finds that he has fallen short, he takes action to improve himself and become a better man tomorrow.

The inferior man sees this exercise as tedious and silly. He doesn't put much emphasis on his thoughts, and as long as his actions do not cause him any issues, he doesn't give them much though either. He simply does whatever occurs to him to be best in each situation, without giving the reason behind his actions much thought. Thus, he merely reacts to each individual situation as it appears.

On the other hand, the superior man acts, instead of reacts. His actions are based on the code which he lives by and not on split second reactions for which he has given little or no thought. The superior man responds; the inferior man reacts.

There is a big difference between responding and reacting. When you respond to something or someone, you are assessing the situation and making a conscious decision about what the correct course of action is, and then you act. Reacting is simply taking action based on your emotions or desires, without really assessing the situation or taking the time to think about what you should do. You just react.

Reacting without thinking is counterproductive to the superior man's ultimate goals. Since he works hard to bring both his thoughts and actions in line with his purpose, he must think before he responds. This ensures that he doesn't go off half-cocked and lose his temper, and does or says things which he will later regret. The superior man understands this and does his best to not allow his emotions to get the best of him by causing him to speak or act without thinking.

When you respond to something or someone, you remain in control, not just of your thoughts, emotions, and actions, but of the situation as well. The superior man responds and maintains control, whereas the inferior man reacts, loses control, and then is left cleaning up his mess later. When a man acts without thinking, it is like shooting for the bull's eye, but not slowing down and taking the time to aim before you shoot.

Responding, instead of reacting, does not come naturally. All men have the same basic thoughts and emotions. The difference is how we learn to control our thoughts and emotions, instead of allowing them to control us. Superior men refuse to allow their thoughts and emotions to control their actions. They make a commitment to themselves to purify their thoughts, control their emotions, and make their actions deliberate, and this leads them to greater personal growth.

Personal Growth

Change your thoughts, and you change your world.
Norman Vincent Peale

Personal growth is vital to the superior man because without daily personal growth, he has no chance of moving towards his ultimate goal of moving closer and closer to the perfection of his character. He seeks out ways to become a better man, not better than his fellow man, but better than he was the day before. Each day, he seeks to improve upon his thoughts and actions of the day before.

He does not look to others to improve his life; he knows that real personal growth, while the seed may be planted by a teacher, coach, or friend, must be cultivated from the inside out, starting with his thoughts. Everything starts with your thoughts.

The superior man is never satisfied with the state of his character; he continually seeks to improve himself. This burning desire to continue to improve himself personally, will not allow the superior man to rest on his laurels and become lethargic in his quest for perfection.

This is not so for the inferior man. He is perfectly satisfied with being good enough. If he has enough in his life to become comfortably numb, then he is more than satisfied. The quest for excellence never really enters his mind, and if it did, he would quickly dismiss it as being unnecessary and too much work.

Excellence is not achieved by accident. There is a reason that men of great drive and achievement are rare – most men are not willing to sacrifice and work for it. It takes discipline and a lot of work. You don't obtain excellence by doing the bare minimum that it takes to get by; you have to constantly endeavor to both achieve it and maintain it.

The superior man understands this, and he makes his own personal growth mandatory. Ordinary is not good enough for him, he strives to be extraordinary. Confucius stated, "The superior man demands it of himself; the inferior man, of others."

The Same but Different

By nature men are pretty much alike;
it is learning and practice that set them apart.
Confucius

The superior man and the inferior man, by nature, are very much alike, but by nurture, they are very different. The man of the code is a superior man. He not only does his best to integrate into his life the virtues that Confucius admired and held in high esteem, but he makes those virtues a part of his very being. He lives them daily. He practices them until they become an integral part of his very being.

He lives life with the purpose of perfecting his character in every way. He carries himself with poise and dignity, no matter what he is doing or with whom he may be associating. The superior man is sincere in his thoughts, words and actions, thus he consistently practices purity of thought and action. He ensures that his intentions are honest and sincere. To profess a belief in something and then not to live it, is dishonest and insincere.

This man values the truth, but at the same time, he is open-minded enough to know that not everyone sees the same truth that he sees. He understands that it doesn't matter whether or not others agree with the truth that he lives by; what matters is that he is true to his principles and his honor. Having such conviction in his way of life, he is self-controlled and composed.

His self-sufficiency comes from knowing that he is in charge of his life, that he will live by his principles, no matter what anyone else thinks or how anyone else lives their life. Superior men are firm in their convictions.

He is kind to those he meets, understanding that everyone has his or her own struggles in life. The superior man is generous and helps as many people as he can, but always puts his own family first. He is competent and thorough in all that he does. This does not mean that he is an expert at everything, but rather that he seeks to do his best at everything which he attempts.

The superior man understands that all men have certain duties, and those duties dictate his priorities in life. He lives by the law of reciprocity and will not take without giving back, knowing that men of honor always repay their debts, whether it is a financial debt or a small kindness that someone does for him.

A man of the code is a superior man, not in the sense that he sees himself as better than the average or inferior man, but in the sense that he lives his life by higher standards than others. He actively develops these character traits by disciplining himself. He molds himself into the kind of man that he alone decides he will be, independent of the opinions or actions of others. His reward is in knowing that, in every situation, he does the best that he can do.

This by no means is meant to say that he is a perfect man. Perfection is what he strives for, but no man ever achieves total perfection. There will be days when he falls short of his goal. There will be times when he loses his temper, when he is out of sorts, when he allows irritations to get to him, but these days become fewer as he continues to work on perfecting his character.

Remember, the superior man is not in competition with anyone else; his competition is his former self, the man he was the day before, the month before, the year before. The point is that he is aware of his weaknesses and strives to improve them, taking inventory of how he is doing along the way and what he needs to improve on. His goal is always just out of reach, but he continues to move towards it daily.

On the other hand, the inferior man rarely thinks about these virtues. I am not saying that the average guy is a bad man, not at all. What I am saying is that the average guy, simply by his lack of discipline, is by definition not at the same level of the superior man. This is not meant to be disrespectful or snobbish, but just factual.

Look at it this way, the average guy may go to the gym a couple of times a week and lift weights, but that in no way makes him equal to a professional bodybuilder. The professional bodybuilder is vastly superior to the average guy, when it comes to his dedication, time, and success in the gym. This doesn't mean that there is anything inherently wrong with how the average guy uses his time. It merely means that when it comes to that area of his life, he is not on the same level as the bodybuilder.

That is how you should look at the superior man. He has dedicated himself to his principles and his endeavors, and to the perfection of his character. Inferior men don't. That is their decision. Some men strive for excellence and some don't; superior men do. It is a personal decision, but one that men of the code take seriously.

How Confucius Distinguished the Superior Man from the Inferior Man:

- Superior men avoid the intoxicated.
- The superior man is satisfied and composed; the inferior man is always full of distress.
- The superior man does not set his mind either for anything or against anything; what is right, he will follow.
- The superior man never trusts in appearances.
- A superior man makes his own decisions; an inferior man follows public opinion.
- The superior man demands it of himself; the inferior man, of others.
- The superior man is in all the circumstances of his life, exempt from prejudices and obstinacy; he regulates himself by justice alone.
- The superior man must always remain himself in all situations of life.
- A superior man first practices what he preaches, and then preaches what he practices.
- The superior man thinks of virtue; the inferior man thinks of comfort.
- A superior man is he whose virtues exceed his talents.
- Superior men are always bold, but those who are always bold are not always superior men.
- The superior man has neither anxiety nor fear.
- In regards to his language, the superior man is never careless in any respect.
- The superior man keeps his mind on his own duties.
- The superior man understands what is right; the inferior man understands what will sell.
- The superior man is quiet and calm.
- The superior man is modest in his speech, but exceeds in his actions.
- A superior man cannot be changed by poverty. An inferior man will do anything when he's poor.

- The superior man considers morality fundamental, follows the proper etiquette in his practice of it, uses humble words to express it, and devotes all his mental and physical energies to attain it.
- The superior man wouldn't recommend or promote a person based only on his words, nor would he ignore a man's words because of his behavior.
- The superior man treats others generously without currying favor. The inferior man curries favor from others instead of treating them generously.

According to Confucius, the superior man is one with ideal characteristics who exemplifies a man of excellence. The above list of teachings, concerning the superior man and the inferior man, is certainly not exhaustive; Confucius had much more to say on the subject. But for our purposes, I believe that this list, and what I have written in this chapter, gives you a pretty good picture of the character of the superior man.

In *Men of the Code*, I will use the terms superior man, man of honor, man of the code, and the real man synonymously. None of these terms are meant to be offensive to those men who do not live their lives in the same way as men of the code.

When I refer to a "real man," I am simply referring to men who have internalized the character traits of what Confucius called the superior man. The real man is the ideal man, a man of honor, character, integrity, courage, and action. He is a man's man, but at the same time, he is a lady's man as well.

The *real man* is the type of man that society idolizes in movies as the classic hero archetype; he constantly strives to improve himself and his character. He is never satisfied with the status quo. He lives his life by the Japanese philosophy of kaizen, which means constant, never-ending improvement. He is a superior man in every way.

In the next chapter, I will summarize the characteristics of a real man. You will notice that most of these character traits are also traits which Confucius attributed to the superior man. Even though they share many of the same qualities, Confucius' "superior man" and the modern ideal of the "real man" are not identical. That being said, the model of the "real man" is most certainly the superior man of our times.

Reflections for the Superior Man

The small man gossips. The average man lets him.
The great man stays silent and allows what
is said of him to make him greater.
Stephen Mansfield

To be pleased with one's limits is a wretched state.
Johann Wolfgang von Goethe

Great spirits have always encountered opposition from mediocre minds.
The mediocre mind is incapable of understanding the man who
refuses to bow blindly to conventional prejudices and chooses
instead to express his opinions courageously and honestly.
Albert Einstein

You must be the change
you want to see in the world.
Gandhi

Eagles fly alone, but sheep flock together.
Polish Proverb

The wisest men follow their own direction.
Euripides

Whenever you find that you are on the side
of the majority, it is time to reform.
Mark Twain

The man who in view of gain thinks of righteousness;
who in the view of danger is prepared to give up his life; and
who does not forget an old agreement, however far back it extends –
such a man may be reckoned a complete man.
Confucius

Adversity toughens manhood, and the characteristics of the
good or the great man is not that he has been exempt from
the evils of life, but that he has surmounted them.
Patrick Henry

Never do anything against conscience,
even if the state demands it.
Albert Einstein

Chapter 4

The Characteristics of a Real Man

Let them know a real man,
who lives as he was meant to live.
Marcus Aurelius

Aren't All Men Real Men?

Excellence is a state concerned with choice.
Aristotle

I would like to start this chapter off by stating that the term, "real man" is not meant to be offensive. It is not meant to say that men who do not live by the principles laid out in this book are somehow not men. As I stated earlier, the term "real man" is meant to be interchangeable with a man of honor, Confucius' idea of the superior man, and with a man of the code, nothing more.

It is not a term that insinuates snobbery or elitism. Real men do not look down on others or think that they are better than their fellow man. It is not about ego gratification or developing a feeling of superiority. The term "real man" as used in this book, is meant to refer to the ideal man, a man who lives his life by his principles, and does so with self-confidence and courage.

At this point, you may be asking, "If a guy is not a real man, what is he?" And that is a good question to ask. A real man is a man that lives his life by a certain code of conduct. He understands who and what he is, and he works daily to improve himself. He is a mature man. By a mature man, I don't mean that he is older; age has nothing to do with being a real man.

I mean that he is mature in terms of his mind and his spirit. He lives his life with a purpose. Real men know what they stand for and what they won't stand for in life.

Being a real man has nothing to do with being male. In the English language, the terms male and man are synonymous, but I would like to challenge you to see the term "man" as having more meaning than simply being a male human being. There are a lot of male human beings which I don't consider to be real men at all. It takes much more than just reaching a certain age to be considered a real man.

We hear the phrases, "Be a man" or "Man up" quite often in our society, but we rarely stop to think about what those phrases actually mean. These two phrases actually suggest that there is more to being a man than simply being born with male sex organs.

Think about it. If you tell another guy to "Be a man," there has to be more to being a man than what he already is. After all, he is already a male human being. If there is not more to being a man than being a male then that phrase is ridiculous, and yet, it has meaning to everyone who hears it.

When you hear someone say to another guy, "Man up and be a man!" what does it mean to you? I bet you answered something along the lines of, it means that he should get some backbone, be tough, be courageous, be brave, and have some self-confidence, etcetera. This is what those phrases mean to most people who hear them.

But wait, what about the argument that if you are a male human being, you are already a man? There is a difference between being a real man and being a male human being. Subconsciously, we know that. That is why we hear the phrase "be a man" to start with, and why when we hear that phrase, we know what it is referring to. There is much more to being a real man than being born a male!

To further illustrate my point, if being a man is simply being a male human being, why do we not refer to boys as men? We refer to young males as boys until after their 18th birthday. Why is that? When he goes to bed, he is a boy; when he wakes up, he is a man. Does this really make sense?

In many cultures, boys are not considered men until they successfully go through a rite of passage. After they complete this rite of passage, they have earned the right to be called men. Becoming a man is not something that just happens because a boy reaches a certain age; he earns it by his actions.

This is something that we have lost in our modern culture. There is no rite of passage anymore. Boys simply become known as men after they turn eighteen. But think about it, what has changed from one day to the next? Is a boy all of a sudden a mature man of character simply because of his chronological age? Well, he is assumed to be in our society.

Once a boy turns eighteen, he is tried as an adult if he commits a crime; he suddenly has legal rights that he did not have the day before, and has much harsher consequences for any mistakes that he makes from that point on. He literally goes from being a boy to being a "man" overnight. There seems to be something missing in that sequence. How could 24 hours make that much of a difference?

What happened to all of a sudden turn the boy into a man? Is there any logic behind this or is it merely a random age decided upon by those who get to make the rules? Is this system even fair to the boy?

These are questions that we should consider. For instance, if a boy is 17 years, 11 months old, and he commits some stupid crime, say for instance he gets arrested for drugs, that charge is wiped off his permanent record in four weeks. If the same boy commits the same exact crime one month later, he is arrested and tried as an adult, and the crime stays on his permanent record for the rest of his life. Is this system fair? What changed in this boy's life, over that four week period, which justifies this difference in punishment?

It seems that becoming a man in our society means little more than being one day older than you were the day before. Is this truly all there is to manhood? Shouldn't there be much more to being a real man than reaching a certain age? In my opinion, there should be, and there is.

This is why I make the distinction between being an adult male and being a real man. There is an ancient Celtic maxim which states, "That which your father conferred on you, earn it anew if you want to possess it." You don't automatically become a man because you are one day older, or because you reach any age at all; that is nothing more than the legal definition of being a legal adult. Being a real man entails much more than that.

The Foundation of a Real Man

To compose our character is our duty.
Montaigne

Being a real man is something that originates in your spirit and in your mind, not something that is automatically conferred on you legally by the government. And it is not something that most boys come by naturally; it has to be taught by someone who understands the foundations of what it means to be a real man.

What are the foundations of a real man? The answer boils down to one thing – the principles by which he lives his life. Real men throughout the world have certain principles or character traits by which they live, and it is their dedication to these principles that separates the real man, or superior man, from boy, or inferior man. These principles are the foundation of all real men. They have internalized these virtues and principles and have made them their own – a part of who they truly are.

Real men are men of the code. They have a code that they live by, even if they haven't physically taken the time to put it into writing. These are men of high standards, and they refuse to lower their standards for any reason, because to do so would be an act of betrayal to themselves and who they truly are.

The real man lives his life independently. His dedication to his principles is not based on the current culture or what is considered acceptable by the majority. He couldn't care less about the majority's opinions, when it comes to the principles that he lives by and the standards that he holds dear; they are not up for debate or discussion.

A man can only have this kind of confidence in his principles if he has a solid foundation, a foundation which must be taught. Ideally, this foundation will be put in place at an early age and reinforced throughout his life. But that doesn't mean that you cannot become a real man if, for whatever reason, you did not have the proper role models in your life when you were younger.

It is never too late to make a firm decision to live the rest of your life as a man of honor. No matter what you have done or how you have lived your life in the past, every day offers you a new chance to start anew. Whether you live your life as a superior man, a man of honor and integrity, or as an inferior man who never lives up to his potential, the choice is always yours and yours alone.

One thing is certain, if you are not the man that you want to be, then *you* have to do something to change that. Nobody is going to do it for you; this is a personal decision that only you can make.

Becoming a Real Man

Stop talking about what the good man is like, and just be one.
Marcus Aurelius

Aristotle stated that, "Men acquire a particular quality by constantly acting a particular way." This is true. Habits are formed by repeating the same action over and over again until that action has formed deep roots in your life. The more you do something, the stronger those roots become. It only takes 30 days to change any habit, or to form a new one.

If you want to become the man that you were meant to be, you have to start developing the habits of a real man. You must start cultivating the character traits of a man of honor. This will take effort and constant vigilance on your part, but the reward is well worth it. Nothing of real value comes without a price.

Being a real man comes from a deep understanding of the virtues which make a man, a man of honor. These virtues or character traits must be cultivated in the same way that you would cultivate a garden. First, you have to prepare the soil (your mind) and make it ready for the seeds that you are about to plant. You have to make a firm decision that you will live your life by your principles, no matter what. After you have prepared the soil (made this decision), you are ready to plant the seeds.

The seeds that you plant in your garden will be the seeds of the character traits that you have decided to live by – honor, integrity, endurance and fortitude, right actions, respect, courtesy, truth, justice, dignity, sincerity, discipline, self-reliance, dedication to what is right, self-confidence, your duties, responsibility, wisdom, knowledge, courage, bravery, kindness, preparedness, insight, filial duty, and loyalty.

These seeds must not only be planted in good soil, but they have to be watered and weeded in order for them to flourish. You water the seeds of virtue by keeping your principles fresh in your mind, by studying them and meditating on their value in your life. You have to nurture them by practicing these virtues in your everyday life. These are not traits that you pick and choose when you will live by them and when you won't. They must become a part of you, who you truly are.

You must also keep your garden weeded; weeds can easily overtake a garden which is uncared for. These weeds that you should watch out for are those vices that you have a weakness for in your life, associating with the wrong people, laziness, selfishness, jealousy, anger, hatred, and being influenced by the opinions of those who do not value your principles.

Study the lives of other real men. Study the wisdom of men of honor and let their teachings motivate you. It takes time, discipline and a lot of persistent work to develop the virtues of a superior man. Building your character is not an overnight project; it is a lifelong mission. You will have good days and bad days, but the important thing is that you never quit.

The vast majority of guys never consider what it means to be a real man, yet they desperately struggle to be different and stand out from the crowd. They want so much to find themselves and to be unique and special, yet their misguided efforts leave them feeling like there has to be something that they are missing.

The character traits of the real man are what they long for, but without a real man to teach them, they rarely figure this out on their own. Dare to be independent and different! Stand out from the crowd and be a real man. Create your own code and live by it every day.

A Man

A man doesn't whine at his losses,
A man doesn't whimper and fret,
Or rail at the weight of his crosses
And ask life to rear him a pet.
A man doesn't grudgingly labor
Or look upon toil as a blight;
A man doesn't sneer at his neighbor
Or sneak from a cause that is right.

A man doesn't sulk when another
Succeeds where his efforts have failed;
Doesn't keep all his praise for the brother
Whose glory is publicly hailed;
And pass by the weak and the humble
As though they were not of his clay;
A man doesn't ceaselessly grumble
When things are not going his way.

A man looks on woman as tender
And gentle, and stands at her side
At all times to guard and defend her,
And never to scorn or deride.
A man looks on life as a mission.
To serve, just so far as he can;
A man holds his noblest ambition
On earth is to live as a man.

Edgar A. Guest

The Manly Man

The world has room for the manly man,
    with the spirit of manly cheer;
The world delights in the man who smiles
    while his eyes hold back the tear;
It loves the man, who when things are wrong,
    can take his place and stand
With his face to the fight and his eyes to the light,
    and toil with a willing hand;
The manly man is the country's need and the moments
    need, forsooth,
With a heart that beats to the pulsing troop of the lilied
    leagues of truth
The world is his and it waits for him, and it leaps to hear
    the ring
Of the blow he strikes and the wheels he turns and the
    hammers he dares to swing;
It likes the forward look on his face, the poise of his
    noble head,
And the onward lunge of his tireless will and the sweep
    of his dauntless tread!
Hurray for the manly man who comes,
    with sunlight on his face,
And the strength to do and the will to dare
    and the courage to find his place.
The world delights in the manly man,
    and the weak and evil flee
When the manly man goes forth to hold his own
    on land or sea.

Author unknown

A Real Man

Men are of two kinds, and he
Was of the kind I'd like to be.
Some preach their virtues, and a few
Express their lives by what they do.
That sort was he. No flowery phrase
Or glibly spoken words of praise
Won friends for him. He wasn't cheap
Or shallow, but his course ran deep,
And it was pure. You know the kind.
Not many in a life you find
Whose deeds outrun their words so far
That more than what they seem they are.

There are two kinds of lies as well:
The kind you live, the ones you tell.
Back through his years from age to youth
He never acted one untruth.
Out in the open light he fought
And didn't care what others thought
Nor what they said about his fight
If he believed he was right.
The only deeds he ever hid
Were acts of kindness that he did.

What speech he had was plain and blunt
His was an unattractive front.
Yet children loved him; babe and boy
Played with the strength he could employ,
Without one fear, and they are fleet
To sense injustice and deceit.
No back door gossip linked his name
With any shady tale of shame.
He did not have to compromise
With evil-doers, shrewd and wise,
And let them ply their vicious trade
Because of some past escapade.

Men are of two kinds, and he
Was of the kind I'd like to be.
No door at which he ever knocked
Against his manly form was locked.
If ever man on earth was free

And independent, it was he.
No broken pledge lost him respect,
He met all men with hear erect,
And when he passed, I think there went
A soul to yonder firmament.
So white, so splendid and so fine
It came almost to God's design.

Edgar A. Guest

Reflections for the Superior Man

He who postpones the hour of living rightly is like the
rustic who waits for the river to run out before he crosses.
Horace

Men acquire a particular quality by
constantly acting a particular way.
Aristotle

Think like a man of action;
act like a man of thought.
Henri Bergson

Know the value of time; snatch, seize, and enjoy every
moment of it. No idleness; no laziness; no procrastination;
never put off till tomorrow what you can do today.
Lord Chesterfield

Whoso would be a man must be a nonconformist.
Ralph Waldo Emerson

Hold yourself responsible for a higher standard
than anybody expects of you. Never excuse yourself.
Henry Ward Beecher

Lay down for yourself, at the outset, a certain stamp and
type of character for yourself, which you are to maintain
whether you are by yourself or are meeting with people.
Epictetus

It is not the critic who counts; not the man who points out how the strong
man stumbles, or where the doer of deeds could have done them better. The
credit belongs to the man who is actually in the arena, whose face is marred
by dust and sweat and blood; who strives valiantly; who errs, who comes
short again and again, because there is no effort without error and
shortcoming; but who does actually strive to do the deeds; who knows great
enthusiasms, the great devotions; who spends himself in a worthy cause; who
at the best knows in the end the triumph of high achievement, and who at the
worst, if he fails, at least fails while daring greatly, so that his place shall
never be with those cold and timid souls who neither know victory nor
defeat.
Theodore Roosevelt

Chapter 5

Character and Excellence

*The man of principle never forgets what he is,
because of what others are.*
Baltasar Gracian

Character and Reputation

If an urn lacks the characteristics of an urn, how can we call it an urn?
Confucius

I have already discussed how the superior man or the real man lives life according to his own principles, and I have touched on some of the virtues which compose the principles by which men of the code live. In this chapter, I want to discuss why it is important to have a code or a set of principles that guide your life, and talk about exactly what character, standards, and principles are.

Character is the distinctive qualities that make a man who he truly is deep down inside. Your character is made up of all the qualities that have been deeply ingrained in your mind and spirit. It is your character that determines how you respond to life's challenges and irritations, to both your victories and defeats.

A man of good character is a man who has developed good character traits in his life and who lives by those traits or virtues. In contrast, a man of bad character is a man who has developed bad character traits and gives little or no thought to developing virtuous character traits in his life.

The specific character traits that you develop, and live by, determine what kind of man you are. Your actions will reveal your character, and the kind of man that you are will determine your reputation for the most part. But reputation and character are not the same thing.

Your reputation is what others think of you; your character is what you truly are. Reputations can be manipulated; character can only be developed. While you have some control over how others see you, you have total control over your true character. You never have total control over your reputation because others can and do lie about other people in an attempt to damage their reputation. You have very little control over what other people believe.

And while your reputation is important, it is not as important as what you are. A man can only control what is in his power to control. You always have control over your character; you seldom have control over what others believe about your character.

D. L. Moody urged us to quit focusing on our reputation and simply take care of our character, stating, "If I take care of my character, my reputation will take care of itself." While this is true in the end, your reputation can take a beating from time to time because other people will maliciously attack your reputation for personal reasons. It is a given that bad people will do bad things, and one of the things that they will do is besmirch your reputation.

Your job is to take care of your character. If your character is solid, then eventually the truth will be evident. Sooner or later your reputation will sync up with your true character. Your actions speak louder than words, and the lies that others tell about you cannot stand up to the truth of your actions. That's assuming that you have developed your character and are living like a man of honor to start with. Bad men have a bad reputation for a reason – they are bad. They have earned their reputation.

Although good men may have their reputation dragged through the mud by those with ill intentions, it is usually only those with questionable character themselves, who actually believe such gossip. Superior men do not trust gossip or malicious hearsay; they take the time to look behind the veil and find the truth. Therefore, they rarely put any stock in reputations, but rather they prefer to observe and make up their own minds.

You may be starting to think that your reputation is not important, but that is not entirely correct. You want to maintain a good reputation, as far as it is in your power to do so, but that is not always possible. What is always possible is to make sure that you deserve a good reputation. As Emerson wrote, "What I must do is all that concerns me, not what the people think."

Both your reputation and your character are important, but they are not equal in value. While it is nice to have a good reputation, it is vital to have a good character. Your reputation is who others *think* you are; your character is who you and God *know* you are. I think it is fairly easy to determine which one of those carries the most weight.

Your character is the foundation of all the other parts of being a man of the code. Without a solid foundation, it is easy for you to veer off track in one way or another. For this reason, it is vital that you adhere to the highest standards. Don't compromise where your character is concerned. Work to build a solid character and maintain a reputation which is true to your nature as a superior man.

This brings us to the question of how you compose your character. How does a person develop a set of qualities or traits in his life that sets him apart from the common man? Where do you start? This can be an especially tricky question if one does not have background knowledge concerning what comprises good character traits, or if one has failed to live a life filled with these positive qualities over the years.

Composing Your Character

For a man of substance, there ought to always be
more on the inside than on the outside.
Baltasar Gracian

The best way to start to compose your character, or to change your character if need be, is to study the traits which you want to incorporate into your life. Study the traits of the superior men of the past. What made these men "men of character?" Why do you admire them? What traits set them apart in your mind? By studying the lives of warriors, sages, and men of character, you can get a good picture of what it takes to be a man of character – a superior man.

These men sought to live lives of honor and integrity. They took life seriously and lived life to the fullest, at the same time, they did so without compromising their character. These men were not perfect. Nobody is perfect. They simply worked at being men of character. They made a firm decision about the way they were going to live their lives and followed through with that decision.

When they found that they had fallen short, or had faults that needed to be corrected or removed, they made the effort to make the necessary changes. Everyone falls short on this quest. The key is to not give up when you miss the mark. When you are sighting in your rifle and you miss the bull's eye, you don't give up; you simply adjust your sights and refine your technique until you are able to place your shots where you want them to be.

The same principle applies to the development of your character. When you miss the mark or find that you have a habit that is not in sync with the person that you want to be, you should simply make the necessary changes to bring your actions into harmony with the character that you want to cultivate.

This is an ongoing process. Although you may develop your character to that of a superior man, you will never reach a point where you will not have to make adjustments from time to time.

Don't give up, even when you fail miserably, and there will be days when you do fail miserably. Losing a battle is not the same thing as losing the war. You have to be in this for the long run. The perfection of your character is a life-long quest, but one which every real man pursues. Voltaire pointed out that, "Perfection is attained by slow degrees; she requires the hand of time." The same goes for the development of your character.

You never quite reach perfection, no matter how much you try. Be patient with yourself, especially when you fail to live up to the standards which you are striving to achieve. Don't allow frustration over your failures to cause you to throw in the towel on your goal to become a man of excellence. We are all human and we all make mistakes.

After you have studied the traits of the superior man, you have to put those traits into action. Study, alone, is useless if it doesn't manifest in positive actions.

You must take the time to decide what character traits are important to you and then start to create your own personal code. *Men of the Code* is the perfect guide to help you create your own code of honor by which you will live your life, but it certainly should not be your only source. There are dozens of books on wisdom and character, and you should continually study them, take what resonates with you for your life, and leave behind what doesn't.

The appendix has several examples of codes that will give you a good idea concerning how to write your own. And by the time you get to that point in this book, you will already have an abundance of information that will have you well on your way to composing your own code.

Aiming for Excellence

Excellence is not a skill. It is an attitude.
Ralph Marston

A man of the code is a man of excellence. Excellence is the quality of being outstanding and superior. That is what men of the code aim for in their life. They aren't satisfied being like the average guy on the street, who just goes through life without any real direction or purpose. Superior men constantly strive to improve themselves.

That is what being a man of the code is all about – being the very best man that you can be. Anyone can just get by in life; that is no great accomplishment. But the superior man has higher aspirations. Ordinary is simply not good enough. He has developed a drive that pushes him to be extraordinary.

Excellence is not for the masses. Most people do not have the drive to constantly endeavor to improve themselves; they are completely satisfied being average, going to work, coming home, eating, watching television, and going to bed, only to get up and go through the same routine day after day until they can retire and do little to nothing with the rest of their lives. This is not the attitude of the superior man.

The superior man knows that every day is another chance to be a better man than he was the day before. Every day brings the opportunity to gain more knowledge, to increase his wisdom, to perfect his skills in his chosen profession, and to once again live life to the fullest.

Pursuing excellence is an attitude that you consciously cultivate. It is not a natural state of being, but a lifestyle that you have to deliberately develop until it becomes your second nature.

As I stated earlier, the Japanese have a term called kaizen, which means constant, never-ending improvement. This is what the superior man should strive for in every area of his life – constant, never-ending improvement. No matter how well you have mastered any skill, there is always room for at least a little more improvement. This is how men of the code approach everything in life.

The vast majority of people in this world merely do the minimum. Their attitude seems to be that good enough is good enough. But good enough doesn't cut it for the superior man; he seeks perfection and excellence. This doesn't mean that everything that he does will be done to perfection, but he will at least try his best to do everything to the best of his ability. He puts his whole heart into whatever he may be working on at the time.

This is something that you must require of yourself. Nobody is going to make you live a life of excellence. Nobody is going to hound you to be the best that you can be in life. This is a choice that you have to make. Excellence is a way of life. Hold yourself to a higher standard than anyone else expects of you.

Holding yourself to a higher standard is a great way to start being a man of excellence. Like I stated, living a life of excellence is a choice, nobody else is going to hold you to this standard; it is totally up to you. You have to be the one that holds yourself to this higher standard. It takes a firm decision that you will live your life, by your principles, regardless of what anyone else thinks about it.

If you continually do this, you will soon find that your life is full of excellence in ways that you may not even realize. Others will see it and recognize you as a man of excellence, and it will become a part of your overall reputation, which is a great reputation to have.

Excellence has to become the prevailing attitude in your life. It actually does have to become a habit, and, as with everything else in life, you have to start from where you are. Start small and continue to build this attitude in your life. You don't decide to start martial arts training one day, and enter the ring with expert fighters the next week. It takes time, it takes work and it takes consistent training. The same principle applies to anything you do in life. Nobody becomes an expert at anything overnight.

Although you can't change overnight, you can start changing immediately. The first thing you have to change is the way that you think. Your thoughts are the beginning of your actions; therefore it is vital that you get your mind straight first. If your mind is not right, you will never be able to become a man of excellence.

Excellence is not something that you fake in order to build your reputation; it is an attitude and a way of life. This attitude of excellence has to be refined over time. There are no short cuts. It is not something that you can buy or that anyone can give you.

It is the way of the superior man, the way of the warrior. Each of the character traits of the man of the code can be traced back to living a life of excellence. The common man lives mainly for his own comfort and gives little attention to pushing himself to go the "extra mile" in order to live a life of excellence. Simply put, he is satisfied living an average life.

The man of the code is always contented with his life, but never completely satisfied. By that, I mean that he is at peace with his circumstances and where he is in his life at the present moment, but he is always motivated to improve both his current circumstances and his life as a whole. He constantly strives to be better.

You have to choose excellence as an act of your will. Choosing to live a life of excellence is pretty simple – you merely choose to do so. Actually living a life of excellence, on the other hand, takes a lot of effort and discipline. The catch is you then have to discipline yourself to actually follow through.

Many people make half-hearted decisions to achieve one goal or another, every year, but very few of them follow through on their resolutions. They start out very motivated, but soon allow distractions to sidetrack them from their goals. Think about it. How many New Year's resolutions have you actually stuck to over the long run?

People that don't complete their goals, never really made a real commitment to follow through; they merely made a decision to try. When you say that you will *try* to do something, you are leaving yourself an out. In the words of the old Jedi master, Yoda, "Try not, do." Don't *try* to live a life of excellence – LIVE A LIFE OF EXCELLENCE.

You have to commit to changing your life and living a life of character and excellence. It does no good to *want* to be a man of the code or to *wish* that you were a man of the code; you have to *be* a man of the code.

Starting with chapter six, I will explore the specific character traits that all men of the code hold to be important. There are certain virtues that men of excellence share. These virtues are found throughout the world, in different cultures and in different time periods. Sages and wise men, from the earliest recorded writings up through the current age, have praised the value of these virtues and the men who incorporate these virtues into their lives.

As I discuss each one of these character traits, it would profit you to think about how you can integrate that specific trait into your daily life. This is part of developing your own personal code. Take notes regarding your thoughts as you read. Highlight anything that resonates strongly with your spirit so you can come back to that passage and reflect further on what it means to you.

If you have not been living a life of excellence, you should read the remaining chapters of *Men of the Code* as if you are constructing your new life, the life that you want to start living from this point forward. That is exactly what you will be doing if you are serious about changing your life. That choice is totally in your hands.

Remember, you only live this life once; don't sell yourself short. Don't allow laziness, apathy, or the distractions of everyday life to cause you to shortchange yourself. Time is very deceptive and passes by much faster than you realize.

Make a decision today to live every single day of your life to the fullest, with honor and integrity. Day by day, you build your character, either good or bad, and that character becomes both your destiny and your legacy. Choose wisely.

Reflections for the Superior Man

Let me tell you something you already know. The world ain't all sunshine and rainbows. It's a very mean and nasty place, and I don't care how tough you are, it will beat you to your knees and keep you there permanently if you let it. You, me, or nobody is gonna hit as hard as life. But it ain't about how hard you hit. It's about how hard you can get hit and keep moving forward; how much you can take and keep moving forward. That's how winning is done! Now, if you know what you're worth, then go out and get what you're worth. But you gotta be willing to take the hits, and not pointing fingers saying you ain't where you wanna be because of him, or her, or anybody. Cowards do that and that ain't you. You're better than that!
Rocky Balboa to his son

Excellence is to do a common thing in an uncommon way.
Booker T. Washington

I pay no attention whatsoever to anybody's praise or blame.
I simply follow my own feelings.
Wolfgang Amadeus Mozart

Every man is the architect of his own fortune.
Sallust

It is no easy thing for a principle to become a man's own
unless each day he maintains it and works it out in his own life.
Epictetus

Every man who is truly a man must learn to be alone in the
midst of all others, and if need be, against all others.
Romain Rolland

For when moral value is considered, the concern is not the actions,
which are seen, but rather their inner principles, which are not seen,
Immanuel Kant

Our true character silently underlies all our words and actions,
as the granite underlies the other strata.
Henry David Thoreau

The quality of a person's life is in direct proportion to their commitment
to excellence, regardless of their chosen field of endeavor.
Vince Lombardi

Chapter 6

Honor

Our own heart, and not other
men's opinion, forms our true honor.
Samuel Coleridge

What Honor Truly Is

Honor is simply the morality of superior men.
Henry Louis Mencken

Honor is an intense sense of right and wrong, and the adherence to the actions and principles that a man deems right. In the past, a man's honor was considered something that had to be defended, even to the death. Men fought duels to the death to defend what they declared to be an insult to their honor, or to put it in today's terms, being disrespected.

Noblemen and warriors, both in the East and in the West, considered it part of their duty to defend their honor, especially if they felt that someone had disrespected them or challenged their honor in some way. And, these men took drastic measures to defend their honor.

In many cases, these duels were not about honor at all, but more about someone's wounded pride. To fight to the death over some small insult or misunderstanding is not truly defending your honor, but rather defending your pride. The vast majority of these duels of *honor* were more about defending the man's reputation, not his honor.

Honor is not something that you have to defend by fighting other men, but you do have to fight for it nonetheless. You have to fight to keep your honor daily. Almost every day of your life, you will have opportunities to turn your back on your honor by choosing actions that are dishonorable in one way or another.

The fight to maintain your honor is an internal battle, not an external one. Honor is not something that anyone else can take away from you, but it is something that you can lose. It is totally up to you to maintain your honor. There is an old saying that if you are willing to sell your honor, you will always find a buyer, and this is very true. There will always be temptations for the man of the code to give up his honor and lower his standards, but the superior man will not give in to these temptations. He values his honor too much to lose it.

As the quote at the beginning of this chapter stated, honor resides in your own heart; other people's opinions about your honor are meaningless. Only you truly know whether you are an honorable man or not. No one else can see into your heart. No one else knows the true intentions behind your actions.

If honor is formed and resides inside of your heart, how can anyone else ever take it away from you? And, if no other man can take it away from you, how is it possible that you would have to defend your honor from others?

The answer to these questions is that no one can take your honor from you and therefore, you do not have to defend your honor. As I stated, honor is something that you maintain internally; it is not something that you have to defend from others. Now, you may have to defend your reputation, but your reputation is not the same thing as your honor.

Your reputation is simply what other people think you are, not what you truly are. It is how people perceive you, which has nothing to do with who you truly are. The opinions of others do not make you a man of the code and they do not keep you from being a man of the code. Your thoughts, actions, and intentions make you a man of the code. And those are all things which you have control over.

Likewise, your honor is solely dependent upon you. You are the only person on this earth who can make the decision to live by a code of honor, and you are the only person who can decide that you will act outside of your code of honor.

Socrates stated, "The greatest way to live with honor in this world is to be what we pretend to be." Men of the code should not have to pretend at all. Their thoughts and their actions should be in sync with each other. They should not think one way and act another in some attempt to impress those around them. Men of honor are sincere in their thoughts and their actions and have no need to impress other people.

Honor originates in your mind. As you think, you become. But you can't just think about being honorable; you have to act on those thoughts. Honor is both in your thoughts and in your actions. If you merely think honorably, but never act on those thoughts, can you truly be a man of honor? Your actions are a vital part of your honor.

At the same time, it is not enough to simply perform the right actions and give the appearance of being a man of honor. A man of honor has to be sincere. His actions not only have to be right, but the intentions behind his actions must be right as well.

Actions, Intentions and Honor

The difference between a moral man and a man of
honor is that the latter regrets a discreditable act,
even when it has worked and he has not been caught.
H. L. Mencken

You have to make up your own mind to live a life of honor. It is this decision which makes you a superior man. Only you know for sure if your actions are truly honorable. Of course there are actions which anyone can tell are dishonorable such as robbing someone in a dark alley. I am not talking about those types of actions. I am referring to actions which only you know your true intentions.

It is the intentions behind your actions which determine whether or not your actions are honorable. Sometimes this is not easily ascertained by other people. Francesco Guicciardini demonstrated this fact very well in the following example from his book *Maxims and Reflections*. He wrote, "There is a difference between a brave man and one who faces danger out of regard for honor. Both recognize danger; but the former believes he can defend himself against it, and if he did not, he would not face it. The latter may even fear the danger more than he should, but he stands firm – not because he is unafraid but because he has decided he would rather suffer harm than shame."

In this example, an onlooker would not be able to visibly see the difference in the actions of these two men. It is only the men themselves who would truly know whether or not their actions were honorable. And it is not just the rare, dangerous conflicts which test your honor.

How you handle the smaller, more common challenges, also reveals your sense of honor, maybe even more so than the more dangerous situations. Compromising your honor in the small, daily conflicts is sometimes more tempting than in the larger, more serious conflicts. It is during these times, that your true character will be tested and you come to realize what honor means to you.

These situations require as much resolve and courage as the more serious ones. I'm talking about times when doing the right thing could cost you money or your job. At these times, your life may not be on the line, but your honor is nonetheless. Your job, your money, your car, and your home can all be taken away from you, but your honor is yours to keep or to lose. It takes a lot of courage to choose your honor over your financial security. During these times you learn how serious you are about your honor.

Many people have honorable intentions to begin with, but when it comes to standing for what they believe, their courage wanes and they cave in, giving up their honor shamefully and freely. If you can't maintain your honor in small things, how do you possibly expect to have the courage to live by your honor when even more is on the line?

There are many whose minds are in the right place, but whose lack of resolve robs them of their honor. It takes courage to stand up for what you believe and to live by your own principles no matter what the consequences may be.

Moreover, there are many who have the courage to act, but whose minds are as insincere as the pitch of a street hustler. On the outside, these people seem to be very honorable men, but on the inside, they couldn't care less about honor. These men act solely to impress and manipulate those around them. They do the right things, but for the wrong reasons. Their intentions are not in sync with their actions.

A great example of men like this would be the stereotypical politician. Politicians try their best to maintain a reputation of being honorable men. They even address each other as the honorable John Smith, etcetera. Externally, these men seem to be outstanding men of honor, but internally, they couldn't care less about honor. Their actions are a dog and pony show, and their intentions have agendas that no one else sees.

True honor requires sincerity. Your thoughts, intentions and actions must all be on the same page. The only agenda that real honor has is to live by your principles and do what is right. It is not meant to impress others or to manipulate others into seeing you a certain way.

True Honor

He has honor if he holds himself to an ideal of conduct
though it is inconvenient, unprofitable, or dangerous to do so.
Walter Lippmann

Men of the code are men of true honor. They have decided exactly how they will live their life, and live it according to their own principles, no matter what. It doesn't matter whether or not others are impressed with their actions. It doesn't matter if it costs them a business deal, a friendship, or some other hassle. They are completely committed to being men of honor.

True honor is independent of the opinions of others. Men of honor are not concerned with how others perceive their actions, but only with whether their actions are right and just. The opinions of others do not sway them. This being said, I must also point out that honor is not black and white. It is not adhering to moral codes which are set in stone, but rather to what is right.

This is where many men go wrong. They think that honor is having certain inflexible moral rules that they must follow completely, but that is not true honor. True honor is based on standing up for what is right, no matter what. It is not about being legalistic or bound by moral precepts.

Men who are legalistic about honor, often do injustice in the name of honor and subsequently walk away feeling superior to others, when in fact they are nothing more than men who did not have the courage to do what was right, because they were afraid of how others would perceive them.

Men of the code, on the other hand, put what is right above all else. If doing what is right means that they have to break the law or go against the moral or cultural norms, they have no problem doing so. Their aim is not to please everyone else, but to do what is right.

These are the kind of men that we all admire. These are the heroes that make us feel motivated and good inside. We admire those who are willing to do what's right, no matter what the cost, but most men do not have the conviction to live like a hero. This comes directly from not taking their honor seriously and a lack of courage.

Don't merely appear to be honorable, but actually be honorable. Take your code of honor seriously. You will be presented with many opportunities to compromise your honor. Don't allow emotions such as fear, greed, or anger to rob you of your honor. Nobody can take your honor from you, but you can lose your honor by giving in to these various temptations. You have to be completely dedicated to maintaining your honor or you will find that it has quietly slipped away, without you even realizing it.

There is a high road and a low road in life. Most men take the low road because it is easier and requires little from those who travel it. But men of honor take the high road, with little regard to whether it is easy or hard. Whether the high road is easy or hard matters not; all that matters is whether or not it is right. If you want to be a man of the code, you must be a man of honor. Only a man of honor is a real man.

Reflections for the Superior Man

Shun any actions that will diminish honor.
Tiruvalluvar

He who lives without discipline dies without honor.
Icelandic Proverb

The glory of great men must always be measured
against the means they have used to acquire it.
La Rochefoucauld

Nothing deters a good man from doing what is honorable.
Seneca

What is left when honor is lost?
Publilius Syrus

The post of honor is a private station.
Joseph Addison

Honor is that which no man can give you and no
man can take away. It's a gift a man gives to himself.
Rob Roy

Guard your honor.
Let your reputation fall where it will.
Lois McMaster Bujold

Honor is harder to master than the law.
Mark Twain

You are a man; do not dishonor mankind.
Jean Jacques Rousseau

Do not lose honor through fear.
Spanish Proverb

Mine honor is my life; both grow in one.
Take honor from me and my life is done.
Shakespeare

Life is light when compared to honor.
Japanese Proverb

Chapter 7

Integrity

It is not what we eat, but what we digest, that makes us strong;
not what we gain, but what we save, that makes us rich;
not what we read, but what we remember, that makes us learned;
and not what we profess, but what we practice, that gives us integrity.
Francis Bacon

What is Integrity?

One of the truest tests of integrity is its blunt refusal to be compromised.
Chinua Achebe

The word integrity comes from the Latin word *integer*, which means whole or unbroken completeness. It can also be defined as a state of being complete and undivided, or incorruptible. Thus, if you have integrity, your commitment to your own personal principles will be incorruptible. If we look at integrity from this point of view, it would mean being true to your beliefs and principles, or as the definition above states, steadfastly adhering to the high moral principles or standards that you have set for yourself to follow.

This is what integrity means to the man of the code who seeks to live a life of honor. Without integrity, it is impossible to truly live as a man of the code. You must first make a firm decision that you will live your life by your principles and then do so with the utmost integrity.

Integrity is being true to your beliefs and sincerely living by the principles that you espouse. If you claim to hold certain principles to be sacred in your life, but do not live your life by those principles, that is not integrity, that is hypocrisy. Integrity is living as your proclaim to live. It is integrating all of the principles, which you have decided to base your life on, into your everyday life.

The man of integrity doesn't just talk the talk; he walks the walk. He takes his principles and integrity seriously. In fact, he would never consider acting in a way that is inconsistent with his principles, for that would cause him to lose his integrity.

Acting with integrity boils down to one thing – doing what's right. The man who, in every situation, does what he thinks is right, even if it is going to be hard on him or cost him in some way, is a man with integrity. He holds his integrity in high regards.

He refuses to compromise his integrity to please others or for personal gain. The man of integrity understands that the appearance of personal gain that he would receive, by compromising his integrity, is nothing more than an illusion. It is a test of his integrity. It is never good for you to compromise your integrity, even if it appears to be good for you on the surface.

Integrity Goes Deeper Than Physical Rewards

Never do anything against conscience, even if the state demands it.
Albert Einstein

Many people falsely believe that they can separate their integrity from certain parts of their life. For example, someone may think that he has personal integrity, but may believe that "business is business" and that cheating someone on a business deal is simply doing business. He might rationalize that this is simply business and that it is up to each person to watch his own back and do his homework. This is a buyer beware type of attitude and is commonly seen throughout the world.

Robbing someone's house would probably never cross this person's mind because that would be totally unethical according to this person's so-called integrity. At the same time, he may consider certain questionable business practices to be totally acceptable, even though purposely cheating someone in a business deal is simply another way of robbing someone. This connection never enters this man's mind. He simply sees one as business and the other as unethical.

Real men do not see personal integrity in this way. They view integrity in terms of their pursuit of living a moral life and doing what's right, which is in line with the character traits of the man of the code. In short, they view actions in terms of right and wrong. This is not to say that the man of integrity sees everything as black and white. There is a big difference between looking at life's choices in terms of black and white, and viewing them in terms of right and wrong.

Most people do not realize this. The superior man's principles are both set in stone and yet flexible at the same time. This in no way means that his personal integrity is situational. He maintains his integrity without compromise. What this means is that what is right guides his integrity, not a rigid set of rules. Many people have a hard time understanding this philosophy. Hopefully the following example will help make this clear to you.

Let's say that one of the principles that you live by is to be truthful or honest. Part of living up to this principle would be that you do not lie. This is a pretty straightforward tenet. Now, someone who lives his life in rigid, legalistic terms would say that it is never okay to lie, that doing so would undermine his integrity. This is a good example of someone who looks at his principles in terms of black and white.

The problem with this is that a rigid view of one's principles can sometimes run crossways with doing what is right. Let's continue to examine this concept by looking closer at the principle of being honest and truthful. I think that we can all agree that being honest is a virtue and one of the traits that someone living life as a real man should adhere to as one of his core principles.

Here's the difference between the rigid adherence to this principle and the man who views his principles from the standpoint of right and wrong. The man who views his principles from the perspective of right and wrong has the ability to be flexible in his principles. No, this doesn't mean that he has the option to lie when it is convenient for him, but he does have the option to bend the truth when it is *the right thing to do*.

The man of integrity looks at life in terms of right and wrong, not black and white. Living as a superior man is not about a rigid adherence to specific rules. It is about having the personal integrity to live your life by the principles you have decided to incorporate into your life, and molding those principles by the concept of right and wrong. Again, remember the words of Confucius, "The superior man seeks what is right."

When a man compromises his integrity, there are consequences. There will be the normal consequences, knowing that you have let yourself down by caving in to the pressure to lower your standards. The conscience of the superior man will hold him accountable for lacking the courage to stand up for his principles and compromising his integrity. But a nagging conscience is not the only consequence.

Whenever you compromise your integrity, you hurt yourself mentally and spiritually. Your compromise can be compared to chipping away at your very foundation. The more you do it, the shakier your life becomes. Each time that you compromise your integrity in some way, it becomes easier and easier to do it again. The next time you are faced with a choice between right and wrong, your mind will start to tell you that you already compromised your integrity, so what is one more small compromise going to matter.

Your mind has a way of justifying and rationalizing your actions. Even the worst criminal doesn't think that he is truly a bad person. This is because he is always able to excuse himself with one excuse or another. He is an expert at justifying his own actions in order to make himself feel better about what he has done. Basically, he has become desensitized to the reality behind his actions. This is simply human nature.

My wife and I went to see the movie *Braveheart* when it first came out in 1995. This is one of my favorite movies, as it demonstrates firsthand the way a man of integrity does what is right in spite of the consequences. I remember after we saw the movie for the first time, my wife was literally nauseous from the graphic violence and all of the blood. She almost had to leave the movie.

As I said, this is one of my favorite movies. In fact, I loved it so much that I wanted to see it again. So we went to it a second time a few weeks later. This time, the movie did not have the same effect on my wife. She enjoyed the movie very much and the bloody violence did not bother her so much.

This is a very good example of becoming desensitized. The first time she experienced the gore in the movie, it affected her greatly, the second time, it had very little affect on her. Now she can watch the movie and it does not affect her at all, not even in the slightest.

This same principle of desensitization works in every area of your life. The first time that you compromise on your principles, it may really bother you. You may not be able to sleep, your conscience may bother you until you go and make things right. And even after that, you will probably feel badly about what you have done for months to come.

But, if you continue to compromise your principles and your integrity, you will become desensitized to your actions. You will begin to stop listening to your conscience and just put the whole matter out of your mind.

This is a very dangerous, slippery slope, and every time that you make another compromise, you will slide down this slope a little further and a little further, until you finally look at where you are and you see how far down you have gone. This slide will continue until you are no longer a man of the code, but an inferior man who really has no personal integrity; your integrity and your honor have been freely given away.

You will feel hollow and empty inside. Your spirit will feel weak. And it will become harder and harder for you to do the right thing when there is any pressure against you at all. The courage to stand up for your principles, which you once had, will have disappeared, and will be replaced by effortless justifications in which you mentally deceive yourself. You will find that you no longer value your integrity as you once died.

All of this will sneak up on you very quietly. You make one compromise, then another, then another, and before you know it, you have fallen so far from being the man that you want to be that you won't even recognize yourself anymore.

Being a man of integrity takes constant vigilance. Every decision matters. When you violate your honor and your principles, you will always pay a price, even it is not obvious to you at the time. Don't give in. Have the courage to stand for what you believe, regardless of what others think and regardless of the consequences.

Having personal integrity does not mean living up to the expectations of others. It means having the self-discipline to live your life according to your own standards of right and wrong. The catch here is that your standards of right and wrong must be derived from the correct principles that guide men of integrity. If everyone on this planet decided for themselves what is right and wrong, we would have chaos.

The difference in everyone deciding for themselves what is right and what is wrong, and the man of honor making this decision, is that the man of principle makes his decision from a place of honor and integrity. His conscience is highly developed to the point of internally understanding what is right and what is wrong. He holds himself to a much higher standard than other people.

For the man of integrity, living life according to what you believe to be right and wrong is not a license to do whatever you may want to do. Rather it means that you put what is right over all other considerations. But, to do so, you must first develop yourself to a point of internally knowing what is right and what is wrong.

In addition, personal integrity means that you will also have to be willing to accept the consequences of your decisions. Doing what you know is right will not exempt you from the consequences, but the man of integrity will do what is right nonetheless because he answers to his own conscience first and foremost.

He does not look to others to justify his actions. He makes his decisions according to the firm, but not rigid, principles by which he lives. It is this dedication to his principles that enables him to live a life of excellence and which sets him above the common man. Furthermore, the man of the code cannot be a man of integrity without the courage needed to always do what's right, no matter what. No man can be a superior man if he lacks the courage to live his life, his way and stand for what he believes is right.

Reflections for the Superior Man

Have the courage to say no. Have the courage to
face the truth. Do the right thing because it is right.
These are the magic keys to living your life with integrity.
W. Clement Stone

Calamity is the test of integrity.
Samuel Richardson

A single lie destroys a whole reputation for integrity.
Baltasar Gracian

Virtue is a state of war, and to live in it
we have always to combat with ourselves.
Jean-Jacques Rousseau

You can fake virtue for an audience.
You can't fake it in your own eyes.
Ayn Rand

Integrity is not a conditional word. It doesn't blow in the wind or
change with the weather. It is your inner image of yourself, and if you
look in there and see a man who won't cheat, then you know he never will.
John D. MacDonald

Whatever the world may say or do, my part is
to remain an emerald and to keep my color true.
Marcus Aurelius

A clear conscience is the greatest armor.
Chinese Proverb

The supreme quality for leadership is unquestionably integrity.
Without it, no real success is possible.
Dwight D. Eisenhower

With integrity, you have nothing to fear, since you have nothing to hide.
With integrity, you will do the right thing, so you will have no guilt.
Zig Ziglar

The high road is always respected.
Honesty and integrity are always rewarded.
Scott Hamilton

Chapter 8

Courage

The bravest are surely those who have the clearest vision of what is before them, glory and danger alike, and yet notwithstanding, go out to meet it.
Thucydides

What is True Courage?

Courage is grace under pressure.
Ernest Hemingway

It is impossible to be a man of the code without courage. Without the courage to stand for your convictions, to live by the principles that superior men live by, you will falter. It takes courage to do what's right when everyone around you is pushing you to do the opposite. It takes courage to stand up for what you believe when everyone else is telling you that you are wrong. Courage is essential to being a real man.

Over the years, different men have defined courage in different ways. Webster's dictionary defines courage as the quality of being brave and having the ability to face danger or difficult situations without being overcome by fear.

The first part of this definition is pretty straightforward – courage is the quality of being brave. But, as you will see, there is much more to courage than simply being brave. The majority of people think that being brave means that one doesn't have any fear. This is not necessarily so. The man with no fear at all, in any situation, is not necessarily brave, but rather a bit unbalanced. Fear is a natural emotion, and brave men, as well as everyone else, feel the emotion of fear.

If you will notice, the definition of courage doesn't state that courage is being brave without fear. It states that courage is the quality of being brave without being *overcome by fear*. There is a big difference between having no fear and not being overcome by fear. Having no fear indicates a total absence of the emotion of fear, which is a scary prospect in itself.

If someone has a total absence of fear, his judgment will be faulty in many situations. A total absence of fear is not a virtue, but rather a mental deficiency. Fear is a necessary emotion, designed to warn us and protect us.

It is only when fear becomes obsessive, and we allow fear to control us, that fear becomes a problem.

Mark Twain wrote that, "Courage is resistance to fear, mastery of fear – not absence of fear." If a man has absolutely no capability to feel fear, then he really has no capacity for courage. Courage is overcoming your fears to do what is right in the face of some danger, uncertainty, pain, or embarrassment.

To call a man, who is incapable of feeling fear, brave, could be compared to giving a two year old boy a hand grenade to play with as a toy. Of course, the young boy would have no fear of the hand grenade because he doesn't have the intelligence to understand what it is or that it could kill him. He doesn't have the knowledge or wisdom to understand what the dangers of this "toy" truly are, so he has no fear of it. It would be wrong to classify this boy as courageous or brave for playing with the hand grenade, when in fact, he is not displaying courage, but merely his own ignorance.

The same principle applies to the man who is incapable of feeling fear. If a man does not have the wisdom to know what should be feared and what shouldn't be feared, his actions cannot be classified as courageous. He is not acting out of courage, but out of his ignorance or lack of understanding.

True courage is being able to control your fear and your emotions, and taking action in spite of them. The man of courage places more importance on doing what's right, than he does on his fears. While he may indeed be shaken to his core with fear, he overcomes his fear and acts anyway. This is the strict definition of courage. It is not that the man of the code doesn't, or can't, feel fear, but that he rises up in the face of fear and is not overcome or defeated by his fear.

All men have fears; that is simply a part of human nature. It is not fear that matters, but our response to fear. If we allow our fears to dictate our actions, then we can't say that we have courage. Let's look at an example of what I mean.

Let's say that you are completely terrified of venomous snakes. Maybe you and your buddy were hiking one day and he was bitten by a rattlesnake and you witness him die in agony. Now, after seeing such a thing, it would only be natural that you would have a fear of snakes. You have seen firsthand what a deadly snake can do and have been through a horrific tragedy involving one of these creatures.

Now, imagine that you are once again hiking and you come across a young lady who has broken her leg and is lying hurt and helpless in a canyon, and she is screaming for your help because there is a huge rattlesnake coiled, just a few feet away, ready to strike her. What you do in this situation reveals whether you have courage or whether you will be overcome by your mortal fear of deadly snakes.

If you are a man of courage, you will move to help the young lady without giving it a second thought. Sure, you are scared of snakes, but your duty as a man requires that you act to help her, in spite of your fear. You man up and do what has to be done. You don't allow fear to dictate your response to the situation.

The opposite response would be to freeze and refuse to help the girl because of your fear of snakes. This would be an example of being completely overcome by your fear. Although you can see that the girl is in dire need of your help, you cannot move to help her because you have allowed your fear to get the best of you.

In this situation, it is very easy to distinguish between the man of courage and the coward who allows his fear to get the best of him. The man, who acts in spite of his fear, who sees grave danger but never considers not helping the helpless as an option, is a man of courage. The man who sees what needs to be done, but refuses to do it because of his fear, is a coward who puts his own fears and emotional needs above what should be done and what is right.

Distinguishing between the man of courage and the coward in the above example is very easy, but there are many times when you can't tell the difference between someone who is acting with courage and someone who is acting out of cowardice.

Courage or Cowardice

Courage is almost a contradiction in terms. It means a
strong desire to live taking the form of readiness to die.
G. K. Chesterton

Courage is one of those traits that many people seem to misunderstand. People also have a hard time distinguishing between courage and cowardice, the opposite of courage. At first, it sounds ridiculous that anyone would not be able to tell the difference between courage and cowardice, but externally, it can be hard, if not impossible, to tell the difference.

Courage comes from rational thinking, from a commitment to do what's right no matter what. Cowardice, on the other hand, comes from faulty thinking, putting more emphasis on thoughts of fear instead of thoughts of what should be done. In the same way, rashness, acting without thinking, is not true courage, but simply impulsive behavior. Courage requires that you see what needs to be done, that you understand the possible dangers and consequences, but that you act anyway.

Cowardice and rashness are indeed the two extremes when it comes to the subject of courage. Cowardice is a lack of courage. It is allowing fear to overcome you and cause you to falter at the time of action. Rashness, on the other hand, is being reckless, impulsive, and moving forward without giving any thought at all to the situation at hand.

The one thing that both cowardice and rashness have in common is that when someone acts from either of these extremes, he is letting his emotions control his actions, not rational thought, and definitely not courage. To be courageous, a man has to be thoughtful. Francesco Guicciardini wrote, "Only the wise are brave. Others are either temerarious or foolhardy. Thus, we can say that every brave man is wise, but not that every wise man is brave."

From this point of view, we can compare courage to honor. It is not easy for an outsider to judge whether or not a man is being courageous, just as it is not obvious whether or not a man is acting out of a sense of honor.

There are some actions which, when initially seen, may seem like acts of cowardice, but when examined closer, were truly courageous acts. At the same time, there are some actions which seem like very courageous acts, but if we were able to see beyond the action itself, we would understand that the action was not truly an act of courage at all. Let's look at a couple of examples.

First, let's look at the man with his buddies, who are about to enter into some type of physical encounter, whether it is a brawl or maybe on the battlefield. The fact that this man follows through and fights alongside his buddies is not necessarily a sign that he is courageous. There have been many men who truly wanted to retreat, to run and hide, but didn't have the courage to do what their mind was telling them to do.

Instead, peer pressure, or the fear of what their friends would think of them, influenced their decision. Thus, the decision was not made from a place of courage, but from a mindset of fear.

On the other hand, let's say you are watching an altercation at a nightclub. Two men are having a disagreement. One guy seems pushy and obnoxious, and obviously wants to fight. The other seems reluctant to fight, no matter how much the other guy pushes him. Ultimately, the man who is reluctant to fight, turns and walks away, amidst jeers from the aggressive man and other onlookers.

To those watching this scene, this man may seem like a coward, and indeed he may be, but the fact that he turned and walked away does not necessarily indicate that this man is a coward. He may have been a true warrior with the ability to take the other man's life at will, but instead chose to end this encounter peacefully instead of hurting the other guy.

An action like that takes a lot of courage and self-confidence. This is a demonstration of self-control and courage, not cowardice, but to the untrained eye, it would probably appear like the man was a coward.

Do you understand the point that I am trying to get across to you? Courage is demonstrated in many different ways. It is not always expressed by simply rushing in and fighting, and many times the man who rushes in and fights is not demonstrating courage. Walking away, being patient, waiting for the correct time and place, and enacting self-control, are all courageous actions.

There are times that we will be able to discern courage from cowardice in others, and times that we will not. To the man of the code, whether or not another man is courageous or a coward is not his concern; his concern is with his own actions, and the intentions behind those actions.

What is important is that you understand what true courage is and that you develop it in your own life. True courage is having the intestinal fortitude to stand up for what you believe to be right, in spite the opposition or danger involved. This courage is a must for the man of the code.

Until you develop this courage in your spirit, you will be in a constant battle to live up to the principles by which you want to live your life. There will always be those who stand against you, who try to sidetrack you, and who will do everything in their power to sway you to lower your standards. It takes a lot of courage to stand against others and live your life in your own way. It takes courage to do the right thing, especially when everyone else is telling you to do something different.

Each time you stand against those who want you to lower your standards, your courage increases; every time you give in, you weaken your courage. Start developing your courage today in small, everyday situations, and it will be there for you when you face the major decisions in your life. As Maya Angelou stated, "Courage is the most important of all virtues, because without it we can't practice any other virtues with consistency." If you are completely and wholeheartedly dedicated to your code, you will find that being courageous will come much easier for you. Be dedicated to what's right and let that fuel your courage. Learn to endure whatever you have to in order to be a man of the code.

Reflections for the Superior Man

Great deeds are usually wrought at great risks.
Herodotus

Courage is being scared to death, but saddling up anyway.
John Wayne

Courage is resistance to fear, mastery of fear, not absence of fear.
Mark Twain

Fate often saves an undoomed man, if his courage holds.
Beowulf

The world has no room for cowards. We must all be ready somehow to toil, to suffer, to die. And yours is not the less noble because no drum beats before you when you go out into your daily battlefields, and no crowds shout about your coming when you return from your daily victory of defeat.
Robert Louis Stevenson

Be brave and courageous,
for adversity is the proving ground of virtue.
Battista Alberti

To see what is right and not to do it is cowardice.
Confucius

The test of courage comes when we are in the minority.
Ralph Waldo Emerson

He is the best man who, when making his plans, fears and reflects on everything that can happen to him, but in the moment of action is bold.
Herodotus

The man of true valor lies between the extremes of cowardice and rashness.
Cervantes

If you wanna live life on your own terms,
you gotta be willing to crash and burn.
Motley Crue

A man with outward courage dares to die;
a man with inner courage dares to live.
Lao Tzu

Chapter 9

Endurance and Fortitude

Endurance is one of the most difficult disciplines,
but it is to the one who endures that the final victory comes.
Buddha

What is Endurance and Fortitude

Understanding is the path to endurance.
Tess Calomino

Endurance is the ability to bear prolonged hardship, exertion, or pain. It is synonymous with survival, because if you can't endure the hard times, then most likely, you won't be surviving. Endurance is having the staying power to deal with whatever life has to throw at you.

Fortitude is having the strength, courage, grit, and resilience to not give up during the hard times, difficult times or painful situations. You have to be able to withstand prolonged hardship and pain, just as everyone must at one time or another in life. If you give up at the first sign of resistance, you will rarely accomplish anything of any value.

In addition, it should go without saying, that the man of the code must be persistent in his quest to live life by his own standards. Without a doubt, the ability to bear up under stress and adverse situations is a must for any man who wants to live his life by his own code. Without fortitude, you will give up at the first signs of resistance or confrontation with those who would like to see you fail.

Endurance and fortitude do take courage. It is extremely tempting to just give up and throw in the towel when hardship and pain become almost overwhelming, but it is precisely at those times that the superior man's fortitude is most needed. During times of persistent hardship is when you learn the most about your fortitude, or lack of it.

You have to train yourself to endure the tough times in order to be successful, no matter what your goal may be. If you give up every time the going gets tough, giving up will become a habit for you. Everyone has tough times. Everyone has periods where everything seems to go wrong and where they hear the tempting voice of defeat whispering, "It is not worth it – just throw in the towel and walk away." The temptation to give in to defeat is felt by everybody at one time or another; a determined fortitude and a never-say-die attitude are vital to your success.

To put fortitude in layman's terms, it literally means, "guts, grit, determination, resilience, and staying power. Obviously, these are traits that all real men should have. All great men have failed more times than they succeeded, but their final victory made all of their previous failures seem like a distant memory in the end.

One of the most famous self-help authors of our times, Napoleon Hill, wrote, "The majority of men meet with failure because of their lack of persistence in creating new plans to take the place of those which fail." A vital part a man's fortitude is the tenacity to not give up when he fails in one endeavor or another. Everyone makes mistakes. Everyone falls short at one time or another. Success is a never-ending process, not a goal that you achieve and then move on to the next goal.

You will fall short in one area or another as you work towards your goals. You will encounter sore muscles, injuries, and setbacks as you go through the process of physical training. You will have days when your thoughts don't seem to want to line up with what you truly believe. You will experience setbacks on the road to success.

The trick is in not giving up. This is what it means to endure, to follow through with determination, to endure exertion and pain. Make a firm decision that you will not give up on your goals, no matter what!

If you find that your plan to achieve your objectives is not working, don't give up; simply create a new plan. To quote Napoleon Hill again, "Patience, persistence and perspiration make an unbeatable combination for success." You will find that many times a little more persistence will turn a seemingly hopeless situation into a success.

Many people give up just before they reach their goal. They can't see any progress and everything looks bleak to them, so they throw in the towel. Little do they know that if they would have held on just a little bit longer, their objectives would have been reached; they would have been successful. But they gave up just before the storm clouds cleared.

I have seen this happen over and over again. Ronald Wayne is probably someone that you have never heard of, but I bet you have heard of his ex-partners, Steve Jobs and Steve Wozniak. Of course these gentlemen were the co-founders of Apple Computer. Wayne gave up on his dream of creating personal computers that would be in everyone's home and sold his share of

Apple for less than $800. Just a little more endurance and dedication to his dream, and he would be one of the world's richest men today, but he gave up on his dream before it had the time to manifest.

You can't see into the future. You don't know how your decisions will ultimately play out, but you can develop the endurance to hold on to your dreams during the hard times. Never give up simply because times are hard. Only change directions when your objectives change or you need to improve your strategy for success.

Why Endurance and Fortitude is Important

Come what may, all bad fortune is
to be conquered by endurance.
Virgil

Napoleon Hill taught, "Persistence is to the character of man as carbon is to steel." When you add carbon to steel, you make the steel harder and stronger. Carbon makes it better. This is what persistence does with your character. Giving up weakens your character; whereas persistently enduring life's hardships builds your character.

Developing endurance and fortitude means more than simply putting up with a bad situation; it means conquering that situation and turning it into a victory. It is one thing to simply survive a prolonged hardship, but it is another thing entirely to take that hardship and turn it into something positive. That is your objective. Survival is the foundation of endurance; complete triumph is the endgame.

You aren't putting up with the frustrations and stress of difficult times merely to prove than you can. You aren't doing it for bragging rights. You are being persistent in your fortitude in order to completely triumph over your challenges and to be successful in your overall objectives.

Yes, developing endurance and fortitude does help develop your character, but this is not your main objective in enduring hardships, challenges, and tough times. Your main objective is to win. Refuse to give up. Refuse to lose. Be so completely focused on winning, or achieving your goal, that you never entertain the thought of giving up, at least not for long.

This not only builds your character, but it also helps solidify your dedication to your code. Think about it. If you give up when it comes to the small frustrations in life, do you really think that you will have the fortitude to stand for your principles when you actually have people pushing you to lower your standards, or if you come against situations that truly tempt you to compromise your principles? If you can't do the right thing when it comes to small challenges, how do you expect to do so in more important issues?

It takes stubborn fortitude to stand for your principles when everyone around you is trying to talk you into seeing things a different way. It takes guts and grit to do what is right, when it would be much easier to do what's wrong and nobody would be the wiser.

This determination has to be fostered and cultivated. And the way that you do this is to develop endurance and fortitude in the smaller challenges, so that you have it available for the large challenges.

Think about it like this, you wouldn't step into a boxing match without first training for that match. If you did, it wouldn't be very long before you found yourself on the canvas. You have to start slow. Spend time training and getting in shape. Spar with other men who are closer to your own level before you step in the ring against a really tough opponent.

That is how your fortitude works. This is why we should try to teach our children not to be quitters. The wise father will not let his son or daughter quit a sport, or anything else that they have started, simply because it is hard for them. This teaches them endurance, fortitude, and resolve. That doesn't mean that our children will always be successful at becoming the best at everything they do, but it teaches them not to give up when the going gets tough.

I want to mention one thing here before I continue. Quitting a team or an activity because you have discovered that it is not what you were looking for, is not the same thing as quitting because it is too hard or because it doesn't come easy for you. These are two completely different things.

If you teach your children that anytime they start something, they have to stay in it until the end, you will discourage them from trying new things. After all, it is a big gamble for them, if every time they try something new, they have to continue with it, even if they find that they hate it.

You want your children to be adventurous and to try new things, but once they have tried something new, and found that they dislike it, don't make them stay with it simply because they aren't allowed to quit. This is wrong thinking.

Quitting something because you don't like it, if it wasn't what you thought it would be, or if you just aren't interested in it anymore, is not the same things as quitting because it is too hard for you. The first is making a conscious decision that this is not for you; you just plain don't like it, but you are glad you tried it and found out. The latter is being a quitter and giving up because the activity defeated you, and that is not acceptable.

Persistence in Working towards Your Goals

Those who endure conquer.
Military Motto

Being persistent and not quitting because of challenges is a good thing, but don't get that confused with continuing to do the same thing over and over again, in a misguided attempt to somehow make what is not working for you, suddenly start to work.

Albert Einstein stated that it is insanity to do the same thing over and over again and expect different results. While you should be persistent, you should also be smart about it. If something is not working for you, change your strategy.

Being persistent doesn't mean that you work nonstop and try to force things to happen; it means not quitting, not giving up. Neither does being persistent mean that you continue to pound away at your challenge using the exact same means. You may have to change your plan and your approach to the problem, in order to ultimately be successful.

Be persistent in continuing to endure and to work at achieving your objective, not at doing the same exact thing. There is a big difference in the two. Everything changes. Nothing remains the same for very long. You have to be willing to change in order to be successful. What worked yesterday, may not work tomorrow.

Many people wrongly think that being persistent means continuing to do the same thing until it starts to work. But, if it didn't work last year, last month, or last week, it most likely is not going to work next week either.

While your core principles should not change, your actions must be flexible. You must adapt your actions to the circumstances in order to achieve your goals, and you must do so without compromising your principles. If one thing is not working, try something else. It is simply unwise to continue to do something, which is not getting results, because you don't want to give up.

Not giving up pertains to your overall goal, not the specific actions that lead to achieving your goal. The specific actions are merely the tools that you use to accomplish your goal. If you are trying to hammer a nail with a screwdriver and not having much luck, change the tool that you are using;

don't give up on hammering the nail! When you change to the right tool, you will find that hammering the nail into the board is not really that difficult.

Your main concern is your overall objective, not your current mode for achieving your objective. Be persistent in your goal, but be willing to change your methods as needed.

You have to endure the storms of life and rise above them in order to reach your ultimate goals. At times, this can take a lot of grit and determination, but the superior man will refuse to give up, unless he finds that it is in his best interest to change his course.

You can't control the storms in life; all you can control is yourself. Know that if you don't panic, you stay calm, and don't give up, the storm will pass, things will get easier, and you will be victorious. You have to respond to the struggles in life, but you don't have to let them beat you. Have the fortitude to endure the storm, wait for the storm to pass, and still be standing when others have thrown in the towel and given up on their goals.

Only men of fortitude will be victorious in the end. You have to till the soil, plant the seeds, continuously weed your garden, and cultivate your plants, before you can enjoy the fruits of your labor. If you decided that the dirt was too hard or that you just couldn't get the weeds under control, you would never be able to reap the benefits of your garden.

In the same way, you have to endure the hard times in order to enjoy the good times. If you give up at the first sign of any struggle or challenge, you will never get to experience the feeling of accomplishment that comes with achieving your goals.

While this may sound like common knowledge, the vast majority of men do not endure. They do not have the fortitude to see things to the end; and therefore, they never get to enjoy the feeling that comes with a hard-earned victory.

See your goals in terms of delayed gratification. Don't take the path of least resistance. If you will develop endurance and fortitude, you will enjoy the fruits of your labor; but if you give up, all of your hard work will be for nothing.

Don't fall into the trap of thinking that your efforts are not working simply because you are not able to see the results immediately. Would you ever be able to enjoy the fruits of your garden if you worked the soil, planted the seeds, and then, after a week, you decided that the seeds must not be growing, so you went and dug them up?

You have to give your garden time to grow, time to mature, and time to produce the fruit that you want. If you continue to sabotage your efforts by being impatient or giving up, you will never succeed in your goals.

This same principle applies to everything you do in your life. Goals worth achieving take time. They take hard work and discipline. Your hard work may not produce fruit right away; you have to endure the lean times in order to get to the good times.

Work to develop endurance and fortitude in your life. Superior men don't throw in the towel at the first signs of weakness or hardship. You must endure in order to see your goals manifest in life.

Reflections for the Superior Man

Endurance is one of the most difficult disciplines,
but it is to the one who endures that the final victory comes.
Buddha

Heroism is endurance for one moment more.
George F. Kennan

Endurance is not just the ability to bear a hard thing,
but to turn it into glory.
William Barclay

The majority of men meet with failure because
of their lack of persistence in creating new
plans to take the place of those which fail.
Napoleon Hill

Continuous, unflagging effort,
persistence and determination will win.
James Whitcomb Riley

Endurance and to be able to endure,
is the first lesson a child should learn,
because it's the one they will most need to know.
Jean-Jacques Rousseau

Chances are, no matter how bad your troubles seem to be,
someone somewhere, with less resilience, has successfully
conquered a more severe version of your problems.
Gary Hopkins

Surrender is a choice, it is never a calling.
Craig D. Lounsbrough

If it doesn't work out there will never be any doubt
that the pleasure was worth all the pain.
Jimmy Buffett

To do anything truly worth doing, I must not stand back
shivering and thinking of the cold and danger, but jump
in with gusto and scramble through as well as I can.
Og Mandino

Chapter 10

Actions

*Every action we take, everything we do, is either a victory
or defeat in the struggle to become what we want to be.*
Anne Byrhhe

Be Thoughtful of Your Actions

Every man is the sum of his own works.
Cervantes

Your actions show the world who you truly are as a man, and what your inner beliefs and philosophy are. Your behavior is constantly revealing something about you to those whom you interact with throughout your life. For this reason, it is vitally important to think about, and carefully consider, all of your actions *before* you act.

The philosophy that your actions reveal the true you, has been taught throughout the ages from some of the earliest wisdom teachings, right up to the present day. Ptah-Hotep taught this, as did Jesus, Buddha, and Lao Tzu. The fact that men of honor should carefully consider their actions and act appropriately, according to their own code of honor, is universally accepted, but seems to be taken less seriously in today's society.

Although most people don't seem to take their actions seriously anymore, the superior man doesn't live like most people. He knows how important it is to carefully consider his every move. Everything matters, even down to the smallest action. Every single action carries with it some consequence, no matter how large or how small.

Even the smallest, seemingly insignificant action carries with it some effect on your life. The affects of your actions could be life-changing or they could be something so subtle that you really don't notice it, but just like the ocean is made up of single, small drops of water which combine together to form something of immense power, those small consequences build up over time and do affect you in ways that you cannot imagine.

It is for this reason that every action matters. Don't take anything for granted. Always think before you act and make sure that every action has both a purpose and conforms to your code. If something does not conform to your code, then you shouldn't do it. If you will consider every action important, you will find it easier to slow down and think before you act.

It is a universal law that what you put out into this world, ultimately comes back to you in one way or another. Whether you want to call this the law of cause and effect or karma, it works consistently either way. Everything that you do, both good and bad, comes back to you in some form. Good actions bring good things into your life; bad actions bring bad things into your life. It is as simple as that.

Many times you can immediately see the consequences of your actions on your life. For example, if you are speeding down the highway and get nailed by a cop, the effect of your action is going to be that you receive a ticket and it will cost you money. Other times, the consequences of your actions are not so noticeable, but they are always there nonetheless.

For instance, you may be having a really bad day and you lost your temper in line at the grocery store. Later, you may feel bad about it, and go back and apologize to the clerk and make things right with her. The clerk may be very understanding and assure you that she understands and that she appreciates you coming back to the store to apologize. She may even applaud your honor for doing so. You feel all better about the situation and pledge never to do something so ridiculous again, and forget about it, thinking that the consequences have been taken care of by your apology.

You may think that this has taken care of the issue, but what you don't know is how your actions affected other people who witnessed your outburst. The impressionable young man, who saw you, may think that what you did was cool, and the way a real man acts when he is frustrated. The elderly lady, in the next lane, may now be even more fearful of going to the store alone, after seeing your anger. The possible consequences are endless, and all unknown to you.

Even if you went back and made amends, the ripples of your actions can still spread far and wide, and the results of what you did may affect people's lives for years to come, without you ever being aware of them. This is just one small example, there are thousands of others.

Think back to a time when you threw a rock into a lake. The ripples from the rock hitting the water traveled in every direction. There wasn't just one ripple that came directly back to you; there were many, and they traveled far in every direction. After you threw the rock, you had no control over how many ripples there were or in which direction that would travel.

In the same way, the ripples of your actions travel in all directions and you never really know how many people they affect or what consequences they have on other people's lives. And, even if you don't know how your actions affect others, that does not excuse you from the law of karma; you are still responsible for everything you do.

You only have control over the consequences of your actions *before* you act. Once you act, the results of your actions are out of your hands for the most part.

Really think about the ripple effect of throwing that rock into the lake. If such a simple action carries so many ripples, in so many directions, how much more so do your actions, which really could have drastic affects on the lives of other people, matter? You never really know for sure what consequences your actions may have, both in your own life and in the lives of others.

Sometimes it may take years to see the consequences of certain actions, and sometimes you may never even know how the consequences of a certain action have affected your life, or the lives of others. But I can assure you that the consequences are there, even if you can't see them at the time. There will come a time when you will be able to look back and see the cause of everything that has happened in your life; then you will understand the reasons for everything. Nothing in this world happens without a cause.

Always think about everything you do. What are the possible effects of your actions? Who will your actions affect? How will your actions affect them? Are you doing the right thing? These are all questions that you need to consider before you act, but not many people think about the answers to these questions until it is too late.

As a man of the code, you should not only strive to make sure that all of your actions are just and right, but you should also endeavor to be a good example for others. When they see you, let them see a man who behaves as a real man should behave, with honor and integrity, with calm confidence and self-control. Be a shining example of how a man of the code carries himself. Keep your emotions under control; think and act rationally.

Do your best to make sure that the ripple effect of your actions bring good things into the lives of other people. You are accountable for the consequences of your actions, even if those consequences were not intended. While we can't always control the consequences of our actions, we can make sure that our intentions are just and pure. Pure intentions begin with your thoughts. If our intentions are pure and just, then we can live with whatever the consequences of our actions may be. Remember, things can't be right on the outside until they are right on the inside.

Your Actions Begin with Your Thoughts

If the heart is right, the deeds will be right.
Japanese Proverb

Your actions begin with your thoughts, so it is vital that you control your mind and your emotions, or you will never be able to control your actions. If you allow your mind to run wild, entertaining any and every thought that pops into your head, then your actions will follow along. You will find that your actions will be random at best.

Superior men think before they act. There is sincerity in their actions that comes from being sincere in their thoughts. Their underlying motives are as noble as their actions. When your thoughts are noble and your intentions are noble, you actions will be noble.

Your thoughts, intentions, and actions must all be in sync; they must be in harmony. No matter how noble an act may seem on the outside, if the thought and intention behind that act is not noble, it is not a noble act. Your intention must be pure. Intention, thought and action must be one.

At the same time, intentions alone are not good enough. Many men intend to do good things, but somehow, never get around to actually doing them. Thinking about turning the stove on won't boil the water. You actually have to take action and turn your intentions into something tangible. But you can't take action without first thinking about what you are going to do. Thought always precedes action.

It is for this reason that the superior man must keep a tight rein on his thoughts. Mold your thoughts to your code. Living up to your code of honor starts by taking control of your thoughts and bringing them in line with the kind of man that you want to be. It is insincere and deceitful to think one way and act another.

You are Judged by Your Deeds

A tree is known by its fruit.
Jesus

Just as it is worthless to intend to do something, or think about doing something, but never actually do it, you also shouldn't say that you are going to do something, but never follow through. Henry Ford stated, "You can't build a reputation on what you are going to do." This is true, but you can build a reputation if you continually talk about what you are going to do, but never get around to doing it. And it won't be the kind of reputation that you want to build. The superior man builds a reputation of being a man of his word, not an empty dreamer.

No one has respect for the man who talks about what he is going to do, but never does it. If you do this, you will develop the reputation of simply being a talker, but not a doer. People won't take you seriously; they will take everything you say with a grain of salt. Don't talk about what you are going to do – just do it.

Too many men feel the need to talk about how they are going to do this or that, in order to impress others. Do it, and then talk about it, if you must talk about it at all. And, if you do talk about it, don't do so in order to impress others or inflate your own ego; doing that only testifies to your own insecurities and the need to have others tell you how great you are. The superior man doesn't need the approval of others; he simply acts.

Responding Versus Reacting

When you react, you let others control you.
When you respond, you are in control.
Bohdi Sanders

You can't always control what happens to you or the situation in which you find yourself, but you can always control your own thoughts and actions. Always maintain control over your thoughts and actions; don't give your power away to others.

When you react to a situation or to another person's words or actions, you are giving that person control over you. When you react, you let others control you. When you respond, you are in control.

Think about it, when you react, you are allowing someone else to guide your actions just like a puppet reacts to the puppeteer moving the strings. The puppet is moving, but it is the puppeteer who is controlling his actions. The puppet is not in control, but is merely being manipulated by the actions of someone else.

Don't allow other people or events to control your actions. Always control your own actions. Don't react to someone else; assess the situation and respond accordingly. While this may seem like nothing more than semantics, there is a huge difference.

Responding to a situation or another person requires that you give some thought to your response. It is not automatic; it is calculated. When you respond, instead of react, you consciously decide what your response will be. That puts you in control of your actions, not the other person.

Look at it another way. If a mosquito is flying around and almost flies into your eye, you will blink. It will happen without you having to stop and think about blinking. It is an autonomic response, a response that is controlled by your nervous system, not your thoughts. You don't have to think about it, your eye lid simply reacts to the mosquito. This would be a good example of reacting to the situation.

On the other hand, if the mosquito is flying around, you notice it and decide to swat it away; that is a response. You assessed the situation and made a conscious decision about how you would respond to it. In some situations, like swatting a mosquito, you can respond very fast because you have experience with how to handle that situation. In other situations, your thought process may take longer. Either way, you are in control.

You can't always control the situation, but you can always control your own actions and your responses. Never give your power to someone else. The superior man always maintains control over his own actions.

Let's look at another example. Think about playing a game of chess. If you are able to think several moves ahead, you can control your opponent's moves. The right move causes your opponent to react to your move. And with intelligent foresight, you can manipulate his moves throughout the game. When a chess player controls the game, he wins; when he allows his opponent to dictate his moves, he loses. It is the same way in life. Make sure you still have your king standing at the end of the game.

What determines if you are a man of the code is not the situation or the circumstances, but how you respond to the situation or the circumstances. And your response is always in your hands.

Get Your Priorities Straight

Action expresses priorities.
Gandhi

Your actions speak to your priorities. I often hear people talk about how they just do not have time to do the things in life that they want to do. This is a cop out. Every person on this planet has the same 24 hours in a day that every other person has. The difference is in our priorities. You give time to what you deem important. If something is not that important to you, you spend your time on things which you consider more important.

Therefore, it is not that you do not *have* time to do what you want to do; it is that you put more importance on other things and thus, you spend your time doing them instead. If you want to do something badly enough, you do it, period. You make time for the things that are important to you. It is just a matter of priorities, and that is the bottom line.

The only person stopping you from doing certain things in life is you. The only person holding you back is the man you see in the mirror; everyone else is just watching or throwing options out for you to see how you will respond. You are the only person who is stopping you from living the life that you want to live.

The thing that you have to do is to get your priorities straight. Decide once and for all what is really important in your life. Decide what will come first and what will be optional. If you say that you don't have time for something, that simply means that it is not a priority in your life.

You always have choices. If you are a martial artist, you have to decide whether you are going to practice your martial arts or whether you are going to watch television. You choose, and your choice expresses your priority at that time. Is your priority to sit back and relax in comfort or to get up, get your gi on, and go get a hard workout? What you do will answer that question.

Every man wants to have certain things in his life. He wants certain skills, certain knowledge, etcetera, but not every man is willing to do what it takes to obtain that skill or that knowledge. It depends on his priorities. Skills and knowledge worth having, take effort. They don't come for free. It takes discipline to develop martial arts skills. It takes discipline to spend hours studying and learning to gain knowledge.

You have to prioritize your priorities and then follow through on your decisions. You can't wait for inspiration to motive you; you have to motivate yourself. You have to constantly remind yourself of your priorities. Remind yourself how short life really is and how much you want to get done while you can. Live life with gusto! Don't just stumble through life half awake and awaken only to find out that it is now too late to do all the things that you wanted to do in life.

There is an old saying that clothes make the man. But men of the code know that this saying is nonsense. Thoughts and actions make the man – period. Your thoughts lead to your actions, and both must be right and be in line with your code of honor. When your thoughts and your actions are right, according to your code of honor, then you have become a man of the code.

In everything you do, you must first think about your final objective. What is it that you really want to accomplish? Once you are able to answer this question, then, and only then, will you know the right actions to take. If you act without first knowing what your final objective is, you are simply shooting in the dark, and you may find that the final outcome is something that you never intended and do not want.

Every action initiates a sequence of consequences which follow that action. You could look at this exactly like a domino effect, where one action causes a consequence that causes another action, and so on.

You never know exactly where your actions may lead or what unexpected and unintended consequences may come from one small action. The guy who throws a cigarette butt out his car window, may not think that it is any big deal, that is, until that one small action ignites a fire that burns thousands of acres and hundreds of homes. You must think about the consequences of your actions.

There is a right way and a wrong to do everything in life. And, even when you know the right thing to do, you can still do the right thing in the wrong way. For example, the doctor may prescribe a certain medicine for your medical condition. It is the right medicine and it will heal your body if you take it as prescribed. But, you can still take the right medicine the wrong way. If you go home and take the entire bottle at one time, you will not achieve your desired outcome. In fact, you will probably achieve the exact opposite of what you wanted - you may die.

Taking the medicine was the right action to take, but if you take the right action in the wrong way, you change the outcome. You can have the right intentions, the right desires, and you can know the right thing to do, but if you take the wrong action, it can nullify all of your efforts. And, if you take the right action, in the wrong way, or at the wrong time, it can also cause you to fail.

A man can compromise in his actions without compromising his principles. You must do the right thing, at the right time, and in the right way. These are the foundation stones of success. If one of those foundation stones is not right, it can cause your whole objective to fail and can even cause unforeseen consequences that can lead to even greater problems than the ones that you were trying to solve to begin with. See things from every angle before you act.

Many times, the right action requires patience in order for it to accomplish what you wanted it to accomplish. You have to wait for the right time to act.

If your timing is off, the results will not be the same. Everything matters; there are no inconsequential details.

For example, let's say you are coaching a football team and your team is playing for the championship. You may have a special, trick, pass play that you want to run. You have studied your opponent's game plans and you have found that in a certain situations, they bring their defensive backs up too far and leave an opportunity for your receiver to get behind them. You know that when they do this, you can fake a run and get them to bite, leaving your receiver wide open.

But, you have to patiently wait for that special situation to occur in the game in order for your pass play to be successful. If you run that play before their defensive backs move up, your receivers will be covered, and there is a very good chance that your trick play may end up backfiring on you.

Always remember that, even when you know the right action to take, there is always a right time to take it. The right action, at the wrong time, is no longer the right action. Likewise, the right action, performed in the wrong way, is just as likely to fail as if you had made the wrong move to start with.

Back to above example, even if the situation is right and the other team's defensive backs move up, your special pass play could still fail if it is not executed correctly. If your quarterback makes a bad throw or the receiver drops the ball, it will fail just as badly as if the defenders were in the right position to stop your play.

Your actions must be right, but they must also be executed in the right way and at the right time. Don't allow impatience or carelessness to turn the right action into a failure. Think things through before you act. Look at all the possible outcomes of your actions and plan your strategy well.

Men of the code understand how seemingly small mistakes can have enormous consequences and can change the whole course of their actions. Take care that your actions are just, timely, well thought out, and are executed right.

Reflections for the Superior Man

Rest satisfied with doing well, and leave
others to talk of you as they please.
Pythagoras

Gardens are not made by sitting in the shade.
Rudyard Kipling

Before you act, consider; when you
have considered, tis fully time to act.
Sallust

Choosing the lesser of two evils only guarantees an evil choice.
Good enough is not good enough.
Bohdi Sanders

Virtue is more clearly shown in the performance of fine actions
than in the nonperformance of base ones.
Aristotle

Let your words correspond with your actions
and your actions with your words.
Confucius

It is not only what we do, but also what
we do not do, for which we are accountable.
Moliere

To do an evil action is base; to do a good action without incurring
danger is common enough; but it is part of a good man to do
great and noble deeds, though he risks everything.
Plutarch

A man's action is only a picture book of his creed.
Ralph Waldo Emerson

The way of the sage is to act but not to compete.
Lao Tzu

They make the greatest show of what they have done, who have
done least...Rest in accomplishment, and leave talk to others.
Do, and do not brag...Aspire to be heroic, not only to seem it.
Baltasar Gracian

Chapter 11

Respect and Courtesy

Conduct yourself in a manner that is worthy of
respect and don't worry about what others think.
Bohdi Sanders

Respect Versus Courtesy

Respect for ourselves guides our morals;
respect for others guides our manners.
Laurence Sterne

Respect is having admiration toward another person. I hear so many people say things such as, "You have to respect everyone," but that is completely wrong. You do not have to respect everyone. In fact, you absolutely should not have respect for everyone. You can, and should, *treat* everyone *with* respect, but that in no way implies that you respect that person.

Should we have respect for psychotic murders or child rapists? Well, I don't know about you, but personally, I have no respect for those people at all. I have respect for superior men, men of honor and character, men whose lives define what it means to be a real man. But I have no respect for the bottom-feeders of this world, and neither should you. That doesn't mean that you shouldn't treat everyone in a respectful way.

I know that this concept is hard for some guys to grasp, so I will explain it in further detail. You can treat someone with respect, without actually respecting that person. That is simply being courteous.

For example, if you are walking down the street of any large city, you will undoubtedly see winos or street bums lying on the sidewalk. Do you really have respect for the drunk lying on the sidewalk? I doubt it. I know that I don't. But does the fact that you don't respect what he has done with his life mean that you have to be rude to him? Absolutely not!

Respect is something that is earned by your actions; courtesy is how you treat a person. You don't have to respect someone in order to be nice to them. I am nice to everyone, unless they have given me a reason not to be nice. Being courteous to someone has nothing to do with whether or not you actually respect him; it is simply good manners. Superior men are courteous, not because other people do or do not deserve their courtesy, but because that is a part of their code. It is how they choose to behave toward other people.

Having respect for another person, is something that the other person earns by his behavior. I have respect for men of character, honor and integrity. I have respect for superior men who live their lives by high standards and principles. I don't have respect for those who prey on the innocent, who hurt others, or who live their lives with no honor or integrity. All of these things have to do with the other person's actions, who they are as a person.

True respect is something that everyone has to earn. It is not something that can be demanded of others. This appears to be something that many men don't seem to understand in today's society. I see young men constantly talking about being "disrespected" or "demanding respect." These guys don't understand what respect truly means. You can't demand that someone else have respect for you. That is like demanding that someone love you. It can't be done.

You can require that others *treat* you with respect, but that has nothing to do with them actually *having* respect for you. That is merely refusing to allow people to be discourteous to you, nothing more.

Young men today are confused when it comes to the subject of respect. They have heard over and over in our schools, that they should respect everyone. So, of course, they are going to think that they have the right to demand that everyone respects them. This is just one of many of the destructive things that our public schools are doing to our young men today.

They should be taught that respect is earned by your actions. It is not a God-given right. Everyone is not entitled to your respect. Who, and what, you respect is a personal decision; not a decision for inept public school officials, or anyone else, to make for our young men.

When young men graduate from our school system, they feel entitled, not just to everyone's respect, but entitled to many other things as well. At the same time, they have no understanding about what real respect is because they have been taught that it is something that everyone is entitled to. And since they are entitled to respect, no matter how they behave, they have nothing to aspire to in life. After all, they already have everyone's respect, right?

This politically correct attitude is doing a grave disservice to our young men. They don't understand that they need to earn respect. These young men are not given a chance to actually earn respect in school, since everyone in that setting is entitled to respect no matter what. What a rude awakening it is for these boys when they leave the school system and find out that, in the real world, nobody owes them anything, much less their respect.

Respect for Yourself

Character – the willingness to accept responsibility for one's own life – is the source from which self-respect springs.
Joan Didion

Men of the code have great respect for themselves because they have earned it. They strive hard to discipline themselves to live by certain principles and they hold themselves to a higher standard than the average guy. When you discipline yourself, and hold yourself to a higher standard than you are required to, it gives you self-confidence, self-esteem and a feeling of accomplishment. You develop respect for yourself because of what you have achieved and who you have become.

True self-respect is only obtainable if you respect how you are living your life. While almost everyone will say that they respect themselves, those who do not hold themselves to a high standard of behavior, really don't respect themselves deep down inside. They may not know exactly why, but they will feel that something is missing, that they are not living up to their highest potential.

All respect is earned, even self-respect. The respect that you have for yourself determines how much you adhere to your principles, and your faithfulness to your principles determines how much you respect yourself. The more you respect yourself, the more you will require yourself to live by a higher standard. And, the more that you discipline yourself to live by your own standards, the more your self-respect increases.

You show the world how much respect you have for yourself by the personal standards that you set for yourself. If you have lower standards for yourself, it shows in your behavior, how you dress, how you speak, and your overall demeanor. If you see someone dressed in dirty clothes, with a profane statement written on his sleeveless t-shirt, no shoes, unbrushed hair, etcetera, it is very obvious that he doesn't have much self-respect.

Don't get me wrong, there are many people who dress in expensive clothes and who drive expensive cars, who don't have much self-respect either. Self-respect doesn't come from anything external, it doesn't come from material things; it comes from inside. It comes from knowing who, and what you are, and living up to your own high standards. It has nothing to do with money. That is simply the way that some people try to achieve self-respect, but it never truly works. Respect can't be bought; it has to be earned. You earn it by being true to yourself, your ethics, your principles, and living your life according to your own terms.

Seeking Respect from Others

Respect yourself and others will respect you.
Confucius

When you have authentic self-respect, others will respect you. They may not like you; they may not show that they respect you; they may even show contempt and hatred for you; but deep down inside, they will respect you. But, in the end, it doesn't matter how others respond to you or what they think about you, when you have true self-respect, the opinions of others is of little consequence.

Never allow the opinions of others to affect your self-respect. Your job is to be worthy of respect, not to expect or try to win the respect of others. The respect of others will come when you are content to simply be yourself and live a life worthy of their respect.

You don't need to compare yourself to anyone else. You don't need to compete with other people or to judge yourself by their standards. People respect men who have enough self-esteem to live their life, their way. They respect a man that has the backbone to live what he believes, regardless of what anyone else does.

Simply concentrate on being a man of honor, character, and integrity, and you will find that you will have the respect of other men. You earn the respect of others by your actions, true, authentic actions that are based on honor and integrity.

Trying to win their respect, by changing to satisfy their expectations, will not afford you their true respect. In fact, they will see you as weak and fickle, since you are willing to change who you are in order to win their approval. When you do this, you actually lose their respect instead of gain their respect.

Think about the characters from heroic movies and novels. Which characters do you respect and which ones do you not respect? Do you respect the hero who has the courage and the backbone to defy those who try to change him or do you respect the characters who play political games to try and win the respect of others? We respect the heroes, the strong men who bow down to no one, those who truly know what they stand for and what they won't stand for. The question is why do we respect those men? What is it that we admire in them and wish we had for ourselves in our own lives? The answer is their character, their independence, their courage, and their honor.

The respect of others comes from what we are inside and how we have the courage to live according to our own beliefs. No one respects a man who is a coward or who changes his ethics according to which way the wind blows.

If you want the respect of others, you must have deep self-respect; you must be independent of their opinions concerning how you live your life. You must stand for what you believe and act on your principles. This is the only way to earn true respect from other people. Respect gained by any other means, is not true respect, but merely political posturing.

At this point, you may be asking why it is important to be courteous if you are not trying to impress others or if you do not really care about the opinion of others. And that is a great question.

The Importance of Being Courteous

As we are, so we do;
and as we do, so is it done to us;
we are the builders of our fortunes.
Ralph Waldo Emerson

I have already discussed the difference between respect and courtesy. While you have to earn respect, courtesy is given; you can't demand respect, but you can demand courtesy.

Back to the question concerning why we must be courteous if we are not trying to impress others, the answer is simple – you aren't being courteous to impress other people; you are being courteous because that is a part of being a superior man.

When we act in a courteous manner, we are teaching others how they are expected to treat us. Do you want others to treat your courteously or to be thoughtless, rude, and crude? If you want to be treated with courtesy, then it stands to reason that you should be courteous to other people. As Emerson stated, as you do, so it is done to you. It is common sense that if you are not courteous to others, they are most likely not going to be courteous to you.

It should be made clear that simply being courteous to other people, does not guarantee that they will be courteous to you. While it is true that there is a much higher chance that if you are courteous, others will be courteous back to you, there are many people who won't be courteous no matter how you act. There will always be rude, discourteous people in this world; that is just a fact of life.

The bottom line is that you aren't being courteous in order to persuade others to be courteous to you; you are being courteous because that is a part of who you are as a man of the code. Courtesy and manners speak to your character, not the character of others. Your actions reflect on you, not those in your company.

It should be a part of your code to conduct yourself in a certain way, no matter how others act. A part of your code of conduct should be to always treat others with courtesy and to use your manners. There are very few exceptions to this. Winston Churchill stated that, "Even if you have to kill a man, it cost you nothing to be polite." There are very few circumstances that are more dreadful than having to kill someone. If you should be polite and courteous when you are in a situation that you may have to kill a man, how much more so should you be courteous in your everyday interactions.

Being courteous is simply a way of showing the world that you live by certain standards, and that those standards require you to be well-behaved, even if those around you are not. Courtesy is both about showing respect to others and showing others that you have respect for yourself. Remember, you don't have to actually *have* respect for someone else in order to treat them in a respectful manner. But you do have to have a certain level of respect for yourself in order to demand that you always act in a courteous way towards other people.

Using manners and being courteous should become an integral part of who you are; it should become natural for you. If this is not natural for you, then practice it until it becomes natural. Manners are like everything else, you have to cultivate them in your life until they become a vital part of who you are. You can develop any habit if you practice the specific action every day for about a month.

If being courteous is something that, for whatever reason, is not natural for you, start consciously practicing using your manners every day until it becomes second nature to you, until it becomes something that is so natural for you that you never have to give it a second thought.

And always remember that your actions tell people who you are. While you are using your manners as a sign of being respectful to others, ultimately, your manners speak to the kind of man that you are. People watch how you speak, how you act, and how you handle yourself overall, in order to know who you are and what kind of man you are. How you treat others speaks volumes about what kind of man you are.

Albert Einstein stated, "I speak to everyone in the same way, whether he is the garbage man or the president of the university." Living your life like this speaks to your authenticity and your sincerity. If you speak to everyone the same way, you are truly being yourself; you are not putting on airs to impress some people, while at the same time, being curt to those who you consider to be lesser men.

Also, when you treat everyone in the same manner, you are showing your self-confidence in being yourself. You are simply you, whether you are speaking to someone of great importance or someone who is not in the position to help you in any way. People respect and admire the man who is comfortable in his own skin, who tries to be nothing more than himself in every situation.

This is exactly what I mean when I say to conduct yourself in a manner that is worthy of respect and don't worry about what others think. Your job is to be a man that is worthy of respect, not to ensure that others respect you. To be worthy of respect, you have to conduct yourself in a certain way. You have to be courteous, respectful, and a man who lives by his own principles. Why would anyone have respect for you if you don't even have enough manners to be courteous to other people?

Many people seem to wrongly associate conducting yourself with courtesy and good manners with being standoffish or snobbish, but nothing could be further from the truth. Someone who thinks that they are better than other people won't take the time to be courteous to them; they simply blow them off. Being courteous is simply treating people as though they matter. It is treating people in a respectful way, which is how you should treat people.

Respect yourself enough to hold yourself to a higher standard of conduct, both with other people and when you are alone. Decide what kind of man you will be and then be that man. Don't allow the actions of others to determine how you will behave. Decide how you will behave and then behave that way, regardless of what other people do or don't do. That is the sign of a man who has respect for himself and others.

Be a man that is worthy of respect and a man who demonstrates that fact to others by how he conducts himself and how he treats other people. You are only responsible for your behavior, not the behavior of other people. Give your sincere respect to those people who truly deserve it. If someone doesn't deserve your respect, the code requires that you still treat them in a respectful way and be courteous. Be courteous to everyone, but never give your respect to people who do not truly deserve it. Remember, respect is not a God-given right, but something that everyone must earn by their own actions.

Reflections for the Superior Man

This is the final test of a gentleman:
his respect for those who can be
of no possible service to him.
William Lyon Phelps

He that respects himself is safe from others.
He wears a coat of mail that none can pierce.
Henry Wadsworth Longfellow

He who does not have the courage to speak up
for his rights cannot earn the respect of others.
Rene G. Torres

Politeness is a sign of dignity, not subservience.
Theodore Roosevelt

Seek not the favor of the multitude; it is seldom got
by honest and lawful means. But seek the testimony
of the few; and number not voices, but weight them.
Immanuel Kant

Knowledge will give you power,
but character respect.
Bruce Lee

If you want to be respected by others, the great thing is to respect yourself.
Only by that, only by self-respect will you compel others to respect you.
Fyodor Dostoyevsky

I cannot conceive of a greater loss
than the loss of one's self-respect.
Gandhi

I acknowledge no man as my superior, except for his own worth,
or as my inferior, except for his own demerit.
Theodore Roosevelt

Life is short, but there is always time enough for courtesy.
Ralph Waldo Emerson

A man's manners are a mirror in which he shows his portrait.
Johann Wolfgang von Goethe

Chapter 12

Truth and Honesty

There are new words now that excuse everybody.
Give me the good old days of heroes and villains;
the people you can bravo or hiss. There was a truth to
them that all the slick credulity of today cannot touch.
Bette Davis

Always Seek the Truth

There is no advantage in deceiving yourself.
Bodhidharma

Superior men always seek the truth in every situation. At first, you may think to yourself that everyone seeks the truth, but that would be jumping to conclusions. That fact is that the vast majority of people do not care enough to really seek the truth. Whether it is because of laziness or apathy, most people are simply content to believe whatever is offered to them as the truth.

Different people have different agendas, each usually based on what is best for them personally. People spin the truth, they exaggerate, they tell half-truths, and they flat out lie, all with reasons that are usually hidden behind carefully constructed misinformation which is designed to make it very difficult for anyone to get to the truth of the matter. Because of this, it takes a lot of time and effort to excavate the truth.

Most people are too busy with their job, their family, and their own life, to take the time to discover the truth, so they simply base their opinions on the word of others, many who do the exact same. And the more those falsehoods are shared, the further from the truth they become.

Think about that game we all have played in school, where the teacher gives the first student some information, he tells the next student, and so on down the line. By the time that information gets to the last student, it doesn't even resemble what the teacher said to the first student at the beginning, and this example is with a simple statement.

Now think about how twisted the truth can get when it starts off as a cleverly constructed lie, professionally covered up by a truckload of misinformation. This is how we get most of our information in today's world. We rarely get the whole truth, if we get any truth at all. Information is put out with a specific purpose, and the majority of the time, it is accepted as fact, and we move on to the next story.

Misinformation and half truths originate from our governments, our news media, different companies and organizations, and private individuals. Then word of mouth does the rest. When all the webs are spun, the truth is completely lost, buried somewhere deep within the muck.

It is easy to see why very few people take the time to get to the truth, but the superior man, knowing that the truth is rarely in plain view, takes the time to dig deeper and get the whole story. He knows that it is impossible to make an informed decision without knowing the truth to start with, thus he looks behind the veil so he is not deceived.

Lying has become so common that we actually expect it from our leaders and our government. It has become a joke. People sit attentively listening to political rhetoric and empty promises, and then turn around and seriously discuss what they have heard as if they have no clue that these people can't be trusted. They seem to put blinders on and simply don't care.

Political lies have become so commonplace that the younger generation has completely checked out when it comes to politics. Our president can stand up and lie through his teeth, and people simply laugh about it, when in fact, he should be humiliated by his never-ending lies. A man of honor certainly would be, but then a man of honor wouldn't be a liar to begin with.

But our politicians' lying is handled as some kind of game or an interesting reality show for the media. No one in the media has the courage to call our politicians liars; instead, they put them on a pedestal, hanging on their every word. And when it is overtly obvious that one of them is lying through his or her teeth, the media smoothes it over by using terms such as, "She misspoke," "He greatly exaggerated," or "He over-simplified."

People have become desensitized to other people lying. It has come to be expected. The days of a man's word being his honor are all but over. Only a small minority of people take their word seriously anymore. To everyone else, lying, and dealing with lies, has simply become their way of life. It seems that no one has a problem with lying if that is what it takes to get their way or to get what they want in a particular situation.

When someone is caught in a lie, they simply shrug it off and move on, and no one seems to think it is a big deal. Our world has become a world of cowards and liars, weak, spineless people who lack the character or intestinal fortitude to speak the truth.

This is simply not acceptable to men of the code. They seek the truth in all things. Lying is not a little thing to them; in fact, they consider it dishonorable and an act of cowardice.

Always seek the truth so that you will be able to make rational decisions which are based on truth instead of lies. If you base a decision on lies, then your decision will be faulty right from the start. Don't merely take someone's word for something. Do your homework and verify everything that is important to you. Don't be like the lazy, apathetic populace, who really couldn't care one way or the other. Be wise enough to see through the lies and the hidden agendas. Care enough about the truth to seek it out.

Superior men take their word seriously; their word is their honor. If they say something is so, you can bank on it. Men of the code are not cowards. They live by the principles that they profess, and those principles are important to them. Be a superior man. If you know the truth, tell the truth; if you don't know the truth, either be silent or say that you don't know.

Truth is not Subjective

Truth does not change because it is, or is not,
believed by a majority of the people.
Giordano Bruno

Truth is not subjective. The truth is the truth, period. It doesn't matter if you don't like the truth, if it upsets you, if it offends you, if you wish it weren't true. None of that matters; the truth is still the truth.

Likewise, a lie does not become the truth simply because many people believe it. If the whole world agrees with a lie, it still doesn't make it true. A lie is a lie and the truth is the truth; there are no grey areas. This statement of fact really irritates many people in today's world. They want to argue that all truth is subjective because of our individual perceptions. But that couldn't be further from reality.

Your perceptions are simply how you perceive the world around you. The only person or thing that your perceptions affect is you. There is no such thing as "your truth" or "my truth." There is only THE truth. Now, you may see things in a different way than I do, that is just the way we function as human beings, but neither your perceptions nor my perceptions change the real truth.

Inevitably, when I teach this, I have people who want to argue about this and ask, "The truth according to who?" That is a meaningless question. The truth is the truth, period. The existence of the truth does not depend on someone's definition or point of view. When someone asks, "according to whom," they are no longer talking about the truth, but rather they are referring to people's opinions about the truth. There is a huge difference.

Let me approach this in a different way. Let's say a man is wearing a pair of rose-colored glasses. The tint in his glasses colors everything that he looks at in a specific way. To his mind, what he is seeing is the truth. The sky has a beautiful, rose-colored tint to it, as does everything else that he looks at. He sees it; therefore he believes it to be the truth.

But, even though he may believe that what he sees is the truth, it does not change the true color of the sky. The sky is still blue, or whatever color it may be at the time. Some people may say that what this man sees is *his truth*, but that is incorrect. It is his *perception of the truth*, not his truth.

There is an ancient proverb which states that the sky is not less blue because the blind man does not see it. As I said, there is no such thing as *your truth* or *my truth*, there is only *the* truth. Everything else is merely personal perceptions. Our perceptions can, and do, lie to us.

Everyone that has ever been taken in by a conman, had the perception that the conman was on the up and up in the beginning. Their perception was that the guy was honest, and their perception was wrong. I can give you hundreds of examples where someone's perceptions were completely erroneous, but to them, at that time, they believed that their perceptions were the truth.

Personal observations change, the truth does not. How you do, or do not, see the world, does not affect the truth; it only affects how you perceive the truth.

Superior men understand that their personal beliefs and their background knowledge can affect how they see things, and they make every effort to see things rationally and with an open mind, instead of allowing their biases to distort reality.

Do the best that you can to see things the way they really are, not the way that you want them to be or the way that you wish they were. It is much too easy to deceive yourself by being lazy. Seeing the truth requires something that not many people want to do today – spend time doing research and thinking about what they find.

It is much easier for people to merely accept the sound bites that are constantly fed to them on the news, social networks, and other media. It takes discipline to pull yourself away from all of the technology and just spend time in thought. This is what is known as thinking for yourself, something that is a novel idea to many in this day and age. The superior man is an independent thinker. He thinks for himself and makes sure that his thoughts are indeed, his thoughts, and not someone else's thoughts which have been carefully constructed and spoon fed to him through the various technological means constantly available in today's world.

Men of the code understand that truth is black and white; it is merely man's ability to comprehend the truth that is subjective. Don't buy into the politically correct notion of "all truth is based on perception." It isn't.

Why People Lie

I never lie because I don't fear anyone.
You only lie when you're afraid.
John Gotti

There are a multitude of reasons that people give for lying, but they almost always boil down to one thing – they are afraid of the consequences of telling the truth. If you aren't afraid of telling the truth, why bother lying?

You may be thinking that the conman who lies to swindle you out of your money is not lying because he is scared of the truth; he is lying because he wants something from you. Well, yes, he does want something from you, but he is scared that he won't be able to get it if he tells the truth. In fact, he *knows* that he won't be able to get your money by telling the truth, so he lies.

Every lie, with one exception which I will discuss later, stems from cowardice and fear. If you have nothing to fear, you would tell the truth. But people are afraid, so they lie.

The things which people are afraid of run the gamut. They may be afraid of getting in trouble. They may be afraid of not getting something that they want. They may simply be afraid of hurting someone's feelings. There are thousands of reasons that people use to justify lying.

Men of honor don't take their word lightly. They understand that the act of lying is an act of cowardice, and they are not cowards. Superior men still live by the concept that their word is their bond; their word is their honor. If you want someone to have confidence in your word, then don't lie. It is as simple as that. When you constantly tell the truth, people know that they can trust you and that they can have confidence in what you say.

Honesty speaks to your character. It should be one of the principles by which you live your life. Have you ever known anyone to truly respect or look up to someone who consistently lies and can't be trusted? I doubt it. For most people, if they know that someone will lie at the drop of a hat, they trust nothing that he says and, if you really get down to the truth of the matter, you would find that they really have no respect for him either.

Men of the code are men who have the backbone to be honest. They don't lie for their own personal gain or to avoid the consequences of their actions. They simply tell the truth.

This is not to say that they are overly blunt or tactless. There is a big difference between being honest and being brutally honest. There is always a way to be honest and to be tactful at the same time. Men who like to brag about how they are "brutally honest" are more times than not, just plain rude.

As a man of the code, you have a duty to be honest and truthful, but you should also be tactful. In the same way that most people do not respect someone who is a liar, most people also don't respect a man who is rude and obnoxious, even if he is telling the truth.

You must set certain standards for yourself and these standards will guide your actions. You can't merely have a couple of admirable qualities, but be lacking in many other areas. The superior man must be the whole package. Be honest, but do it in the right way. If you can't be honest and tactful at the same time, simply be silent. Always speak the truth, but if you can't speak the truth, don't lie. Silence is far better than rudeness and rudeness is better than lying.

When Lying is Acceptable

Sometimes you have a higher duty than telling the truth.
Bohdi Sanders

As with most things in life, there is an exception to always being honest. Men of the code not only have to understand and live by their principles, but they also need to understand the hierarchy of their principles. If you have a choice between two individual principles, you must know which one is the most important.

Say for example, that you lived in Nazi Germany and you were hiding two Jewish girls from the Nazis. If Nazi soldiers came to your door and asked you if you were hiding those girls, would you have a higher duty to protect the innocent girls or to be honest to the Nazis?

There are times when life will present you with these kinds of decisions, so it is important to make sure that you understand the hierarchy of your principles, which ones are most important. In the example above, you would have a higher duty to protect the innocent than to be honest with the criminals. It would not be an act of honor to have given the girls over to men who would have killed them. So, in the particular circumstance, telling the truth would have been an act of cowardice, and lying an act of courage.

Most things in life are not black and white; there are shades of grey. This is not to say that you should live by situational ethics; that is merely justifying your actions. You shouldn't live by situational ethics, but at the same time, you shouldn't be rigidly bound by a strict set of rules. Yes, I know that this sounds like an oxymoron, but it isn't.

For the superior man, one thing guides all of his actions – what is right. He lives by a specific code, but he is not rigidly bound by that code. His code is a guide that directs his actions, but underlying everything in that code is the one thing that is non-negotiable – doing the right thing.

If doing what is right means that he has to do something that he normally would not do, then he doesn't think twice about it; he does what is right. What truly makes an action right or wrong is the underlying intention behind the action. Going back to the example above, lying to the Nazis was not a selfish action, but a courageous action. His intentions were honorable, therefore his actions were honorable.

It is not only important to do the right thing, but to do it the right way and with the right intentions. Telling someone the truth with malicious intentions can be just as bad as lying, and lying to someone, because of honorable intentions, can be more honorable than telling the truth. For many people, this is a hard concept to grasp.

Rigidity is the source of many evils in this world and always has been. Men, who put their rules, or the law, first place in their life, do many unjust deeds and justify them by pointing to their rules or the law. Never trust a man who is not willing to bend the rules in order to do what is right.

There is a time and a place for everything. What is important is that you do everything in your power to do the right thing in every situation. Consider your code, but never put your code above what is right. When there is a question about the right course of action to take, always ask yourself, "What is right?"

Lao Tzu taught, "Highly evolved people have their own conscience as pure law." Superior men should be highly evolved. They should develop themselves to the point of having a thorough understanding of right and wrong. What is right should always be your trump card.

Reflections for the Superior Man

Hard truths can be dealt with, triumphed over,
but lies will destroy your soul.
Patricia Briggs

It is hard to believe that a man is telling the truth when
you know that you would lie if you were in his place.
Henry Louis Mencken

The important thing is not to stop questioning.
Albert Einstein

It does not prove a thing to be right
because the majority say it is so.
Friedrich von Schiller

No statement should be believed
because it is made by an authority.
Hans Reichenbach

If you add to the truth, you subtract from it.
The Talmud

Instead of thinking how things may be, see them as they are.
Samuel Johnson

Throughout your life, choose truth and your words
will be more believable than other people's oaths.
Isocrates

Look beneath. For ordinary things are far other than they seem.
The false is forever the lead in everything, continually dragging along
the fools; the truth brings up the rear, is late, and limps along in time.
Baltasar Gracian

Weigh the meaning and look not at the words.
Ben Johnson

The truth is for the few; the false is for the populace.
Baltasar Gracian

When you shoot an arrow of truth, dip its point in honey.
Arabian Proverb

Chapter 13

Justice

A just man. He stands on the side of the right with such conviction,
that neither the passion of a mob, nor the violence of a despot
can make him overstep the bounds of reason.
Baltasar Gracian

What is Justice

Being good is easy, what is difficult is being just.
Victor Hugo

Men of the code are men of justice. What is just and what is right are synonymous. Justice is based on fairness or reasonableness in the way people are treated. It is based on good, sound reason and requires wisdom and insight.

Many people get confused when it comes to issues of justice. As I said, justice is based on fairness, but what exactly is fairness? What does the word "fair" actually mean?

Misunderstanding the true meaning of the word "fair" is where many people get confused when it comes to the subject of justice. The word "fair" implies being reasonable or unbiased. It does not, however, mean what most people think that it means. Most people, when they use the word "fair," use it to mean "the same or equal," but that is not always the case.

While the word "fair" can mean being treated equal, it doesn't have to mean equal. Is it fair to hold the mentally retarded man to the same standards as the man with an IQ of 160? Of course not! This would not be acting in a reasonable way; there would be no wisdom in that. This would be ridiculous and highly unfair, but it would be treating the two men the same. Treating people fairly is not synonymous with treating them exactly the same.

True justice means that the right thing is done in every individual situation, not that the *exact same thing* is done in every specific situation. There is a big distinction between doing the *right* thing in a specific situation and doing the *same* thing in a specific situation. Real justice takes effort, insight and wisdom; it is not a cookie cutter process. The problem is that too many people in today's society do not understand this.

Real justice is customized for each individual person and each individual circumstance. A "one-size-fits-all" mentality is not true justice, but rather legalistic and systematic. This is what is happening in our schools today. They proudly boast of their "no-tolerance" policies, as if they are something to be proud of, when in fact, no-tolerance policies would be more appropriately named "no-justice" policies.

Most schools today have a no-tolerance policy towards fighting, weapons on campus, and drugs on campus. At first, these sounds like great policies. These policies make it sound like we will finally get our out-of-control schools, which have been run by incompetent administrators for decades, under control. But is that really what these no-tolerance policies do?

In reality, these policies lack any semblance of justice and fairness. For example, if a bully is bullying a young boy and that boy manages the courage to fight back, he is automatically suspended from school. This is not just and it is not fair; it is merely legalistic. Young men today not only have to muster the courage to stand up to the bully, but they have to do so, while at the same time, having the courage to get in trouble with the inept administrations which run most of our schools.

The same goes for the no-tolerance policies about drug and weapons on campus. The administrators cannot be troubled to take the time to be wise and just, so they use the time-saving crutch of their no-tolerance policies. If a boy brings his prescription allergy pills to school in order to take one when and if he needs it, he is suspended just as if he would have brought some illegal drug to school.

If his mom packs a plastic knife in his lunch box in order for him to cut his lunch, the school administrator only sees a knife; he doesn't take into account the circumstance. Again, the boy will be suspended. This is not justice; it is idiocy.

This did not happen when I was in school because we had administrators who cared about developing young men of character, not mindless sheep. Every situation is different and justice in each situation requires that you take the time to understand both the situation and the intentions of those involved. People used to know this, but our new and "enlightened" societies have exchanged true justice for time-saving, one-size-fits-all policies that serve the system, not justice.

The modern idea of justice is little different than lynch mob mentality. Lynch mobs have no desire to get to the truth of the matter or understand the reality of the situation; they merely want to punish someone, get it over with, and move on. It would take too much effort for them to take the time to stop, gather information, and make a rational decision concerning what justice is in each situation; so they just hang them high and move on.

This has nothing in common with true justice. Justice is having the courage to ensure that the right thing is done, in spite of the overriding consensus or emotions involved. It has nothing to do with what is the quickest or easiest way to handle the situation. It has nothing to do with making sure that everyone is treated in exactly the same way. Justice is ensuring that right is done in every situation.

The Corruption of Justice

Often man is preoccupied with human
rules and forgets the inner law.
Antoine the Healer

All man-made laws are subject to abuse. They are made by men who are less than honorable, although they revel in using "honorable" as their title. Many times they are enforced unfairly and for reasons other than justice.

Our society is so fast-paced that most people will not slow down enough to understand specific situations well enough to ensure that justice is carried out. God help the innocent man that is drug before a jury in today's world; his future might as well be determined by a coin toss.

Justice in today's world has become nothing more than a game played by law enforcement, prosecutors, defense lawyers, and judges, most of who couldn't care less about bona fide justice, but rather about the game and the financial system which it supports.

You may be shocked to learn that our legal system today is more about money than about justice. It's true! Our justice system is no longer about justice, but rather it is about revenue. Since this book is not about the abuses of our legal system, I will not delve into too much detail here, but I will give you just a few statistics to think about.

Today, the prison system in the United States is big business. Its estimated turnover is around $74 billion and eclipses the gross domestic product of 133 nations. Let me repeat that. Our prison system produces around 74 BILLION dollars a year! It is a money-making machine! In fact, it is so profitable that many prisons are now privately owned. That is big business, not justice!

The prison privatization boom began in the 1980s, under the governments of Ronald Reagan and George Bush, but reached its height in 1990 under the Clinton administration. These private prisons bring in billions of dollars a year, and to top this off, you are paying for it. That's right. This money comes from the American taxpayers.

According to a 2012 Vera Institute of Justice study, the number of people incarcerated has increased by over 700% over the last four decades. And, the cost of this new business to the American taxpayer has been in the billions.

Think about that for a minute. The incarceration numbers have increased by over 700% while, at the same time, our politicians continually tell us how the crime rate has dropped over the past years. Does that make sense to you?

And these numbers do not include the revenue generated by our court system, our police, those who work in our legal system, or the lawyers! If you are arrested and have to go to court, even if you are innocent, you have just lost thousands of dollars. And all of this is just touching the surface!

Traffic tickets alone are a multi-billion industry. They have basically nothing to do with highway safety. Do you think that the cop hiding on the side of the road is there for your safety? Of course not! He is there for one reason, and one reason only – to bring in money. It is all about money. It is estimated that government agencies and insurance companies bring in 7.5 to 15.5 billion dollars annually from traffic tickets alone.

I could go on and on about the business of our "justice" system, but that is a whole book in itself. I will just wrap this section up by stating that a legal system which puts more importance on revenue than it does on ensuring justice, has more in common with the mafia than it does with a system of justice. Men of honor will not play this game.

Superior Men Value Justice

The superior man enacts equity;
justice is the foundation of his deeds.
Confucius

Superior men always put justice, what is right, over popular opinion and the law. They understand that individual circumstances must be taken into account in order to truly understand a situation or to know what action is right and just.

There is no such thing as absolute law when it comes to the law of man. The only absolute laws are laws of the Universe, not laws made by men. This is true regardless of the law, but it is even truer when those laws have the hidden agenda of making money, not ensuring justice. When considering a law, consider the righteousness of that law.

Most people today do not take the time to understand what is going on with our justice system. They are naïve and too trusting. As I stated in an earlier chapter, men of the code take the time to get to the truth; they don't merely believe something because it is stated by the government or those in authority.

If you want real justice, you have to work for it. You can't be lazy. The truth in most circumstance is not obvious; you have to take the time to uncover the truth in order to ensure justice. Not doing so means that justice is not really that important to you, so you simply trust that you are being told the truth and act on what you are told. By now, you should understand that acting on what you are told is not wise. You must find the truth for yourself, as it is more often than not, hidden.

Superior men act on what they *know*, not what they think or what they are told. They understand that, from the beginning of time, people have lied and tried to cover up the facts in order to manipulate specific situations to their advantage. Acting on information without verifying it, is foolishness.

While we can't control everything, we can do our best to make sure that justice is served. It is your commitment to justice that makes your actions righteous, not the outcome of your actions. Your job, as a man of honor, is to be committed to justice, to be committed to what is right. Make sure that your actions are right and just, and let the chips fall where they may.

For the superior man, being just is not a matter for debate. Every action is either right or wrong, just or unjust. A door is either open or shut; it has to be one or the other. It can be almost shut, but almost shut is still technically open. In the same way, there are no grey areas when it comes to justice. An action is either just or it is not just, period.

Many people are more than willing to be unjust if that is what they perceive to be best for them. Superior men do not see that as an option. Men of the code hold themselves to a higher standard. Their every decision is based on right and wrong. Justice is the cornerstone of their every action. Justice is an integral part of their lives; it is their priority.

Hold yourself accountable for all of your actions. The Bible states, "He that is unjust in the least is unjust also in much." Don't allow any situation in life to cause you to be unjust. Be a man that stands out from the crowd and who stands for justice, no matter what the odds. Always do what is right, no matter what anyone around you does.

Reflections for the Superior Man

Don't appear just; be just.
Aeschylus

The voice of the majority is no proof of justice.
Friedrich von Schiller

To avoid action when justice is at stake
demonstrates a lack of courage.
Gichin Funakoshi

Extreme law is often injustice.
Terence

If thou wouldst seek justice, thyself must be just.
Stephen R. Lawhead

You can also commit injustice by doing nothing.
Marcus Aurelius

Highly evolved people have their
own conscience as pure law.
Lao Tzu

The just man is not one who does hurt to none, but
one who having the power to hurt, represses the will.
Pythagoras

Justice will not be served until those who are
unaffected are as outraged as those who are.
Benjamin Franklin

Truth never damages a cause that is just.
Gandhi

Right is right, even if everyone is against it,
and wrong is wrong, even if everyone is for it.
William Penn

No man is justified in doing evil
on the grounds of expediency.
Theodore Roosevelt

Chapter 14

Dignity and Sincerity

Be mild with the mild, shrewd with the crafty, confiding to the honest, rough to the ruffian, and a thunderbolt to the liar. But in all this, never be unmindful of your own dignity.
John Brown

Carry Yourself with Dignity

Nothing is so essential as dignity.
Time will reveal who has it and who has it not.
Elizabeth Gilbert

Dignity is a sense of pride and self-respect in yourself. Your dignity shines through in the way that you carry yourself in every situation. Men of the code should conduct themselves with dignity at all times. This doesn't mean that they are always stern and serious, but that they never lower themselves to a level where their dignity is compromised.

Real men maintain their dignity no matter what situation they may be in. You must maintain your dignity at all times. To some, this statement may imply that they have to go through life avoiding fun and being serious at all times, but this is because they have a false idea about what true dignity is.

True dignity comes from your internal attitude about yourself, and this attitude comes through in your actions. It originates in your thoughts. Dignity is what makes you worthy of respect and honor. It is all in how you carry yourself and present yourself to others. And, as with all actions, that begins in your mind.

Dignity is the sense of self-worth that you present to other people. It tells them what you truly feel about yourself, and that cannot be faked, at least not for long. True dignity has to come from a place of sincerity.

You can always tell the difference between someone who is faking self-esteem and someone who truly has a good sense of self-worth. Those who are trying hard to portray themselves as having dignity come off as elitist and snobby; those who have true dignity come off as down to earth and noble.

You want to be careful about the image that you portray to others. Be sincere in how you portray yourself, but at the same time, make sure that you act appropriately for the situation. You want to build a reputation and an image of dignity and nobility, but do so with sincerity. Don't fake it; live it.

Having dignity means that you are worthy of honor and respect. While you can never demand that others respect you, you can always ensure that you deserve respect. You do this through your actions. Self-respect is the belief in your own integrity and dignity. How can you truly have self-respect if you don't carry yourself with dignity, or if deep down inside, you don't truly think that you deserve respect?

This is something that must be cultivated and can only come from the inside. There is no self-respect without self-discipline. Your sense of dignity becomes stronger and stronger as you discipline yourself to live by the standards by which you have decided to live. A lack of standards is one of the main causes of low self-worth. When someone does not live by any standards, or lives by low standards, he loses respect for himself. How can you respect yourself when you don't live by your principles and don't carry yourself with dignity?

It is only by living in accord with our own personal standards that we feel good about ourselves and start to develop self-respect. You can be very successful, at least externally, and still lack self-respect if you are not living by the standards which you know inside that you should be living by. Dignity is not something that you can fake. Your conscience knows whether or not you are living up to your standards, and it will not let you off the hook if you have thrown self-discipline to the wind and lowered your standards.

For the man of the code, this means that you develop more and more self-respect as you discipline yourself to live according to your code of honor. The more you discipline yourself to follow the strict standards by which you live, the more concrete your self-respect, your dignity, becomes. You start to respect the fact that you have the fortitude to stand by your beliefs.

You know that living as a man of the code requires great discipline, and you respect the fact that you have the discipline that it takes to walk this path. This leads to dignity. And when you have true dignity that comes from sincerely knowing that you deserve the respect of others, it will manifest in your actions; you will carry yourself with dignity at all times.

As I stated, true dignity starts with your thoughts. When you know beyond the shadow of a doubt, that you deserve to be respected, that you have earned respect by your efforts and actions, a sense of dignity will rise up inside you. This confidence, which comes from truly knowing that you are a man worthy of respect, will show through in everything that you do.

You will start to feel better about yourself. You will respect yourself and therefore you will know, without a shadow of a doubt, that you deserve to be respected by others, whether they respect you or not. Their actions and opinions don't matter. You know the truth; and that truth, that respect for how you live your life, will shine through.

You Must Be Sincere

With sincerity, there is virtue.
Shinto Maxim

The superior man should be a man of dignity, not merely appear to be a man of dignity. This means you must be sincere. You must be free from hypocrisy and develop honesty of mind, which means that you have to monitor your thoughts. No one respects a hypocrite. A hypocrite is someone who pretends to have admirable principles or beliefs, but doesn't back them up with his actions. He pretends to be something he is not. He is a fraud. This is not the way of the superior man, but rather the way of the charlatan.

Sincerity is a very important part of being a man of the code and it is vital when it comes to being comfortable in your own skin. If you are simply pretending to being a man of honor, or a man of dignity, your counterfeit dignity will be found out sooner or later. It does you no good to pretend to be someone or something that you are not.

Be who you are. This doesn't mean that you don't take pains to improve yourself and make yourself a better person, rather it means that you should be relaxed and comfortable letting people know who you truly are and what you stand for – be sincerely you. Don't worry about what everyone thinks about you, or if they approve or disapprove of who you are; just be yourself, be a man of dignity and honor. Let them see what a true dignity is through your actions.

The key here is being sincere, not simply appearing to be a man of honor. Be honorable to your very core. When you truly are the person you want to be, you do not have to be shy about being yourself. It is only when you are pretending to be someone other than who you really are, that you become unsure about allowing others to find out the truth.

For many people, depending on your personality, this can be a difficult thing to do. Most people desire the approval of their friends and family, and they can worry that if they allow others to see who they truly are, they will not approve of what they see. This is one of the main reasons that people hide who they are, and more or less play the part of an actor in public or around their friends and family. This usually boils down to one of two things.

First, either the person is lacking in overall self-confidence concerning who he is or how he lives his life and fears that his peers, friends, and family will not be accepting of who he truly is or how he lives. The second factor is that he wants so much to be liked or admired, that he is hesitant to take the risk because he fears that showing his real face will cost him the respect and admiration of his friends and family.

Both of these boil down to a lack of self-confidence in who he truly is as a person. While he may feel, deep down in his spirit, that he is living as he should, he has a deep-seated fear that others will not understand or approve of who he is or how he lives his life. It takes courage to live your life your way, without worrying about what other people think of your choices. It also takes sincerity and making up your mind that, in the end, you are going to live your life in your own way, no matter what anyone else may think about your choices.

This may seem like a weird statement considering the fact that we are talking about men who live a life of honor and dignity. After all, who doesn't respect a man of honor?

The reason that some men of honor worry about how others will perceive them is because so many do not live with honor in today's world. Therefore, those who do carry themselves with honor and dignity find that they stand out. It can be a scary proposition for some men, especially until their self-confidence is totally developed, to stand out or be different from their peers. For this reason, it is essential that you develop a sense of pride and self-respect in yourself and the life that you have chosen to live.

You have to be completely sincere about who you are and the principles by which you have chosen to live your life. Unless you are sincere about living life as a superior man, you are only fooling yourself, and this will not lead to permanent changes in your life. You have to be sincerely devoted to your beliefs and the principles in your life. If you are merely pretending, sooner or later that will come to light. As Aesop taught in his famous fables, "Those who pretend to be what they are not, sooner or later, find themselves in deep water."

Being sincere means having confidence in your decisions and who you are, or who you are becoming. You develop this confidence by meditating on who and what you want to be, then sincerely working to become that person. At this point, I need to make a distinction between pretending to live life as a man of the code and pretending to be who you want to be. These two actions may sound the same, but they are miles apart.

Pretending to live a life of honor and integrity, while at the same time really being the opposite, is merely being a hypocrite. Acting like the man that you want to be, as you work to develop the qualities that you sincerely desire to develop, is part of the process of becoming the person you want to become. If you want to be a man of honor, act like a man of honor until you sincerely have become that person. This is not being a hypocrite, but rather one of the techniques that one uses to change his character. Do you see the difference in the two?

Furthermore, being sincere means that you aren't competing with others. You are merely doing the best that you can do to improve your own life. It doesn't matter where anyone else is in the process of becoming who he wants to be; it only matters where you are and what you are doing to improve your own life. It is okay to use others as examples or as role models, but not as someone that you have to compete with in order to achieve your objectives.

Sincerity means that you truly believe in the life that you are striving to live. If you truly believe in something, with all of your heart and mind, why would you be embarrassed of standing out or being different?

Have the self-confidence to live your life with dignity, no matter how anyone else lives his life. Don't allow the fact that the majority of men don't live a life of honor and dignity, cause you to lower your standards or stray from your own path.

Allow them to see the true you. If you are truthfully living your life with honor and dignity, I promise they will respect you for what you are, and maybe secretly want to be the kind of man that you are, even if they don't let you know it. All men respect a man of true dignity, a man who has a sense of pride and self-respect.

Men of the code carry themselves with dignity in every situation of life, and do so sincerely. Their dignity is not for show; it is not to impress those around them. It is simply their way of life, who they truly are. And they do stand out from the crowd. That is a good thing, especially when you consider how the majority of men carry themselves in today's society. If you are not standing out from the crowd, you are doing something wrong.

The majority of men do not carry themselves with dignity or sincerity. Let them live as they will. You have decided to go beyond the ordinary and live a life of excellence. You have decided to be a man of the code, why would you be moved by those who live by lower standards? Just carry yourself with sincere dignity and don't worry about what others think about it. Your goal is not to be superior to others, your goal is to be superior to the man that you were yesterday.

Reflections for the Superior Man

Self-respect is the fruit of discipline; the sense of
dignity grows with the ability to say no to oneself.
Abraham J. Heschel

His words are his bonds, his oaths are oracles; his love sincere,
his thoughts immaculate; his tears, pure messengers sent from
his heart; his heart as far from fraud, as Heaven from Earth.
William Shakespeare

Dignity consists not in possessing honors,
but in the consciousness that we deserve them.
Aristotle

The whole dignity of man is in thought.
Labor then to think right.
Blaise Pascal

Insincerity is always weakness;
sincerity, even in error, is strength.
George Henry Lewes

The weak cannot be sincere.
La Rochefoucauld

Sincerity is impossible, unless it pervades the whole being,
and the pretence of it saps the very foundation of character.
James Russell Lowell

The shortest and surest way to live with honor in the world is to be in all
reality what we would appear to be; all human virtues increase and
strengthen themselves by the practice and experience of them.
Socrates

Sincerity is an openness of heart that is found in very few people.
What we usually see is only an artful disguise people
put on to win the confidence of others.
La Rochefoucauld

No man can produce great things who is not
thoroughly sincere in dealing with himself.
James Russell Lowell

Chapter 15

Discipline

He who conquers others is strong;
he who conquers himself is mighty.
Lao Tzu

Why is Discipline Important?

We must all suffer one of two things:
the pain of discipline or the pain of regret and disappointment.
Jim Rohn

Discipline is vital to living life according to your code. None of the other virtues or traits of the superior man will ever be developed to their full potential without discipline. It takes discipline to control your spirit, mind and body, bringing them all in line with the standards by which you have decided to live. Without discipline, you cannot live a life of excellence.

So, why is discipline so important? The answer lies in knowing what it takes to actually live according to higher standards than those around you. It takes a lot of time and constant effort to integrate these principles in your life. Living as a man of the code takes work and dedication – it's not the easiest lifestyle. If it was, everyone would live this way.

Without self-discipline, you will barely get out of the starting gate before you find yourself starting to make excuses for not living up to your code. If you really want to live a superior life, you must learn to discipline yourself. You must take control of your mind and body, and discipline them to meet your goals. If you don't, you will find that somewhere down the line, you will experience the pain of regret and disappointment for not following through with your goals. It's that simple.

Discipline is a form of delayed gratification. Either you discipline yourself now for future rewards, which you will be proud of and which will mold you into the person you want to be, or you live foolishly, only doing whatever your mind and body dictate to you. If you choose the latter, you pay for it in the future when you find your goals have never come to fruition. It is up to you to decide what the future holds for you. Will you discipline yourself and live a life of excellence or will you allow laziness and malaise to rob you of the discipline is important to virtually every part of your life.

To achieve anything worthwhile, you have to discipline yourself. If you continually put off honing your skills, in any area of life, you will find that your skills will not develop. Not only will they not develop, but they will regress.

It doesn't matter what the skill is that you want to perfect, if you don't work at it, it will fade away. This goes for everything from your martial arts skills to golf. Whatever skills you want to perfect in your life, you have to discipline yourself to work at them, and if you don't, you will eventually find yourself envious of those who had the discipline to continue to work and perfect their skills.

If the price of excellence is discipline, then you must have discipline to live a life of excellence, and living a life of excellence is what being a man of the code is all about. Therefore, discipline is vital to being a superior man.

You must discipline yourself to prepare in order to successfully meet future challenges. It doesn't matter what you want to accomplish in life, if you don't take the time to prepare yourself to meet future challenges, you will find that you will fall short.

Yet, so many people let discipline slide and still feel that they are prepared to meet life's challenges. This is merely self-deception. You must prepare yourself today to meet the challenges of tomorrow. If you wait until tomorrow, it will be too late, and all you will have is regrets over what you didn't do today.

You have to train yourself to do what it takes to compose your character, to control your mind and emotions, and to build your physical skills. It takes dedication and hard work, and many times your mind and your body will be screaming at you to do something besides work on your training. You have to have the discipline to overrule your mind, take control, and follow through to achieve your goals. This is what self-discipline is all about.

It does no good to only concentrate on the training that you enjoy or that you are good at, and which you find easy; you have to work on the areas that need improvement. You have to push yourself to train and improve your weak points, even if you find that training disagreeable and unpleasant. Life is not always about what you want to do, but what you need to do.

Whenever you find yourself tempted to be a couch potato instead of working on something that will improve your life, remind yourself what you really want. What is it that you want to achieve? What kind of person do you really want to be? Ask yourself these questions, and then ask yourself what you need to do to achieve those objectives.

You can look at your goals like a garden. In essence, you are cultivating all of the qualities that you want in your life by giving them continual attention. Just like a garden, you have to give your goals daily attention to see them come to fruition. If you start a garden and don't continue to tend to it, your goal of a good harvest will not be fulfilled. You have to discipline yourself to do the garden work in order to have a beautiful, striving garden, even when you had rather be doing other things.

The parts of your garden that are growing well and weed free will require less work; the parts that have weeds growing and are not thriving, will require more of your time. This same principle can be applied to the development of your character traits and the principles that you want to integrate into your life. You have to maintain the areas that you have developed well, and you have to work harder on the areas that seem to be problem areas for you.

By now, you should be starting to comprehend that self-discipline begins with your mind. You have to learn to control your mind in order to train your body to do what is needed to achieve your goals. If you can't control your mind, you will find that your self-discipline is weak. Discipline your mind, and your body will follow. It is your mind that controls your body.

The more you bring your mind under control, and force both your mind and your body to do what is needed to become the kind of man that you want to become, the more confident you will become in your ability to continue to develop self-discipline. It is like a continuous cycle where the more you discipline yourself, the easier it becomes to discipline yourself. And, as you continue to take control of your mind, and develop more self-discipline in your life, the more your self-confidence, self-respect, and self-esteem grow.

Self-discipline is just like everything else. The more you practice it and the more you work at it, the easier it becomes. Eventually it becomes almost automatic. This is the point that you want to get to in your life. Make self-discipline a habit in your life. Do not let your mind, emotions, or body dictate to you how you will live your life. You decide what kind of person you want to be, and then you tell your mind and body what they *will do* and force them to do what is needed to become the person that you want to become.

It is your dedication to becoming a superior man that will motivate you to develop this kind of self-discipline. Nobody can do this for you; it is totally in your hands. If you consistently discipline yourself, you will reap great rewards. Start to cultivate self-discipline in your life and take control of your world. The rewards are well worth it!

Reflections for the Superior Man

What lies in our power to do, it lies in our power not to do.
Aristotle

What we do upon some great occasion will probably depend
on what we already are; and what we are will be the
result of previous years of self-discipline.
Percy Bysshe Shelley

No man is free who is not master of himself.
Epictetus

By constant self-discipline and self-control,
you can develop greatness of character.
Grenville Kleiser

Discipline is the bridge between goals and accomplishments.
Jim Rohn

The price of excellence is discipline.
William Arthur Ward

Discipline is remembering what you want.
David Campbell

Self-discipline is an act of cultivation. It requires you
to connect today's actions to tomorrow's results.
Gary Ryan

Self-discipline begins with the mastery of your thoughts. If you don't
control what you think, you can't control what you do. Simply,
self-discipline enables you to think first and act afterward.
Napoleon Hill

A disciplined mind leads to happiness,
and an undisciplined mind leads to suffering.
Dalai Lama

Discipline is a bridge built through everyday action.
J. R. Rim

You can't achieve major goals with minimal work.
Rob Liano

Chapter 16

Self-Reliance

Prepare yourself for you must travel alone.
Book of the Golden Precepts

Self-reliance is reliance on one's own capabilities, judgment, or resources. Basically, it is your independence. Being self-reliant in today's world is a tall order. Is anyone truly self-reliant without owning their own farm or ranch, and being independently wealthy? And even if you do have the finances to be independently wealthy, you will still need to depend on others to some extent for your medical needs, supplies, etc. In short, very few people on this earth are completely self-reliant.

Nonetheless, it is important for the superior man to be as self-reliant as possible. Real men have independent spirits. They don't like having to depend on anyone else. If you are dependent on someone else, that person has some control over you, and as a result, he could possibly put you in a situation in which you don't want to be.

Self-reliance is basically relying on yourself for your needs instead of relying on other people. While it is true that everyone in today's world needs money to survive, or at least needs money to survive in comfort, you can still strive to be as independent as possible. Most people depend on others for their income; they have a job and work for someone else. While there is nothing wrong with that, it certainly puts you in a position where you are dependent on someone else, at least where your finances are concerned.

Although, as I said, there is nothing inherently wrong with working for someone else, it can place you in a difficult position at times. Let's look at an example. Say that your boss is not a man of character and he asks you to do something for his business that is not ethical. That puts you in a difficult moral position. On one hand, you need the money to support your family, but on the other hand, you want to stay true to your code of honor. Refusing to do as your boss wants could cost you your job, but complying will go against your own personal beliefs.

This is just one example; I'm sure you can think of dozens more. There will always be these kinds of conflicts when you depend on someone else instead of being totally self-reliant. These kinds of conflicts can put you in the difficult position of having to choose between making the money that your family needs to survive and living up to your own principles, and that is not a position that you want to find yourself in as a man of the code.

This is just something that the majority of us have to learn to live with and to work around. Unless you own your own company or business, you have to work for someone else to earn a living and to take care of your duties and responsibilities. You may be thinking that the answer is simple – just start your own business. And this is a viable option, but it is not as simple as it sounds.

Starting your own business is definitely easy; making a good living from your business is a whole other matter. There are thousands of people who own their own business and who are not beholding to someone else for their income, or are they? Even if you have your own business, you are still relying on other people to either purchase your products or your services. In essence, you are still relying on others for your income; the only difference is that you are in control of how you do it and the ethical practices of your business.

For example, an author is in the business of writing books or articles. He can decide what subject he will write on and can write whatever he wants. He has a lot of freedom, especially if he publishes his work himself. You may think that he is totally self-reliant for his living, but you would be wrong. Even if he publishes his own work, he will not make a penny if readers don't buy his books. He is still dependent on other people for his income. Are you starting to get the point? It is not easy to be totally self-reliant.

Therefore, self-reliance for the superior man becomes less of an absolute term and more of a relative term. Most people will most likely never be totally self-reliant, but you should strive to be as self-reliant as possible. Being self-reliant is not an all-or-nothing proposition. You can work to be as independent as possible, although you may not be totally self-reliant.

What you want to do is to become as independent as possible, in as many areas as you can. This doesn't just apply to the physical parts of life, but also to your mind and spirit. The more you take control over your own life, the more independent you become. For example, you may have to work for a company to make money, but you can use that money wisely by saving and investing; the more that you save, the more financially independent you become.

This principle works in every area of your life whether it has to do with your health, your home, or other areas. If you want to be more independent where your health is concerned, start to learn how to eat healthy, learn about holistic health cures instead of running to the doctor for every little thing. If you want to be more independent with your home, learn to do home repairs instead of having to always call a repair man to do the work for you. There are hundreds of examples concerning becoming more independent.

As I stated above, becoming self-reliant doesn't just relate to finances or the physical aspects of your life; being self-reliant concerns every single area of your life – physical, mental and spiritual. Actually, becoming independent in the mental and spiritual areas of your life is much easier and can be wrapped up in a simple statement: Think for yourself!

If you want to be independent, it is vital that you think for yourself and not let anyone else do your thinking for you. Don't let others tell you what you should think, how to think, or what to believe. There are many physical aspects of self-reliance that you have very little control over, but you have total control over your mind and your spiritual life. The only person that can stop you from being independent, where these two areas are concerned, is yourself.

Don't be lazy. Think for yourself at all times. Do your homework on whatever topic you may be mulling over, and think rationally. Your mind is your own, don't give anyone else control over what you think or how you think. It doesn't matter whether or not anyone else actually likes what you think or agrees with what you think; it is none of their business. Taking control over your mind is actually the first step in becoming self-reliant. If you can discipline yourself to become mentally independent of others, it will be easier for you to become independent in the other areas of your life.

You are not responsible to any man, as far as your thoughts and your spiritual life go. Your self-reliance is up to you, starting with becoming mentally independent. Start by making your mind independent, and then move on to as many areas as you possibly can.

Becoming mentally independent doesn't mean that you never listen to anyone else. There are a lot of wise men on this earth. You should listen to their wisdom and learn from them, but at the same time, you should think about what they say, not just take their words as gospel. Use what the wise men say, but always think about what is being said and seek the truth for yourself.

Why should you seek to be self-reliant? The answer lies in two words – freedom and safety. Being self-reliant gives you more personal freedom to live the way that you want to live. The more self-sufficient you become, the more freedom you have. If you don't want to be betrayed, trust only in yourself. Make self-sufficiency one of your main goals and continuously work towards it.

Reflections for the Superior Man

You may always be victorious if you will never enter into any
contest where the issue does not wholly depend upon yourself.
Epictetus

Recognize that if it's humanly possible,
you can do it too.
Marcus Aurelius

Depend on others and you will go hungry.
Nepalese Proverb

Each individual is responsible for his own evolution.
Lao Tzu

Depend not on another, but lean instead on yourself.
True happiness is born of self-reliance.
The Laws of Manu

It is thrifty to prepare today for the wants of tomorrow.
Aesop

Individually free is he who is responsible to no man.
Max Stirner

The greatest fruit of self-sufficiency is freedom.
Epicurus

Trust God, but tie up your camel.
Hadith

Those who live by the plow live in self-sufficiency.
All others lean on them to simply subsist.
Tiruvaluvar

More satisfying far, that many depend upon you,
than that you depend upon anybody.
Baltasar Gracian

If a man does not keep pace with his companions, perhaps it is
because he hears a different drummer. Let him step to the
music which he hears, however measured or far away.
Henry David Thoreau

Chapter 17

Self-Confidence to do What's Right

Never let your sense of morals get in the way of doing what's right.
Isaac Asimov

Self-Confidence is Essential

The moment you doubt whether you can fly,
you cease forever to be able to do it.
J. M. Barrie

Men of the code always strive to do what is right in every situation, because of this, they have to develop the self-confidence to do what is right. It takes a lot of self-confidence to do what is right, especially when everyone around you are urging you to do what you consider to be wrong. You must develop enough self-confidence to listen to your own conscience and to uphold your code, in spite of any opposition.

The more that you act on what you know is right, especially in the face of tremendous resistance, the greater your self-confidence will become. It is like doing anything else; the more success you have, the greater your confidence grows.

There will always be those who come against you when you take a stand for what is right. People have different ideas about right and wrong. Some will have a completely different opinion about what is right than you do, and others simply couldn't care less about whether their actions are right or not. Either way, don't allow their actions or opinions affect you.

The superior man knows what is right, at least in most situations. He spends time studying the difference between right and wrong, studying the wisdom of the sages, and has used what he has learned to develop his code. His code guides him in all of his actions, and thus the arguments of those who oppose him fall on deaf ears. He cannot be moved from what he knows to be right. He is completely dedicated to what is right.

What is "right" changes according to each individual situation. What is right in one situation may not be right in other circumstances. The superior man's code is not a rigid set of rules which he applies to every situation in life, but rather a set of principles which guides him to make the right decision in each situation. But even if you have the right set of principles, it does you no good if you don't have the self-confidence to act on them.

Your code will guide you, but you must have the self-confidence to move on what you think is right. Without confidence in your own actions, your code is all but useless.

How to Develop Self-Confidence

Believe you can and you're halfway there.
Theodore Roosevelt

Self-confidence comes from being successful. Think about playing football. When you first learned how to catch or throw a football, you probably did not have a lot of self-confidence when it came to that skill. Your self-confidence grew a little more each time you successfully made a catch or threw a good pass. As you continued to play, your self-confidence in the sport continued to grow until you didn't have to wonder whether or not you could catch a football or throw a good pass; you just did it.

Your self-confidence works the same way in anything that you do. You have to develop it slowly; the more success you have, the more your self-confidence grows. It works the same way when it comes to making decisions concerning right and wrong.

As you learn to trust in your code, and in your intuition, your self-confidence increases. Each time you make the right decision, even when it comes to small decisions, you become more confident in yourself and your ability to make decisions and to do what's right.

You have to have these small successes in order to build your self-confidence to be able to stand up for what is right when others are standing against you. It takes a lot of courage to do what is right when everyone else is doing what is wrong. You need to practice being courageous in small situations so that you have the experience that you need when it comes to more important situations.

If you wanted to play basketball for a living, you wouldn't start out in the NBA; you would start in high school, and then move on to college, developing your skills and self-confidence as you practiced. You wouldn't start out being a professional basketball player.

It is the same way when it comes to making decisions concerning right and wrong. You start off with small decisions. When you see a guy accidently drop a five dollar bill, you pick it up and go give it to him instead of putting it in your pocket and calling it a good day. When you see a kid bullying another kid, you step in and stop it. When you are tempted to do something that you want to do, but that you know you shouldn't do, you walk away. Each time you successfully do what is right, you develop more self-confidence in your ability to do what is right the next time. Each time you resist the temptation to do something that you know you shouldn't do, your self-confidence grows stronger.

By holding yourself accountable in these small situations, you are strengthening your self-confidence for the bigger situations. And you have to continually work at keeping your self-confidence high. Your self-confidence will fluctuate.

You have to consistently maintain it. You maintain your self-confidence by consistently doing things successfully. Success builds self-confidence. You may have high self-confidence when it comes to throwing a football, but not much self-confidence when it comes to racing motorcycles. You have to practice something consistently to continue to have confidence in that activity.

Therefore, it is important that you consistently do what's right. Don't only do it when it is convenient for you or when it is profitable for you; do what's right all the time. Be completely dedicated to what's right. Look for ways to increase your self-confidence and take advantage of them.

Discipline your mind to support your self-confidence. Don't allow negative thoughts to take root. Don't think badly of yourself, even when you have a lapse in judgment. Self-confidence is critical to your success, so don't take it lightly. Confidence is one of your most important qualities; without self-confidence, you will accomplish very little in life.

Always remind yourself of your successes and of the fact that you have what it takes to do what's right, no matter what. When you hold to what is right, you not only build your self-confidence, but you set an example for others who may be observing you.

Circumstances never excuse wrong actions. The greatest actions are done in times of great adversity. Always be satisfied with having done right, no matter who is for you or against you. Never apologize for doing what is right; never allow fear to prevent you from doing what is right.

Develop your self-confidence to such a level that no one can make you doubt your actions. Remember, everyone has an opinion, but not everyone's opinion matters. Protect your self-confidence and continue reinforce it daily.

Reflections for the Superior Man

Nothing gives one person so much
advantage over another as to remain always
cool and unruffled under all circumstances.
Thomas Jefferson

To be yourself in a world that is constantly trying to
make you something else is the greatest accomplishment.
Ralph Waldo Emerson

Be decisive. You must train day and night
in order to make quick decisions.
Miyamoto Musashi

As soon as you trust yourself,
you will know how to live.
Johann Wolfgang von Goethe

Public opinion is a weak tyrant
compared with our own private opinion.
Henry David Thoreau

In the darkest hours we must believe in ourselves.
Terry Goodkind

Concentrate more on your achievements than your failures.
Learn to take the failures as opportunities to rectify your errors.
Stephen Richards

Calm mind brings inner strength and self-confidence.
Dalai Lama

Nothing builds self-esteem and
self-confidence like accomplishment.
Thomas Carlyle

Self-confidence is the first requisite to great undertakings.
Samuel Johnson

One important key to success is self-confidence.
An important key to self-confidence is preparation.
Arthur Ashe

Chapter 18

Roles, Responsibilities, and Duties

*Men have many roles to play in life and the best men take their duty in
each role seriously, for how he fulfills each, defines him as a real man.*
Bohdi Sanders

A Superior Man's Responsibilities

Not for ourselves alone are we born.
Marcus Tullius Cicero

Men of the code wear many hats. Most are protectors, friends, husbands,
and fathers, or some combination of those roles. We take our roles seriously
and do our utmost to be the best that we can be in each of those roles.

These roles comprise our main duties as men of the code. When we enter
into some type of relationship with another person, we have accepted certain
responsibilities and duties that come along with that relationship. If you are
not willing to accept those responsibilities and duties, then you should never
enter into that relationship to start with. It is that simple.

But, once you have made the commitment to enter into one of these
relationship roles, you have a duty to fulfill. And even if you never enter into
the role of a husband, friend, or father, superior men still have a duty to
themselves and to be a protector of those who deserve their protection. I will
discuss this later in this chapter.

Real men take their duties seriously. They don't merely attend to them
when it is convenient or beneficial to them; they are a top priority in their
lives. Fulfilling their duties is a major part of their code and they would no
more blow off their duties than they would lie, cheat or steal.

No one forces you to assume any role in life. As a man of the code, you
choose your own path and you accept the responsibilities that come along
with the path that you have chosen, just as when you chose a lady to spend
your life with, you accept everything that comes along with that decision.

There will be many good, enjoyable things that come along with your
decision to be married to someone, and other things that are maybe not things
that you necessarily enjoy, but you accept them all nonetheless. After you

have assumed the role of a husband, you don't get to pick and chose what aspects of your wife's life you'll be a part of; you made that choice when you married her. Real men accept the fact that they have made a commitment to step into that role and they do their duty to the best of their ability.

I am going to discuss each of the more common roles that men take on in life and get into more specific details concerning each one. You will notice that these roles do overlap and that they are not totally independent of each other. They are not compartmentalized in your life, but rather they are an integral part of who you are as a man of the code. Now let's look at some of the most common roles and the duties that come along with them.

Your Role as a Warrior/Protector/Hero

The Art of War teaches us to rely not on the likelihood
of the enemy's not coming, but on our own readiness
to receive him; not on the chance of his not attacking, but
rather on the fact that we have made our position unassailable.
Sun Tzu

One of the main roles of superior men is that of the warrior, protector, and hero. You are the protector of your family, your wife and your children. No one cares as much about your family as you, and certainly no one is going to take the responsibility for their safety the way that you should. Your family depends on you to look out for their best interest and to be their protector and their provider. In short, you should be the hero of your family. It is your duty and your responsibility.

Your responsibility, as a protector, does not end with protecting your family. Men of the code are the protectors of everyone with whom it is in their ability to protect – the elderly, the weak, and those who are in their presence and deserve their protection. This is simply what real men do; they look out for those who can't look out for themselves.

Does this mean that you have to take on the responsibility to protect the whole world? Of course not! Your duty is to protect those around you, and those who deserve your protection. You are not the guardian of the galaxy. It is not your job to take on the consequences for everyone else's actions.

For example, if you and your wife are leaving a restaurant at night and walking back to your car and you see two scumbag gang members fighting in the parking lot, it is not your duty to intervene. Your duty in that situation would be to keep your wife safe. That fight is none of your business. It is neither your duty, nor your responsibility, to try to make peace between two thugs in the parking lot.

On the other hand, if you are leaving the restaurant and you see some thug harassing an elderly couple in the parking lot, you would have a duty to step in and help them.

The difference is that some people deserve your help and your protection, and some do not. You have a duty to protect some people but not a duty to protect everyone. That is the duty of the police, not your duty.

Every man should be able to defend himself and his family. Taking care of your family is your number one duty as a protector. Real men are warriors. They resist those who are their enemies and protect those that they cherish. There are things worth fighting for in this life. The warrior spirit is a vital part of being a real man.

Defending those who both deserve your protection and who cannot defend themselves, is a moral imperative for real men. This is a vital part of standing up for what is right. There are situations that call for violence and real men do not shy away from those situations, especially when their duty to protect their loved-ones is involved. There is no room for pacifism when the lives of your family members are at stake.

As a warrior/protector, you must not only be *willing* to protect those you love, and those who deserve your protection, but you must also be *able* to protect them. How can you protect others if you can't even protect yourself? How can you protect those you love if you are in poor shape and can't even run across the street? I think that you know the answer to those questions.

When you look at your physical fitness and your health in this light, it becomes evident that staying in shape is about much more than looking good or feeling good; it is part of your duty as the protector of your family. You must be in shape in order to protect your family. Otherwise, you are simply relying on luck. Many men deceive themselves when it comes to this area of their lives.

They wrongly believe that because they are willing to protect their family, and would give their life to stop a predator from hurting their family, that they are also *able* to do so. The two are not synonymous. You can have the will to defend your family, but not the ability.

This is why it is vital for you to stay in good condition, at the very least. It would be even better if you learned some self-defense skills and become proficient in the art of self-defense. As George Washington stated, "Let him who desires peace, prepare for war."

Take your self-defense skills seriously. While it is fine to take martial arts classes as a fun activity or a sport, that is not your goal as the warrior/protector of your family. Your goal is to ensure that you have the skills and the courage to keep your family safe, no matter what. A man that is not willing to protect his family is not a real man.

You must cultivate a calm resolve to do whatever it takes to protect your family. Always maintain your calm. Even when things get violent, you should maintain a calm spirit. Remember that force is overcome by force. Don't count on the other person to be merciful. You must prepare yourself in times of good fortune for the bad times. As the old samurai maxim goes, "Tomorrow's battle is won during today's practice."

In order to truly be the protector of your family and those around you, you must learn to overcome your fear. Fear can be paralyzing, especially if you aren't prepared to deal with someone who is big, muscular, and violent.

As the protector of your family, you have no choice; you must overcome your fear and be prepared to deal with any threat which comes your way. You must learn to deal with the effects of the fight-or-flight response. I won't get into that subject here, but there is a very good discussion on that, and overall self-defense, in my bestselling book, *Modern Bushido: Living a Life of Excellence.*

Learning self-defense cannot be a hobby for you; your duty requires that you have good self-defense skills in order to protect your family. Because of this, you must make sure that you are prepared. You must know how to handle any attack that comes your way and you must be able to protect your loved-ones. Anything less and you are shirking your duty as their protector.

The great general, Sun Tzu, who wrote the now famous book, *The Art of War*, stated, "He who lacks foresight and underestimates his enemy will surely be captured by him." Have the foresight to prepare now to keep your family safe and never underestimate your enemy. There are some very bad people in this world, people who do not think like you do, and those people will give no more thought to assaulting, murdering, and destroying your family than you do about stepping on a spider.

If you aren't prepared to deal with these kinds of people, then you are not fulfilling your duty to keep your family safe. Don't be lulled into believing the politically correct train of thought that says that everyone is simply doing the best that they can in life. That is a complete lie. There are some people who live to prey on others. They are hunters, and good, law-abiding people are their prey. Remember, the hunter can make many mistakes and still live to hunt again; it only takes one mistake for the hunted to lose his life. You must be prepared!

You are your family's warrior and protector. It is your utmost duty in life. Take this duty seriously and prepare yourself. Success is not gained through idleness. If you aren't sure that you can defend your family today, now is the time to change that. Take steps right now to learn self-defense, to secure your home, and to become the protector that your family deserves.

Your Role as a Husband

A real man loves his wife, and places
his family as the most important thing in life.
Frank Abagnale

When you decided to get married to that special lady, you made a commitment to her. You have entered into a sacred pact with her and from that point forward, she should be the most important part of your life. You swore an oath to God that you would cherish, love and protect her, and real men always uphold their oaths.

I know that this is a rare way of looking at the role of being a husband in our society, but superior men are rare men. We live and think differently than most. Our word is our honor. Once you have sworn an oath, be man enough to keep your word.

No one put a gun to your head and made you marry your wife; you made that decision yourself. It was an act of your free will. You made your choice, now be man enough to cherish her and make her happy.

As a husband, you have a duty to protect and provide for your wife. Do your best to make her happy. Surprise her with unexpected gifts, flowers, and most of all, the gift of your time and attention. If you want a happy, fulfilled marriage, it takes work, it takes time, and it takes your attention.

Too many men think that their work is done after they have wined and dined a woman enough to make her fall in love with him. After the wedding, they feel as if they have their wife and no longer have to try to impress her or win her heart and they turn their attention elsewhere. This is not the way of the superior man, and it does not lead to a strong marriage.

If you are no longer willing to go out of your way to make her feel good about herself, to make her feel special, to continue to touch her heart and let her know that she made the right decision when she agreed to marry you, then I can guarantee you that there are thousands of other men out there who are waiting to do just that.

The superior man never stops flirting with his wife. He never stops making her feel loved and special. In fact, he goes out of his way to do so. Real men know what they have when they have found the perfect woman, and they are intelligent enough to know that it takes effort to keep her.

Keeping your wife happy is like staying in shape. You don't get in shape and then never work out again because you have accomplished your goal. That would be ridiculous. As soon as you stop working out and eating right, you start to regress. The same principle applies to your marriage.

You don't stop flirting, treating your wife special, giving her attention, taking her out, and spending time with her, simply because you have won her heart. If you do that, the connection that you both have will start to grow weaker, and weaker. That doesn't create a strong, lasting marriage; it creates a void, an emptiness where both you and your wife will feel something is missing. This is not what you want.

You must continue to work at making your marriage stronger, just like you have to continue to lift weights to keep your muscles strong. Be creative and find ways to strengthen your marriage. Continue to date your wife, even if that means cooking a special dinner for her and spending some quality one-on-one time with just you and her. Continuing to court your wife doesn't have to cost you an arm and a leg; just be creative. I can assure you that she will appreciate your efforts, even more so than just going out to dinner and a movie.

Your wife should be first place in your life, ahead of work and ahead of your hobbies. She should be first place, period. This doesn't mean that you have to neglect your work or give up your hobbies. Just make sure that you are putting her first and giving her the time she needs. If you will do this, everything else will fall into place.

Be the man that she needs you to be, the man that she deserves. She needs to feel secure and protected. While today's woman can take care of herself and provide for herself, she does like to be taken care of and to feel secure. If you aren't willing to be a real man and provide her with the life that she deserves, you shouldn't have married her to start with.

Real men take care of their wives. They make them feel safe and secure, not just financially and physically, but secure in their relationship as well. No woman wants to doubt her husband's loyalty or fidelity. While a little jealousy may make you feel good about yourself, giving her reasons to feel jealous will only weaken your marriage in the long run.

Your loyalty should be unquestionable. Your wife should never have to wonder about your fidelity, as a man of the code would never cheat on his wife. Infidelity is a betrayal of trust; it is a betrayal of everything that a man of the code holds dear and sacred. It is dishonorable and dishonest. It should be something that is never an option for you, because you are a man of your word, a man of honor and integrity.

When your wife understands that this is the way that you feel, jealousy will no longer be an issue in your marriage. Her confidence in you will be strong and unquestionable. This is what you want. You have to build this confidence in your precious wife. You have to let her know by your words and your actions, that your character is unquestionable, that you are indeed a man of the code, a superior man, and that she never has to worry about your heart wandering. She needs to feel secure in every way, and when she does, you will find that all of your effort will be well worth it.

The average man doesn't see the value in putting forth so much effort after he is already married. He becomes lazy, quits taking care of his body, gains weight, becomes sloppy, and takes his marriage for granted. He expects all of the benefits of a great marriage to simply happen automatically, merely because he is married. That is wrong thinking and is one of the reasons that so many marriages end in divorce today.

Neglected marriages cannot be strong; they cannot be full of love and happiness. Nothing in this world happens without a cause. Good marriages grow strong because two people put in the effort to make them good; bad marriages happen because of neglect.

A man of the code should be one of the best husbands that any woman could hope to find. He values honor, character and integrity. He knows how to treat women with respect and honor. He understands how to make women feel special and valued. And he uses this knowledge to build trust in his wife and to build a strong marriage.

Good husbands see marriage as a partnership, but they have the courage to step up and be leaders in their marriages. They play an active part in their marriages and head off any conflicts before they can grow into real problems.

This takes insight and attention. Give your marriage the attention it deserves, just as you would your own business or your favorite pastime. Never neglect your marriage. Work at building a marriage that will last a lifetime. Be the best husband that you possibly can be.

Look at your marriage like a fire. You don't simply build a fire and expect it to burn forever without attending to it. You must constantly add more fuel to it or it will burn out. If you neglect it, the flame will disappear. Cherish your marriage and make sure that you keep the flame burning bright!

Your Role as a Father

It is easier to build strong children that to repair broken men.
Frederick Douglas

When you make the decision to have children, and you do make that decision, even if it was unplanned, you have entered into a lifetime commitment. You will always be that child's father, no matter what. You have brought another life into this world and it is up to you to be his or her father, to guide and teach your child, to raise a man or woman of character, honor, and integrity. This is one of the most sacred duties that you will ever have in your life, and you never get a second chance to raise that child as you should and to instill the values and principles of your code in their life so that he or she will grow to be a well-balanced adult.

If you blow it, your failure will have long-lasting consequences, not only in the life of that child, but in his or her children, and their children. Becoming a father is taken too lightly in today's society. It seems that every couple wants to have a baby, but very few ever stop to consider how that child should be raised or the sacred duty and responsibilities that comes with becoming a parent.

When you become a father, you now have a sacred duty to protect, educate, and train your child to become either a man of the code or a woman of character. Too many fathers fail in this duty. Their father neglected this duty, and so they have no idea about what it means to be a real father. This sad cycle continues from generation to generation, unless someone takes the time to teach fathers how to be real fathers and not just sperm donors.

Men of the code take their roles as a father seriously. The job of a father is not to be your child's best friend, his buddy, or his pal; it is to be their role model, his teacher, his protector, and his guide. After your duty to your wife, it is the most important duty you will ever have. Take it seriously! You only get one chance.

While it is true that you may have more than one child, and therefore, you will have more than one chance to perfect your skills as a father, you only have one chance with each child. And that one chance is of the utmost importance. Your actions as a father will directly affect the direction of your child's future and the kind of life that he or she will lead. The kind of father that you are will determine the kind of man or woman your child grows up to be. I can't think of any responsibility that has more riding on it than being a father.

Yet so many "fathers" take this responsibility for granted. They spend little or no time thinking about how to be a good father. Many feel that as long as they provide a roof over the child's head, put food on the table, give his child clothes and shoes, and make sure he or she goes to school, that they have done their job. Nothing could be further from the truth.

You should start teaching and training your child from the earliest age. Raise your sons to be men of honor; raise your daughters to be strong women of character. Teach them to be wise and to think for themselves.

You are the king in your family and your children depend on you to do what is best for them. Don't let them down. Can you imagine a king entrusting his children's development and education to anything less than the best instructors and the best teachers? Can you, in your wildest dreams, envision a king sending his children to be educated by a teacher who despises what he stands for or the values that he wants to instill in his children? That would be idiotic. Then why would you do that? Are your children any less important that the children of a king?

Hopefully, you are starting to see how important your role as a father actually is. There is an old saying that a teacher affects eternity; he can never tell where his influence stops. A father and mother should be the child's main teachers. You are in charge of your children's education and their future; you truly don't know where your influence will end. If you do your duty as it should be done, your influence will last for generations.

Lead by example. Never count on your children listening to you if they can't see that you walk the walk. "Do as I say, not as I do," does not work, and it is hypocritical. It is your duty to pass on your knowledge and wisdom to your sons and daughters. And it is also your duty to be a man that they can admire and look up to. Be the man that you would have liked your father to be. I will discuss your duty as a father in more detail in a later chapter. For now, I just want to impress on you how important that role actually is.

Your Role as a Friend

The wicked have only accomplices; voluptuaries have companions in debauch; self-seekers have partners; politicians attract partisans; the generality of idle men have attachments; princes have courtiers; but virtuous men alone have friends.
Voltaire

Only men of character can be a true friend, everyone else is merely an acquaintance. I know that his may sound like a very strong statement, but it is a fact, whether you agree with it or not. In addition, you don't have many friends; you can probably count your true friends on one hand. Don't buy into the Facebook philosophy that you have hundreds of friends; you don't.

These statements may sound very opinionated and harsh, especially in world where everyone seems to think that they have hundreds of "friends" because of all the different social medias available on the computer, but I have news for you, those people aren't really your friends; they are your acquaintances.

True friends are those people who will stand by you through thick and thin. When the whole world is against you, they stand by your side. Even if you are in the wrong, their friendship remains strong. These are the people that you can count on, no matter what. Now, is that how you would describe all of your hundreds of friends on social media?

It takes honor, courage, and loyalty to be a true friend, all character traits of superior men. When you have given your hand in friendship, you have entered into a pact. Therefore, you should be slow in offering other people your friendship. It is dishonorable to turn your back on a true friend.

Men of the code are true friends. They take friendship more seriously than other people, and once you have made friends with a superior man, you have a friend for life, unless you break it off or betray him. You must choose your friends wisely. As Plato stated, "The word friend is common, the fact is rare."

True friendship doesn't happen overnight and it certainly is not developed without ever even meeting the person face to face. It takes time and trust, trust which must be earned over years, before you can really know that you have a true friend. That kind of trust is not easily given. It must be earned; it must be proven.

I am sure that you have heard the old adage, there is no friendship among thieves, but have you ever stopped and asked yourself why there is no friendship among thieves? The answer is that it takes a man of honor to be a real friend.

If someone has no honor, they cannot be a true friend. They will turn their back on their "friend" whenever the friendship becomes inconvenient or when things get intense. People like this do not have what it takes to be a real friend; they are only there for the good times, but quickly disappear when the going gets tough.

As a man of the code, you don't have the option to turn your back on a true friend. You have given your hand in friendship and must honor that relationship. To do otherwise is dishonorable. It is an act of betrayal. You should never betray another person, much less a true friend.

Be the kind of friend that you want your friends to be. Never be the first to break off a true friendship. Be a reliable, true friend. Anything less is below your standards that you have set for yourself. I will discuss the topic of friendship, in more detail, in another chapter; I merely want to touch on the topic here because it is a vital role for men of the code.

Your Duty to Yourself

Try not to become a man of success
but rather to become a man of value.
Albert Einstein

In addition to the roles and duties that I have already discussed, as a man of the code, you have a duty to yourself. You have a duty to be true to the standards and principles by which you have sworn to live your life. If you can't be true to yourself, you can't be true to anyone else.

Your foremost duty to yourself is to uphold your code and be true to the kind of man that you want to be. No one is going to *make* you live up to the code that you have decided to live by. In fact, most people will try to talk you out of living your life by your code of honor because they will see it as too restrictive and it may get in the way of certain things that they would like you to do. Stay true to your code anyway.

Your true friends will always support you in your lifestyle; false friends are only concerned with having company in their folly. When your chosen lifestyle interferes with their fun in some way, they will try to convince you that your choice is wrong. They will use every argument that they can come up with to persuade you to set your principles aside, if not forever, at least for "tonight."

This is nothing more than the Universe tempting you to see how serious you are about living a life of honor. If you are serious, you won't give in to peer-pressure. Just remember, if these people were truly your friends, they would never try to talk you into walking away from your code.

Once you have decided to walk the path of the real man, you have a duty to yourself to be true to your path. Living a life of honor is not something that you only live when it is convenient for you. You can't just set your code aside for a night and live as lesser men do and then come back to it when it pleases you. Doing so only weakens your resolve and makes it easier for you to set your code aside the next time something comes up. That is not honor;

that is not living as a man of the code. You have to make a firm decision about how you will live and then stick to it.

You have a duty to yourself to be true to your code, to your principles. At times, this will take a lot of resolve and courage, but that is just a part of being a real man. Real men don't compromise on their principles because someone else wants them to. They take their principles seriously and don't mind walking alone at times, if that is what maintaining their principles requires. Never compromise your principles to please someone else. If you do, you will regret it afterwards.

Your Duty to Your Family

As iron as worn away by frequent filing, a family's
strength is eroded by incessant inner frictions.
Tiruvalluvar

I have already discussed your role as a husband and a father, and your duties as a warrior and protector, but you also have a duty to your family as a whole. You have a duty to your immediate family to be the head of the household. This means that it is your duty, along with your wife's duty, to ensure that you have peace and tranquility in your family. You need to be aware of what is happening with each family member.

It is extremely easy to get so caught up in your own life, focusing on improving your life, working to perfect your principles, making a living, and being a good husband and father, that you don't notice problems that other family members may be dealing with.

You have a duty to your family to be aware of what is happening in their lives. This means that you must take the time to communicate with your wife and children. You can't deal with issues when you are unaware of the existence of any problems.

If there is a problem between siblings or between one of your children and your wife, it is part of your responsibility to help mediate that problem and help each person find a solution. Notice that I didn't say it is your responsibility to solve the problem for them. Everyone has to take responsibility for solving their own issues. That is just a part of learning and growing, but you certainly can, and should, help them and guide them.

What you don't want to do is allow these issues to worsen and become bigger problems within the family. Remember, you are supposed to be teaching your children, and teaching them how to resolve their issues in an honorable way is part of your duty.

I have already discussed your duty to protect, guide, and provide for your family. This should be evident, so I will not go into depth on that subject here. I do, however, want to make sure that you are clear on another point though. I don't want to give the impression that I am saying that you have all the responsibilities of making sure the household runs smoothly.

You and your wife are a team, but every team needs a leader. Your duty to your family is to be that leader. Although movies, television, and politically correct organizations would like you to believe that you should be an irresponsible, overgrown boy, you shouldn't be.

Men of the code are not boys, they are not irresponsible, and they do not buy into that lie. They are real men and they are leaders. If you are dumping all the responsibilities of raising your children, running the household, and taking care of any problems around the house, on your wife, then you are not fulfilling your duty as the head of the household, as the leader of your family.

That is not being a real man, and it is certainly not being a man of the code. Man up and be a leader for your family. You may or may not be a leader at work or a leader among your friends, but you should be a leader at home.

In addition to your duty to your household, you have a duty to your extended family as well. You should see to it that you parents are well cared for in their old age. This is your filial duty, meaning your duty to your parents.

Other cultures take this duty more seriously than our culture, and even our culture doesn't take it as seriously as we did years ago. But as a man of the code, it is your duty to see to it that your parents have what they need in their old age. They cared for you when you were younger and you couldn't care for yourself, and it is your duty to make sure they are cared for when they are older and can no longer take care of themselves.

Duty to Those around You

Wherever I walk, everyone is a little bit safer because I am there. Wherever I am, anyone in need has a friend. Whenever I return home, everyone is happy I am there.
Robert L. Humphrey

Men of the code also have a duty to those in their presence who are in need, and deserve, their help. I am sure that you have seen news clips of someone who is being attacked, or someone who has been hit by a car, or some variation of this, and people simply ignore their cry for help and walk on by. This is disgraceful and is something that a man of the code would never do.

People, who ignore a cry for help when someone is truly in need, are cowards. They do not care about their fellowman and do not have the intestinal fortitude to do what's right. They prefer to pretend that they never heard the cry for help and that they never saw the person in need. Confucius stated, "To know what is right and not do it is the worst cowardice," and he was exactly right.

There is not much that is more cowardly than to see an elderly person getting mugged and refuse to help. It would never cross the mind of a superior man not to stop and help someone in such a situation as that, but as proven time and again by hidden cameras, people do that all of the time. How someone can be so cowardly is beyond me, but they are. This is not the way of the superior man.

The superior man is courageous. He puts what is right ahead of what is convenient. Of course it would be more convenient to just walk on by, we all have busy lives, but is that the right thing to do? What would you hope someone would do if it were your elderly dad who was being mugged or who had just been side-swiped by some reckless driver?

A man of the code will always step in to help those in need when it is in his ability to do so. It is the right thing to do, and that should end any question about whether or not to do it.

When a superior man sees a situation like the ones described above, he jumps into action. He knows that he has a duty, as a man of the code, to help in whatever way he can. To just ignore the situation would be unthinkable.

Would intervening possibly be dangerous? Of course! Would it be the right thing to do? Absolutely! This is why most men of the code practice some form of self-defense. You just never know when you may be called upon to defend those you love or some stranger in need. You should be prepared for such a situation as this.

If the right thing to do would be to intervene and you have made a decision to always do what is right, then you had better be prepared to step up when you have to do so. As I stated previously, it would be wise to learn some self-defense.

Superior men do not go through life only thinking of themselves. They live life differently than most; they also consider their duties to others, whether it is their family, friends, or a perfect stranger in need. Every great man throughout history has sacrificed a part of his life for others. Only those who are completely self-centered focus merely on their own life and their own pleasure.

Helping others should be included in your code. There are certain situations where it is absolutely your duty to help others, and other situations where it is simply the right thing to do. The roles that superior men play, and their responsibilities and duties, encompass much more than their personal lives; they live for something much greater than their own personal desires – they live for the code.

This chapter has been a short overview of a superior man's duties and responsibilities. Each of these subjects could be a whole book on their own, but hopefully you can see that being a man of the code encompasses much more than developing your own ethical standards. Being a real man is taking on responsibilities that many men today prefer to avoid. Only real men are willing to step up and fulfill all of the duties that are required of them; others simply dodge their duties and live their life selfishly.

Reflections for the Superior Man

Our grand business is not to see what lies dimly
at a distance, but to do what lies clearly at hand.
Thomas Carlyle

A hero is a man that does what he can.
Romain Rolland

The man who has nothing for which he is willing to fight,
nothing which is more important than his own personal safety,
is a miserable creature and has no chance of being free unless
made and kept so by the exertion of better men than himself.
John Stuart Mill

As circumstances change, the ways
of dealing with them alter too.
Han Fei Tzu

A father – He should make himself worthy of respect by his virtue and
abilities, and worthy of love by his kindness and gentle manners.
Montaigne

In prosperity our friends know us;
in adversity, we know our friends.
John Churton Collins

Many kiss the hand that they wish cut off.
George Herbert

Trust in today's friends as if
they might be tomorrow's enemies.
Baltasar Gracian

Be slow to fall into friendship, but when
you are in, continue firm and constant.
Socrates

Make friends only with those
gentlemen who are superior men.
Confucius

Let cold deliberation take the place of sudden outburst.
Baltasar Gracian

Chapter 19

Relationships

It is better to be alone than in bad company.
George Washington

General Relationships

Keep away from people who try to belittle your ambitions.
Small people always do that, but the really great
make you feel that you, too, can be great.
Mark Twain

You will have to deal with hundreds, if not thousands, of different people over your lifetime. It would be wise to have at least a rudimentary understanding of people and how to successfully keep yourself in good standing with the majority of them. How people respond to you has a lot to do with what you know and how you use what you know. There are entire books written on this subject, so I obviously can't cover everything in this short chapter, but I do want to give you a general idea about how to successfully deal with the people in your life.

First impressions are very important in every new relationship. Most people make up their mind about whether or not they like you within the first one or two minutes after you have met them. That first impression can be hard to remove from their mind. Therefore, it is vital that you keep this in mind and always do your best to make a good first impression.

Have an idea in your mind about how you want others to perceive you and then take steps to make sure that you get that idea across to them on the very first meeting. You should always be aware of what image you are portraying to others. The image that they have of you will largely be based on the image that you give them.

Insecurity never makes a good impression, whether you are around men or women. Men will see it as a sign of weakness and that you are a possible easy mark; women will simply see it as a turn off. Always represent yourself as being very self-confident, but not overly self-confident to the point of being an ass.

Try to see yourself through their eyes. How will they look at you? What are they thinking about you? Are you coming across as friendly, yet confident, good natured, yet firm, honorable, yet fun loving? When you look at yourself through the eyes of another, it gives you plenty of feedback about what you are doing right and what needs to be tweaked.

Try to mentally put yourself in the other person's shoes. Learn to pick up cues and hints about how he thinks, what he believes, and how his mind works in general. When you can piece together that puzzle, you can easily move yourself into his good graces.

People like to talk about themselves, but that is not the wisest thing to do. Let the other person talk about himself and learn from the information that he freely gives you. At the same time, participate in the conversation in a friendly manner, but avoid revealing information that is too personal.

You also don't want to appear to be hiding anything; often this gives an impression of being nervous or shady. It is always better to listen and learn, than it is to talk too much and give away information that should remain private. Just be yourself, but be smart about it at the same time.

Be empathetic to the other person's feelings. There is no better way to foster good feelings than to really listen to what the other person is saying. Ask him questions about whatever subject he is talking about and show that you are interested. Another helpful technique is to restate what the person said in your own words in order to make sure that you really did understand what he was saying. Actions such as yawning and looking at your watch are great ways to show that you are bored and have no interest in the conversation at all; avoid things like that.

Men of the code are trustworthy; learn to keep confidential things private. This is not only honorable, but a good practice to build confidence between yourself and the other person. Let them know that they can confide in you and that you are a man to be trusted.

Never try too hard to win over someone who is unfriendly or not on your side. When you go overboard trying to win someone's approval, you end up both, not getting his approval and losing his respect. Be confident enough in yourself that you are just as happy whether the other person approves of you and wants to develop a relationship or whether he appears to completely dislike you. The superior man's self-worth is not dependent on the opinions of others. If someone doesn't want to play ball, be content to take your ball and go play alone.

Praise people when they have done something deserving of praise. People don't hear enough good feedback; most of what they hear is negative. They are starving for approval, and if you are willing to give them sincere praise, that will ingratiate them to you. Praise carries the most weight when you praise in public. Always try to praise someone in public, but correct them only in private. Correcting others in public causes them to lose face and they will hold that against you, even if it doesn't show at the time.

As long as I have touched on the subject of things which can cause hard feelings, I might as well address the topic of cynicism and sarcasm as well. While many people enjoy joking around and being sarcastic, many others are easily offended by sarcasm. You can very quickly take joking too far and that will cause hard feelings, even to the point of turning someone into an enemy. Be very careful when using sarcasm or joking around.

While having a good sense of humor is a very good thing, it is safer to save your humor for other people's jokes. People in today's world have become so politically correct and sensitive that joking around with them too much can be like playing Russian roulette. It only takes one offensive comment to completely destroy a relationship. Be careful.

As a rule of thumb, it is wise to stay away from subjects that people have very strong feelings about, such as religion, politics, race, etc. We no longer have an open-minded society where issues can be debated with an open mind and where people can disagree without being disagreeable. People tend to draw battle lines when it comes to certain subjects and those who are on the other side of those lines are considered enemies.

Always tread carefully when it comes to subjects like these. As I said earlier, it is always better to be quiet, listen, and learn, than it is to reveal too much personal information. In most cases, there is very little upside to revealing your personal feelings on these issues, but the downside can be big. In gamblers' terms, that is always a bad bet!

Cultivate the reputation of being honorable and honest with everyone. Keep your promises to other people. It is best to simply let your word speak for itself and not make concrete promises, but if you do make a promise – keep it. Men of the code keep their word. Their word is their bond. When they say that they will do something, they do it.

It is also wise to learn to read people. Many people say one thing, but mean something else. Never assume that because you live by high standards, other men do too; many people don't. You have to be aware of when someone is not being truthful to you, when they are trying to con you or get the best of you in a business deal. You have to pay attention, not only to what they say, but to how they say it, to the meaning behind their words. Remember, things are not always as they seem to be.

Watch their body language. Listen to how they say what they say. Pick up on the little hints which alert you that something just doesn't feel right about what someone is saying to you. Some people are experts when it comes to sweet talking people. They know all of the ways to make someone feel at ease and comfortable, and to get into their head and manipulate them.

You have to deal with everyone with your eyes, your ears, and your mind wide open, and your tongue restrained. Look for the angles and ask yourself why it is important to the other person to convince you to see things his way. Try to see the whole thing through his eyes and ask yourself, "What's in it for him?"

Never give out too much information, even when you trust the other person. Always keep something in reserve. Be warm, friendly, and attentive, but always maintain a little mystery about yourself. Never allow anyone to completely see everything there is to see about you or to completely understand all of your thoughts.

Always make eye contact, but I caution you to be aware of other cultures. This is an Anglo-European standard, which is not the case for all. The eyes will tell you a lot about a person. Not making eye contact makes you seem nervous or submissive; it gives the other person the upper hand, which is something that you never want to do. Be confident, relaxed, sincere, and look him straight in the eye, but don't stare him down. That makes the other person uncomfortable. While you may know that you are "the man," overtly proving that point will not gain you favor in the other person's eyes or help you obtain your goal, at least in most cases.

Learn to be charismatic and use a little charm when you are interacting with others. As long as you are being sincere, you have no reason to feel that being charming and charismatic is being phony or flattering to the other person. There are plenty of sincere things you can find to compliment someone on, you don't have to use flattery. Most people can tell when they are being flattered. Remember, flattery makes you seem insincere and will raise questions concerning your honesty or your real agenda.

Do your best to remember people's names. There is nothing more pleasing to someone else than to know that other people know them and remember their name. The easiest way to do this is to make a conscious decision when you meet someone to remember some distinct characteristics about that person and then connect those characteristics with some anchors or pegs.

An anchor or a peg is a concrete way to remember names, information, or facts. For example, if you meet someone and his name is Dan, you may picture this guy in your mind, with no legs, sitting on a shrimp boat, and anchor his name with Captain Dan from the movie *Forest Gump*. Our mind remembers images much better than it does names. When you connect a concrete image with anything it makes it much easier to remember, this is especially helpful with someone's name.

Another useful way to remember people's names is to write them down. Keep a book that is solely for networking. As soon as you can, after you leave that person's presence, write down his name and some details about that person. This not only allows you to remember his name, but it refreshes your memory for the next time you meet this guy.

There is no way you will remember all the things that you talked about, but if you write down some of the important things, such as his wife's name, his hobbies, etcetera, the next time you meet him, you will be able to ask him personal questions about his wife's health, his golf game, his boat, or whatever it may be. This is a great way to ingratiate yourself to him and it makes a big impression.

The world works on relationships. The more connections that you have, the more you can get done in this world. Even if you can do it all yourself, it is still much easier with some good connections. It is important to make and maintain a good network of quality people. Never burn bridges unless you have to, and then, never without a very good reason. You never know when your path may take you back to that same bridge again, and if it isn't there, you will have to go the long way around.

Although it is best not to burn bridges, there are times when the superior man does need to sever a relationship. We are, after all, men of character, not lap dogs. Our patience does have limits. The point here is that you should think about it long and hard before deciding to burn any bridge, but when you have gotten to that point, burn it completely, knowing that when you do so, you have made a lifelong enemy. I will discuss dealing with your enemies later in this chapter.

This has been a quick summary of how to deal with the people in your life. There are many books which go into detail on the subject of dealing with people and I highly recommend that you take the time to read a couple of them.

Courtesy and Manners

A man's manners are a mirror in which he shows his portrait.
Goethe

No matter who you are dealing with, or what kind of relationship it may be, it is always in your best interest to be courteous and use your best manners, even with your closest friends.

As I have already discussed, men of the code conduct themselves with good manners, not because we are trying to impress anyone with our behavior, but rather because that is a part of who we are as superior men. Good manners tell other people something about ourselves, how we conduct our lives, and whether or not we have respect for other people.

Being courteous to other people is simply the way of the superior man. I am not going to even attempt to discuss all the different areas of etiquette in this small section; there is just way too much to cover. There are quite a few books on the market on etiquette and even several on etiquette for men. I strongly urge you to grab one and read it, if only for a refresher.

In this section, I simply want to re-enforce to you the importance of being courteous and using good manners in your various relationships. It is very easy to set your manners aside when you are together with a group of guys, especially guys that you know well, but this is a mistake.

Even when you are hanging out with some of your best buddies, you should still conduct yourself with good manners. Being rude and crude may seem appropriate when a group of guys are hanging out, but it isn't. Men of the code do not lower their standards, even if those around them do.

I'll bet that if you pay attention, not all of your buddies participate when the guys start being rude and obnoxious. Some will not lower themselves or forget who they are. Oh, they may laugh at the jokes or the crude behavior, along with everyone else, but if you pay close attention, you will see that they are not really participating in that behavior.

Superior men conduct themselves with class and tact, even among those who don't. You have to decide, once and for all, what kind of man you want to be and then be that kind of man, regardless of how others act.

You may think that I am being a little too rigid now, but I will remind you that men of the code always hold themselves to a higher standard. There is rarely a time when you should be discourteous or rude to other people.

And, if you should be polite and not set aside your good manners with your buddies, how much important is it to be polite and courteous when you are in the company of ladies? It is very important!

Good manners show respect for those who are in your company. You should always show respect towards ladies. Just conduct yourself like a gentleman; it's really not that hard to do. It costs you nothing, but the payoff can be tremendous.

Remember, you want to guard your reputation. You want to cultivate a reputation of being honorable and a real man. Would a real gentleman act like an obnoxious, crude, foul-mouthed jerk in front of ladies? Would those actions truly demonstrate that you have respect for the ladies in your presence or would it demonstrate that you really have no more respect for them than you do for the wino down on the corner?

If you want respect, you have to conduct yourself in a respectful way. If you want others to respect you, give them a reason to respect you. Remember, respect is earned, it is not a birthright. Being courteous and using good manners shows others that you have respect for yourself and respect for those around you.

Many men complain that they are not able to find a woman of character, that women have lowered their standards to a point that they are not even ladies anymore. Well, you are not going to find a woman of character when you act like an uncivilized brute. What lady in her right mind would be attracted to someone who is discourteous and lacks manners?

If you expect to find a woman worth having, you have to be a man worth having. Don't buy into the images of men that are being put on television and movies, where the man is a unmannered jerk, but the beautiful, sexy woman wants him anyway because he is just such a "man's man." That is another bogus lie promoted by those in Hollywood – pure fantasy.

Classy women worth having are looking for classy gentleman worth having, not for unmannered, rude men with no class and little, if any, tact. Use your manners and be courteous, and not just when you are at special events or around people who appear to be higher class people, but all the time, around everyone you meet.

Make good manners and courtesy an integral part of who you are as a man of the code. Whenever you are tempted to set your manners aside, remind yourself that superior men do not set their code aside, no matter how anyone else is behaving. Their bad behavior is not a license for you to behave badly.

I will end this section with a quote from Woodrow Call from *Lonesome Dove*, "I hate rude behavior in a man. I won't tolerate it." Well Captain Call, you don't have to worry about that with real men. Real men hate rude behavior as well and you won't catch a superior man being rude. He may be blunt from time to time, but being blunt is different than being rude.

Women

The way to love anything is to realize that it may be lost.
G. K. Chesterton

Since I just finished discussing courtesy and manners, I will cover that part of a romantic relationship first. Always be courteous to women. Help them with their bags. Open doors for them and let them enter first. When you are walking down the street, you should walk on whichever side may present any possible danger, so that you stand between your lady and any danger. I am not going to cover every specific form of etiquette for you; as I stated earlier, if you are not familiar with appropriate etiquettes, there are many books out there will catch you up.

The point here is that you should always be courteous to women. And yes, even if they claim that they do not want you to, and even if they are rude about it. Again, you must make etiquette a part of who you are. You aren't behaving in this way to impress the women, or anyone else; you are behaving in this way because it is how men of the code behave.

Don't buy into the garbage that radical feminists try to push on men. Some women will actually be rude to you if you open a door for them or treat them like a lady in any way. Just ignore their crass behavior and be a superior man anyway. Why should you always be courteous to women, especially since so many seem to be unappreciative of your efforts? This is a good question, and one I hear quite often.

Those women are overwhelmingly in the minority, although they would like everyone to think that their rude behavior is the standard. Most women truly appreciate, and are flattered by, real men treating them with respect and courtesy, and using manners in their presence. And those who don't, well, are they really the kind of women that you care about making an impression on anyway? I doubt it.

Men of the code live their life by a higher standard, not to impress others, but because they have made a firm decision to live by a certain code. As I have said before, they live by their principles regardless of how others live or how others react to their behavior.

Don't be afraid to be chivalrous to women in your presence. I have had hundreds of men write me and make comments about how they simply won't open doors, or treat women chivalrously anymore, because women are rude, ungrateful, and snotty about their attempts to treat them special. My response to them is to do it anyway. There will always be rude, classless people in this world, both men and women; you shouldn't allow them to influence your actions. You should behave in the way that you know is right; their response is not your responsibility.

The more masculine you behave around women, the more feminine women will feel in your presence. And women do like to feel feminine, no matter what some may say. Be a real man and you will discover that most women, not all, but most, will respond in kind by acting like a real woman, and not one of those radical feminists which no real man is interested in.

Chivalry is not dead; it still resides in every real man. The problem is that real men are becoming a rarity in this world. Being chivalrous is simply a way of treating women with the upmost respect. The chivalrous man feels a deep duty to follow through with the standards that he has set for himself concerning how he will treat women. That is really all the modern day chivalry truly is – following that part of your code.

It is not cowering down to women. It is not bending over backwards to always give them their way. It is not putting her needs before yours or trying to buy her love and affection. It is not allowing her to be disrespectful to you or putting up with her rude behavior. In short, it has nothing to do with being a doormat; it is simply being a real man in the way that you respect and treat women.

Real women, women of character, and those who really understand who they are as a woman, not only love to be treated with respect and courtesy, but they require it. They don't have much respect for men that buy into this politically correct garbage, or for the radical feminists who are pushing it. They want to be real women and act like women, not men. This is the kind of woman that you want to find; these are women of character. And this is the kind of woman that the rest of this section pertains to. I am not interested in women who think they are in competition with men, but in those women who enjoy womanhood and everything that goes with it.

Women love confidence in men. They love it when they see a man that is willing to stand up for what he believes is right, a man that stands up for himself and for others. They are looking for a passionate man who knows what he wants, what he stands for, and has character and standards. This is what women of character are looking for.

If you want to impress a quality woman, you have to be a man of character. Be chivalrous and courteous; be a real man. Your character is what makes her love you in the long run. Always remember, quality women are looking for quality men. Just as men of the code are not willing to lower their standards, neither are quality women. If a woman is not is not interested in your character, save yourself some heartache and move on.

Women are looking for security in a man. This doesn't mean that she is helpless and needs a man to look after her, far from it. She is more than willing to take care of herself, especially if she can't find a man of character like she longs for. Quality women are strong women. The media would have you think that strong women are those who act manly, have contempt for men, and always want to compete with men, but this is a lie.

Strong women don't want to compete, they don't have contempt for men or want to act manly; they are simply not willing to lower their standards and accept an inferior man as their life partner, nor should they be. But they do want to find a man who can provide them with security and a good, happy life. That is what all women want, if they are being honest, but many simply don't know how to find such a man because quality men are hard to find.

You must develop real self-confidence in yourself and your abilities. Become confident in your ability to make rational, intelligent, and wise decisions. Learn to control your emotions. Women don't want a man who can't control himself or who has little to no self-confidence.

Be decisive and strong. This not only demonstrates your self-confidence, but it helps develop your self-confidence as well. Quality women do not like indecisive, anxious, scared, timid men. They like bold, self-confident men who believe that they can take care of any and every situation.

If you find that past situations, events, or circumstances have caused you to lose your self-confidence and have made you anxious and timid, now is the time to change that. Men of the code decide who and what they will be. They decide, not past events, bad relationships, or bad memories. It is time to take control of your life and become the man that you want to be.

Practice being bold and assertive! Many men complain that women don't like nice guys and that they only go for tough guys and thugs. And a lot of women do, because they are looking for some of the character traits that those men portray, like self-confidence, assertiveness, boldness, toughness, and the fact that they act more like real men than some doormat.

Does this mean that you should act like a thug? Of course not! But there are some character traits that the tough guy has that you should have as well. You can be a nice guy and a bad ass at the same time. The two are not mutually exclusive.

Women do not want the nice guy who is a wimpy, pushover type of man. They want a bad ass that is also nice, courteous, responsible, and dependable. In fact, you don't have to be a bad ass, just simply man enough to stand up for what is right and have some backbone. Not every man is going to be a combination of Bruce Lee, James Dean, and John Wayne, but every man can develop the backbone to stand up for what he believes in, even if it means that he has to deal with one of those tough guys.

These tough guy types do have the self-confidence, the assertiveness, the boldness, and the toughness that women want to see in a man, but they lack the character, the chivalry, and the honor that women really want. That is why so many women end up with these tough guy types, only to later get divorced and become jaded where men are concerned. Quality women want the whole package; they want a complete man.

They want a man that they can respect, in every way. They don't respect a nice guy who is a wimp and gets pushed around all of the time. Neither do they respect a brutish thug who has no manners and thinks of nothing but his own image or reputation. Quality women want a real man who has all of the qualities of a man of the code, not just a few of them. Unfortunately, most women end up settling for what they can get, because true men of the code of hard to find.

Never put being nice ahead of what is right. Don't be a "yes man." To women, this demonstrates a lack of courage and resolve. Be assertive and bold, but do so in the right way. You can disagree without being disagreeable or without raising your voice and yelling. Raising your voice all the time shows a lack of self-control, which does not impress women at all.

She wants a leader, a rational man of sound judgment and self-control, someone she can put her trust in, not a man that she never knows when he is going to lose control and explode. She doesn't want to have to walk on glass around you or be afraid of you. Control your emotions! Respond, don't react. Think before you speak.

Never lose your composure. Be calm and collected, no matter what kind of situation you are in. Every time you respond in this manner, you build a little more confidence in her that she has a real man and that she should support you.

Practice making decisions. Don't be one of these guys who can't make up his mind because he is afraid to make a mistake. What kind of confidence does that instill in women? Look at all the angles, do your homework, and then make a confident decision and stick to it. And after you have made your decision, take the responsibility for that decision. That is something that women can respect, not a guy that is so unsure of himself that he can't even make up his mind.

Another thing that women find very unattractive and annoying is men who constantly complain. If you constantly complain and criticize she will lose respect for you. Doing so makes you look like a victim, not a secure man who is in control of his own destiny. She is looking for a real man, a man that takes action, not a man who sits in the safety of his own home and complains about everything under the sun, but who never does anything about anything.

Never act like a victim; always act like you can handle anything and that you are in control. Never panic or lose control over any situation. Real men remain calm and rational, even in the face of death. If there is some emergency situation, simply take care of it. Do what you can do. Panicking never does anything to make the situation better; it only makes everything worse. Show her that she can depend on you to take care of any situation. Never panic!

It may sound like I am saying that you are not a real man unless you are a bad ass who can handle anything and everything in life, who is almost like a super hero, but that is not the case. What I am presenting to you is the ideal. There is no such thing as the perfect man. We all have flaws and fall short in one area or another.

You may not have the genes to handle any muscle bound thug who threatens your family, but you know what, you can develop the self-confidence to stand up against such a thug anyway and figure out how to handle him. You may naturally be shy, but you can take steps to develop your assertiveness and self-confidence. You may have a bad temper, but that doesn't mean that you can't learn to control it. Do you see what I am getting at? You may not have the complete package, but you can always work to improve who you are and make yourself a little better each day.

I don't want any man to think that what I am teaching does not apply to them. The traits of the superior man apply to every man who wants to be a man of the code, who wants to better himself and become a better man.

A quality woman understands that there is no such thing as the perfect man. The intelligent woman is not looking for a perfect man, but rather the man who is perfect for her. You can be that man.

Don't be afraid to date a lot of women. Going out with more women allows you to get to know more about women in general. And the more that you know about women, the more you understand how to please women and what they are really looking for. Also, the more that you go out with different women, the more comfortable you will become around women, and the more your self-confidence will grow. I am not encouraging you to become a womanizer. That is not the point. You can date and socialize with many different women without being a womanizer.

What I am saying actually applies to everything in life – the more that you do something, the better you become at it. When you go on lots of dates, you get better at being comfortable with women, you better understand women, and you learn how to please women. You also learn what you do and don't want in a woman, which makes it easier for you to find the perfect woman to spend your life with. So don't be shy; when a lady catches your eye, be confident enough to ask her out and get to know her.

I do want to point out that you shouldn't use women though. Never lead a woman on or play with her heart. That is not being a real man, but a player. Players are sleazy, heartless guys who never think of women's feelings, only their own pleasure and desires. These guys are part of the reason that so many women are jaded today. They have been misled by some player and now find it hard to trust men at all. Players make relationships harder for every man. Don't lower yourself to be like one of these guys.

As long as I am on the subject of dating, I should point out a couple of things. When you go out on a date, you are responsible for the safety of your date. She may or may not need your protection, but as a man of the code, she has it. When she, or any other lady, is in your presence, you should take the responsibility of ensuring their safety. Be aware of your surroundings and make sure that she not only feels safe, but that she is safe.

Always use your best manners and treat her special. Open the car door for her. Of course she is capable of opening the car door for herself, but at least for that night, she is with a real man, and you should treat her as such. Just treat her special. Really listen to her when she talks. Get to know her and respect her, even if you know early in the date that she is not the right girl for you. Relax and have fun.

And, after your date is over, walk her safely to the door. This doesn't mean that you have to give her a good night kiss or anything else. It is simply a part of your duty. You ensure that she is safe while she is on a date with you and you see her safely all the way back to her home. It is classless to just drive up on the street, tell her goodnight, let her get out of the car, and then drive away.

Also, on the subject of driving up to her house, never, and I do mean NEVER, show up for a date and honk your horn. That is about as classless and disrespectful as you can be. Get out and go to the door and greet her properly. It always boils down to respect and courtesy.

When you ask a lady out, you need to be able to discern what she is saying to you with her answer. Know the difference between someone who is flirting and playing hard to get, and someone who is truly not interested. If she is really not interested, it makes you look like a loser if you continue to try to change her mind. There are millions of available ladies in this world; if you are not someone's cup of tea, for whatever reason, thank her for her politeness (if applicable), and move on.

No woman respects a man who has to beg for her attention. If a lady is not interesting in you, leave it at that. If she is someone that works with you and she has turned you down a couple of times, she is not interested. Have some self-esteem. You are a man of the code, a good catch for any woman. If she can't see that, she is not good enough for you. Move on.

If you ask a woman out and she has some excuse for not going, use the *Brad Pitt test*. Would she give Brad Pitt the same excuse if he were in your shoes and asked her out? If you can't answer yes to that question, then she is probably not interested.

When you are in a relationship, whether you are in a seriously relationship or married, do not cheat. If you are not ready to settle down with one woman, let her know this up front. If you are going to date other people, you should be man enough to let anyone who is getting more serious about having a relationship with you know this fact. And, if you are not ready to exclusive, don't expect her to be exclusive either.

No matter what the circumstance is, men of the code do not cheat on their girlfriend or their wife. That is despicable and shows both a lack of character and a lack of self-control. If you are interested in dating other ladies, discuss it and work it out. If your marriage is done, then end it and move on. But do not be such a coward as to slip around and cheat on her.

Think about how you would feel if your wife or girlfriend, who you loved or cared deeply about, cheated on you. Be empathetic to the feelings of others and be honorable in *all* of your actions.

One last thing on dating, if you have been going out with someone for quite a while and you find that she is just not the woman for you, break up with class. Leave her feeling lucky that she got to know you and to have spent so much enjoyable time with you. Leave her feeling good, not just about you, but about herself as well.

This doesn't mean that you make up some flimsy lie and flatter her. If she is a quality woman, and that should be the only kind of women that you ask out, then she deserves to know the truth. Be honest, but not brutally honest. Be straightforward, but kind and loving. Tell her the truth, but do it in a way that honors her and respects her feelings. And for Pete's sake, be man enough to do it in person, not on social media, a text message, or on the phone.

This woman has spent a part of her life with you, whether it was a few weeks or a few months, honor that. Be a man of honor. Tell her the truth, but always spin it in a way that puts it on you, not her. I don't mean that you simply use the cliché that, "It's not you; it's me." But never just put all the blame on her and crush her self-esteem and leave her feeling dejected.

If she was good enough for you to date for several weeks, months, or years, then she must have something special. Make sure she knows that and realizes that you two were just not a right match, but that you think very highly of her. Address what needs to be addressed and take your leave. There is no need to draw out an awkward situation.

The main thing is that you take care of this situation with class and respect. As I said before, never play with someone's heart or emotions. Leave her knowing that you are a good man, a man of honor and character.

Women and men are different, no matter what the media and the radical feminists want you to believe. Learn as much as you can about women. The more you understand women, the better armed you are to be able to please them, relate to them, and get along with them. And it is important that you know how to please women.

Little things make a big difference to women. Don't feel that it is unmanly to pamper your lady. Do small things such as run her a bubble bath, bring her flowers, even if they are out of your garden, cook a special dinner for her, or give her a massage. Many men wrongly feel that doing these kinds of things makes them less manly, but that is wrong thinking. No woman wants a man who is too insecure about his manhood to show his soft, caring side.

Also, it is not unmanly for you to help in the kitchen, to help do the dishes, to clean the house, to make up the bed, in short, help do some of the boring work. Doing these things can really mean a lot to her. She probably doesn't like doing these things any more than you do; that is why they are called chores. Be man enough to help out.

There are many little things that you can do to show her that you care. Be creative and come up with your own ideas. You can clean out and detail her car for her or just surprise her by gassing her car up and running it through the car wash. The small ways to show her how much you care are endless.

Doing nice things for your wife does not make you less of a man. I am a 6th degree black belt and I have colored my wife's hair many times. It is not something that I like doing, but it is something that helps her and makes her know how much I care about her. Does that make me less of a man? Not in my book.

Also, don't become lazy in your relationship. It is very easy to just want to stay around the house when you don't have to work, but you need to take the time to take your wife or girlfriend out and do fun things together. This is another area where you can be creative. You don't have to always spend a ton of money to go out and have fun together. Go hiking, go walking together, go for a drive, the possibilities are endless.

Don't consider it unmanly to go out of your way to learn how to treat a woman. It's not unmanly; it's wise. Your wife or girlfriend is important to you; learn how to please her and make her feel special.

Friends and Enemies

You do not really know your friends from
your enemies until the ice breaks.
Icelandic Proverb

Friends

One is known by the friends he keeps.
Baltasar Gracian

You always have a choice of who you decide to befriend and that choice is vitally important. A true friend is worth more than gold, but a fake friend is often worse than a hated enemy. It takes time to develop a real friendship. It is an investment of both time and trust, and if you don't invest wisely, your time will have been wasted and your trust betrayed. Never enter into any friendship lightly.

There are no guarantees when it comes to developing a friendship. The best that you can do is to evaluate the other person's character to the best of your abilities and then be the best friend that you can be. And you should be the best friend that anyone can ever imagine ever. You must be the kind of man that you want for a friend.

Think about all the qualities that you would like to have in your best friend. What kind of man would you like him to be? What qualities would he have? How would he treat you? How dependable would he be? Would he be someone that you would bet your life on? Think about the answers to these questions, and then you will know what kind of friend that you should be.

Good friendships don't just happen anymore than good romantic relationships just happen; you have to work at them and cultivate them. It takes a lot of time and effort to develop a strong friendship, but it is worth the effort. Once you have the friendship of a superior man, you have a friend for life. The trick is, truly knowing when you have that friendship.

Many of man has believed he had a true friend, only to find, when the chips were down, that he had no friend at all. Never trust someone with too much information, or with anything vitally important, until you know for a fact that he is truly your friend. Trusting someone too much, too quickly, has cost many men in ways that they could not have imagined.

While you should have many acquaintances, your true friends should, and will be, very few. Your acquaintances may run the gamut of different types of people, but your friends should only be men or women of quality. Confucius urged us to, "Make friends only with those gentlemen who are superior man." There are several reasons that you should make sure that your true friends are superior people.

People will judge you by the quality of your friends. If your friends are kind of sleazy, what does that say about you? Why would a man of honor have friends that are not honorable men? Moreover, you can only trust men who are men of honor; therefore only men of honor can truly be real friends. If a friend is someone that you need to count on when your back is against the wall, then his loyalty should be unquestionable. Again, this can only be said of superior man.

Once you have given your hand in true friendship, you should be your friend's true friend. You should be the best friend possible and this includes treating your friend with respect and honor. Too many people take this for granted and don't treat their friends as well as they do strangers.

Don't neglect your friendship. Make sure that your friend knows that he can count on you and that you will always be there for him. You cannot do this by mere words; you have to prove this by your actions. Actions always speak louder than words. You must prove, over years of friendship, that you can be trusted and that you will always be there for your friend, in good times and in bad.

Building a friendship takes a lot of effort. Today, everyone is very busy, running in many different directions. It takes effort to maintain that connection with your friend when you are tired and just want to do nothing. Emerson addressed this when he wrote, "Go often to the house of your friend, for weeds choke the unused path." A true friendship will lasts a lifetime, but until you have developed that true friendship, you have to cultivate it, just as you have to cultivate a new fruit tree.

When you first plant a fruit tree, it requires a lot of attention to establish it. You have to water it often, keep it mulched, check it for problems, give it fertilizer, and protect it. It may take several years before it starts to produce any fruit, but when it does, all of your hard work will pay off and it will produce fruit for a lifetime.

Building a friendship works in much the same way. You have to give it more attention in the beginning. You have to work to keep it alive and to make it strong. If any problems or challenges develop, you have to address them and not allow them to destroy what you have worked for. And after it has developed strong roots, your friendship will provide you with a lifetime of pleasure and a strong relationship. It will become a relationship that you will be able to count on through thick and thin, for the rest of your life.

You do, however, have to watch out for problems. Just because you are friends, that doesn't mean that there are necessarily no boundaries. You must respect your friend's boundaries, just as he must respect yours.

Don't wear out your welcome. Your friend needs his private time, just as you do. Being friends doesn't mean that everything that your friend does is your business. Don't stick your nose where it doesn't belong. Be careful when giving advice. Although there are times when you may have to step up and give unasked for advice, as a rule, it is best not to give advice without first asking he if would like some advice on the situation. And, when you do give advice, if he doesn't want it or doesn't agree with it, drop it. Don't badger him about it.

Never speak for your friends. That is definitely overstepping your boundaries. When you speak for your friend, you are showing a type of disrespect. Your friend has his own mind, it is not your place to make decisions for him or speak for him. That is simply being presumptuous and should not be done.

There are times when your friendship may require you to be pushy, such as if your friend is doing something that you know for a fact is a big mistake, or something that will really hurt him, but as a rule, don't be overly pushy with your friend. Just because you are friends, that doesn't mean that you both don't have your separate lives and personal business. If your friend doesn't want to share something, or talk about something, drop it.

Do your best to help your friend in every way. Build up his self-esteem and his confidence. Praise your friend when he deserves praise. And, if you can praise him in public, it's all the better. On the other hand, never criticize or reprimand your friend in public, always make that a private conversation. And don't make a habit out of that either. Pointing out something that you don't agree with should only be done if you feel it is absolutely necessary.

If he has a need and you can help him with it, help. If he needs a hand with something, lend a hand. Be there when you friend needs you to be there. Don't wait until he is dead until you show how much you appreciate him and his friendship; do it often.

Never be the first to end a true friendship, no matter what. Once you have given your hand in friendship, do your best to keep that rare bond. Cultivate your friendship and it will last a lifetime and serve you both well.

Enemies

Keep your friends close and your enemies closer.
Sun Tzu

You have enemies, whether you know it or not. Everyone does, even if it is nothing more than the office worker who is so jealous of you that he is willing to do anything to see you fail. An enemy is not always the person that harms you, but the person who would like to harm you, or would like to see you fail.

Enemies come in many shapes and sizes, and from places that you may not expect. Always be on guard for new, unknown enemies, as they are the ones who will blindside you. This is especially true in today's world. With most everyone having easy internet access, it is very easy for your enemies to attack you online, without you even knowing where the attack came from or why. Never underestimate your enemies; they can, and will, do things that you would never imagine.

Many times, your enemies will be motivated by jealousy. Unchecked jealousy soon turns to hate, and long-held hate can manifest in malicious actions. This is why you need to be aware of even the smallest comments of a jealous nature. When you know that someone is jealous of you, keep your eye on them; they can potentially be trouble.

Every enemy has the capability to disrupt your life, some in a small way and others to a much larger capacity, but not that many of them go to the effort to cause you harm. The fact that you don't openly see enemies attacking you physically, verbally or discreetly behind your back, doesn't mean that you do not have any enemies. It simply means that your enemies are not malevolent enough, or energetic enough, to make the effort to cause you harm, but their lack of effort should not be mistaken for a lack of malevolence toward you.

As Democritus taught, just because a man does you no harm, it doesn't mean he is not your enemy. You have to look deeper than that. You have to read between the lines. Someone doesn't have to wrong you to be your enemy. Your enemy is the man who is happy when you are hit with misfortune, the man who celebrates your downfall. He is the man who wishes you calamity, even if he doesn't have the courage to openly state the fact.

Be careful who you trust. You don't always know who your enemies are. They are not always those who openly oppose you. The enemies of a good man are usually not men of character and backbone. They are more likely to be men of low character who lack the courage to openly come against you. Instead, they find it easier to simply sit back and think malicious thoughts of your ruin, awaiting their opportunity. Be wise and learn to read people's spirits.

Many of your enemies will attack you anonymously in a cowardly attempt to cloak their actions and protect themselves from any reprisal. These cowardly enemies can cause as much problems as the man who attacks you out in the open, and sometimes even more problems. They are the type of enemy that will write things about you on the internet under fake names or who will drop anonymous "information" about you to your boss. Always be very aware of this type of enemy.

Sometimes you have no doubt about who your enemy is. When you know without a doubt that someone hates you and wishes you malice, then you should do what you can to make sure that he doesn't have the opportunity to harm you in some way. Always make sure that your defenses are strong. One way to do this is to make sure that you have no skeletons in your closet. If you are a man of honor, and all of your actions are just, then that leaves very little ammunition for your enemies to us against you.

Whether you are referring to war or business, if you want to win, you need to be able to counter your enemy's strategy. You first need to know exactly what your enemy's strategy is, in order to attack it. Don't just shoot in the dark. You need factual information concerning what he plans to do. Take the time to do a little research and find out who your enemy is and what makes him tick. You must know your enemy. Know his weaknesses and his strengths. Know what his goals are, what he wants to achieve and why. Gather as much information on him as possible.

Once you know your enemy well, you are ready to start thinking of ways to disrupt his strategy and defend yourself against his malicious attacks. Only after you understand your enemy, can you begin to devise a plan to attack his strategy. Attacking your enemy's strategy without doing your homework can backfire on you. You must be able to understand what is going on in your enemy's mind in order to plan your own strategy. You must know who he is and how he thinks in order to predict how he will react and what his next move will be.

Things are not always as they appear to be on the surface. In fact, they are seldom what they appear to be. You must work hard to get through all the layers of deception and find out what your enemy's true purpose is, and why. Don't just discover his strategy, but look deeper and find out why he has developed this strategy. What is his motivation? What is his ultimate objective? Once you know what his motivation is and what his objectives are, you are ready to develop a plan to counter your enemy's strategy. Knowledge is power; ignorance is dangerous.

Always remember, the friend of your enemy is also your enemy. Never trust your enemy's friend, even if he claims to be friends with both of you. A true friend will not befriend your enemy or remain friends with your enemy after he knows that your enemy is in the wrong and is a man of poor character. If he claims to not want to choose sides, he has already chosen a side. Sometimes refusing to make a choice is making a choice.

Don't deceive yourself into thinking that you don't have enemies; you do. Even the best of men have enemies who hate them with a passion. If you truly have no enemies, that is a bad sign. That means that you are doing very little with your life. Every man who honestly states his opinion, or stands for something, has enemies. It has always been that way and most likely always will be.

The best defense against your enemies is to make sure and be the man of honor that you should be. Give them nothing to use against you. Make sure that you don't let your guard down. It is better to make sure that your enemies can't hurt you, than to hope that they won't hurt you. Make sure that you keep your affairs in order and keep an eye on what your enemies are up to. Never give them an opening.

A lack of attention can have disastrous consequences. When you know who your enemy is, you must take him seriously and keep an eye on him. It is always better to be safe than sorry.

Reflections for the Superior Man

The word friend is common, the fact is rare.
Phaedrus

The company of just and righteous men
is better than wealth and a rich estate.
Euripides

If you have one true friend, you have
more than your share comes to.
Thomas Fuller

The greater man is one of courtesy.
Lord Tennyson

Our friends show us what we can do,
our enemies teach us what we must do.
Goethe

In planning, never a useless move;
in strategy, no step taken in vain.
Sun Tzu

The most painful thing is losing yourself in
the process of loving someone too much,
and forgetting that you are special too.
Earnest Hemingway

Your acquaintances must fill the empire;
your close friends must be few.
Chinese Proverb

The unwise man imagines a smiling face, a friend.
Surprised to find how little support he musters at a meeting.
The Havamal

Rare though true love may be,
true friendship is rarer still.
La Rochefoucauld

Trust in today's friends as if they might be tomorrow's enemies.
Baltasar Gracian

Chapter 20

Wisdom and Knowledge

*It is not difficult to know a thing; what is
difficult is to know how to use what you know.*
Nah Fei Tzu

Obtain Knowledge and Wisdom

Preparation is the key to success.
Alexander Graham Bell

Every man of the code should do his best to add to his wisdom and knowledge daily. Don't count on others; don't be lazy; do the leg work and obtain knowledge for yourself. The more knowledge that you have, the better off you are. There is no such thing as too much knowledge or bad knowledge. Never be afraid of acquiring as much knowledge as possible, on as many subjects as possible. The more you know, the better armed you will be.

Simply put, the more you know, the better off you are. You can never tell when you may need a certain piece of knowledge. Prepare yourself with as much knowledge as you can. Make it your business to know what is going on in this world and how things work. Keep yourself aware of what is happening in your country, your state, and your community. Learn as much as you can. You must educate yourself; don't depend on others.

You can learn something from everyone you meet. Everyone knows something that you don't know. Always be open to learning from others. Never consider someone to be worthless, as far as knowledge is concerned.

It is wise to study and acquire knowledge from history, as well as the people that you meet in life. History teaches us much about human nature and the way that the world works. Those who will not learn from history are doomed to repeat the same mistakes.

Study wisdom from the sages of the past. The sages and wise men of the past have so much to offer us. Never think that their wisdom is outdated and doesn't apply to today's world. It does. True wisdom is universal and is not restrained by cultures or time. What was true about human nature 500 years ago, is true about human nature today. If you don't believe me, take the time to study some of the experts in human nature from the past and see for yourself whether or not it still applies to people today. You will find that these wise men could have just as easily written their teachings last month, instead of 400 or 500 hundred years ago. My book, *Defensive Living*, delves into these teaching and shows how they are just as relevant today as their ever were.

You can gain wisdom and knowledge from both good and bad people. As I said before, you can learn something from everyone. Good people will teach you how to live a better life, whereas bad people will provide you with lessons about how not to live your life and the consequences of certain actions.

In every situation, look at it and ask yourself, "What can I learn from this situation? What knowledge can I take away from this experience?" If you approach every situation with this attitude, you will find that everything is a learning experience. You can even turn the worst circumstances into something positive and walk away with knowledge that you couldn't have obtained in any other way.

Every situation is unique and offers the opportunity to learn unique lessons, but you have to be open to those lessons. Next time something bad happens in your life, instead of ranting and raving over what happened, look for the lesson in that incident. Take a bad situation and use it to your advantage by gaining wisdom from it.

In today's world, everyone can be as educated as they want to be. You have more information at your fingertips than any generation that has come before. We have libraries full of information. With the internet, you don't even have to leave home to increase your knowledge. There is knowledge to be found on television, if you make the right choices.

All you have to do is take the time and put in the effort to learn what you want to learn. But you do have to apply yourself. You have to quit numbing your mind with all of the distractions available today and spend your time improving your mind. It takes work to increase your wisdom and your knowledge, but it is well worth the effort.

Another thing to keep in mind, especially in today's world, is that you don't necessarily have to know everything about everything in order to be knowledgeable. You simply have to know how to get the knowledge that you need, when you need it.

If you know how to find out what you need to know, then most of the time, that is as good and knowing it. There will be times when it will benefit you to already have the knowledge you need, but let's be honest, we can't know all there is to know about everything in our world. But if you have the knowledge about how to get the information that you need, you will be far ahead of the game.

The More You know, the Better Off You Are

Survival favors the prepared mind.
Robert Crowley

The more you know, the better off you are, *if* you know how to use what you know. True knowledge is much more than just knowing a bunch of facts; you have to know how to use that knowledge to your advantage, how to put that knowledge to work in your life.

You could have the all of the food that you could possibly want and still starve to death if you didn't actually use it. Simply having something does not make you better off; having it and *using it* makes you better off. Think of it in a different way. You could be a billionaire, but having all the money in the world wouldn't do you any good if you didn't actually use it.

It is definitely good to acquire a lot of knowledge and wisdom, but that is just the first step. Acquiring wisdom and knowledge is your preparation, but to actually benefit from it, you have to put it to use in your life. Acquiring wisdom and knowledge, without ever putting it to use in your life, is exactly like having millions of dollars in your bank account, but never spending any of it. It does you no good.

You have to not only acquire knowledge, but know *how* to use it as well. This takes more than being able to memorize facts or quote some sage; it takes a thorough understanding of what you have learned. It takes experience, failures and successes, and it takes perseverance.

Without the understanding of how to use what you know, your knowledge does you little good. You must put your knowledge to work in your life. You must use what you know.

Learn everything you can. Learn to distinguish between good and evil, right and wrong, and the ways of the superior man. The wisdom of those superior men, who lived before you, can help to keep you on the right path. Many have lived by the virtues of wisdom. Study their wisdom!

Acquire all the knowledge that you can and put it to use in your life. Governments, con artists, and people in general, take advantage of the ignorant. They have no problem using what you don't know against you. The only way to counteract this is to educate yourself. Your ignorance is their power.

Nobody cares about your family, your success, or your wellbeing like you do. Most people are out to get whatever they can, anyway they can. Knowledge and wisdom are your defense against these people. If you neglect to increase your knowledge and use your wisdom, you are a sitting duck for those who would take advantage of you.

Be smart and increase your knowledge daily. Don't just read wisdom, but truly study it and integrate it into your life. Never forget the importance of knowledge and the wisdom to put it to use in your life.

One of the best ways of obtaining knowledge, and truly understanding it to the level that you are able to use it, is the Trivium method. There are three parts to the Trivium method of educating yourself: general grammar, formal logic, and classical rhetoric. Don't panic, I will explain this in very simple terms and you will find it very beneficial.

The first part of the Trivium method of education is general grammar. This basically means that you discover and get a good handle on the facts that comprise basic knowledge. In simple terms, you ask the right questions about whatever subject you are studying. The essential questions that you should ask are: who, what, when, and where.

You should try to answer these questions first, whenever you are trying to understand a new subject or you are trying to obtain more knowledge. By answering these basic questions you will have a good foundation about the subject you are studying, but you still need to go deeper and ask "why?"

Asking "why" takes you to a better understanding of the subject. It helps you understand the reasoning behind what you have learned. Answering "why" helps you to establish a valid relationship between the facts, and also allows you to discover when there is no valid relationship between the facts. When you can't discover a valid relationship between the facts that you have uncovered, that might be a reason to doubt that your facts are true.

The third part of Trivium knowledge consists of learning *how* something works. This is where you actually learn to apply the knowledge. This is an important part, because as I stated earlier, knowledge is useless unless you can actually put it to use in your life. When you know *how* to use what you have learned, that knowledge has been transformed into real wisdom.

When I was teaching writing in school, I would use this method to teach my students how to organize their writing. This is a simple way of looking at the Trivium method. I taught my students to always answer these questions in their essays and their essays would be complete. I gave them a check list to ensure that they answered who, what, when, where, why, and how. If you think about it, that pretty much covers it all.

This is important to you in obtaining new knowledge for the same reason. If you can answer all of these questions about a subject, you will pretty much have all the information that you need to know, where that subject is concerned.

Use your critical thinking skills when evaluating information. Make sure that you can answer these basic questions about whatever the subject may be, *before* you accept what you have heard or read as truth.

There is so much propaganda in today's world that it is wise to question whatever information comes your way. Never just accept something as the absolute truth before you have done your homework and checked it out.

It is very important that the man of the code is well-informed and has an abundance of knowledge and wisdom. But, at the same time, you must make sure that your knowledge and wisdom are based on fact, not opinion or even worse, pure propaganda.

Do your best to educate yourself on many subjects and stay up to date on what is happening in your world. You never know when the knowledge that you learn, or the wisdom that you acquire, will come in handy or be vital in your success.

Reflections for the Superior Man

A man may learn wisdom even from a foe.
Aristophanes

It is the mark of an educated mind to be able
to entertain a thought without accepting it.
Aristotle

It is possible to store the mind with a
million facts and still be entirely uneducated.
Alec Bourne

I never met a man so ignorant that I couldn't learn something from him.
Galileo Galilei

Study the past if you would define the future.
Confucius

When you cannot be deceived by men,
you will have realized the wisdom of strategy.
Miyamoto Musashi

To know the road ahead, ask those coming back.
Chinese Proverb

Do not seek to follow in the footsteps of the men of old;
seek what they sought.
Matsuo Basho

The reverse side also has a reverse side.
Japanese Proverb

Never dare to judge till you've heard the other side.
Euripides

Knowing yourself is the beginning of all wisdom.
Aristotle

Any fool can know. The point is to understand.
Albert Einstein

He who knows all the answers has not been asked all the questions.
Confucius

Chapter 21

Mental and Spiritual Strength

What the mind of man can conceive and believe,
the mind of a man can achieve.
Napoleon Hill

Developing Mental Strength

Human beings, by changing the inner attitudes of their minds,
can change the outer aspects of their lives.
William James

In our world, it is vitally important to develop mental strength. You will find that, during your lifetime, you will have a vast variety of different sources of stress. What determines how well you will handle those different types of stress is how well you have developed your mental strength. As with every kind of strength, mental strength must be cultivated now for when you need it later. You can't wait until you have a crisis to develop your coping skills; they must be built day by day, just as you build muscle in the weight room.

You must train your mind how to respond to certain situations. Most people never think about this fact; they simply react as they go, to whatever situation they may be in at the time. This is not the way of the superior man. The superior man responds; he doesn't react. Although the dictionary list these two terms as synonyms, there is a big difference between the two. Learning this important distinction will be most valuable to you.

As I stated earlier, when you simply react to a situation or another person, you are allowing that event or person in control you. When you respond, you make a conscious decision concerning what you will do in that situation. Responding puts you in control of your mind and your actions. But, to be able to do this, you must be prepared ahead of time. You must have some set of guidelines that guide your responses.

These guidelines help you develop your mental strength. Without them, you are very much like a boat drifting on a lake. You simply move in whatever direction you are blown at the time. Your code is your rudder. Your guidelines put you in control and give you the power to make rational decisions based on who and what you are – a man of the code.

When you truly understand who you are, what you are, and have internalized the code by which you live, you will find both mental strength and mental calmness. This simplifies your life. You don't have to deeply debate every decision or every action. You simply use your code as a guide by which you make your decisions, and you stick to it.

Although this sounds very simplistic and easy, it is also very easy to forget this principle and get caught up in whatever situation you may be dealing with at this time. You have to constantly remind yourself to respond instead of react, at least until it has become second nature to you.

Your emotions will try frantically to take control of your actions and cause you to react instead of allowing you to respond. It is vital that you learn to control your emotions if you are ever to develop true mental strength. You must make your principles and your code your foundations for your mental strength. Never allow your emotions to dictate to you what you will and won't do, or how you will respond.

This is only possible through the development of your mental strength and self-confidence in your decisions. Resolve beforehand, how you will and will not respond to certain situations. This requires some effort; if it were easy or happened naturally, everyone would respond instead of allowing their emotions to take over and control their actions. It is not easy. You have to work at this constantly; but this is one of the main ways that you will develop mental strength.

Once you have developed mental strength, you can deal with whatever life throws at you. There is nothing that can completely overwhelm you. You begin to think rationally instead of emotionally. Mental strength puts you in the driver's seat. If you don't control your mind, your mind will control you. It is your duty as a man of the code to take control of your mind, your will, and your emotions. Giving up this control can be likened to leaving your life to chance or simply being in a rudderless boat; you are merely adrift without any direction.

A huge part of developing mental strength is learning to control your thoughts. All of your responses, your words, and your actions start with your thoughts. Control your thoughts and you will take control of your mind, your responses, and your actions. Allow your thoughts to run wild, and you will start to find that all of these will start to spin out of control and cause you problems.

When you start to take control of your thoughts, you may begin to feel that you are being insincere. After all, you can't help what you think about something, you simply think what you think, right? Wrong!

Your thought pattern has been developing since you were born. It has been molded and shaped over the years to the place where it is today. Someone or some thing has guided your thinking for your entire life, either consciously or unconsciously. You have been taught how to think, whether you know it or not.

Some people have been taught, or guided, well, and others haven't been. Either way, you can begin, where you are now, to start to take control of your thoughts. It is not an easy process, but it is vitally important.

If you have a son, you wouldn't simply allow him to develop his mind on his own, simply hoping that somehow he learns how to think like a superior man. You would teach him how to think for himself. You would give him the guiding principles which would guide his thought processes, or at least this would be the ideal way of raising your son.

The problem is that many parents have either, not understood this process, not cared enough to do the work, or simply did not care, period. Therefore, we have a world full of men who have never learned to discipline their mind and control their thoughts. The good news is that it is never too late to change and start to take control of your thoughts.

The Power of Your Thoughts

Change your thoughts, and you change your world.
Norman Vincent Peale

Your thoughts control everything that you do, from when and how you wake up, to your attitude throughout the day. Different thoughts actually produce different results in your life. Your thoughts control your emotions, your words, and your actions. Your thoughts can also control your body chemistry, aid in healing, and control your happiness. Now if that isn't power, I don't know what is.

Many people have a problem believing these facts. They think that your thoughts are random and that there is nothing that you can do about what you think. Well, that is true to a point. You really can't stop a specific thought from popping into your mind, but you can choose which thoughts you entertain and which thoughts you allow to dwell in your mind. A random thought is not going to hurt you; it is how you handle your thoughts that makes a difference in the long-run.

For example, if you have had someone you trusted really stab you in the back, you may have thoughts of revenge that randomly pop into your mind, at least until you have taken control of the situation and let it go. Those random thoughts of revenge are not going to have any effect on you *unless* you allow your mind to dwell on them. The more attention you give those thoughts, the more you allow those thoughts to take root in your mind, the more problems they will cause you. They will start to cause your emotions to run amuck. They will start to affect your health, your attitude, and your body chemistry. Soon you will find that you have literally been overtaken by hatred and anger.

I had someone, who I thought was a friend, who allowed his jealousy to overcome his rational thought process. He was a fellow author, but his books did not sell very well because they weren't very good books. He started to dwell on the fact that my books well flying off the shelf and his were basically dead in the water. The more he dwelled on this fact, the more envious he became.

He continued to dwell on his jealousy and his envious thoughts until they started to control his emotions and his actions. His jealousy turned to anger and hate, and eventually those thoughts started to control his actions as well. Instead of focusing on how to improve himself or write better books, he started focusing on how to stop me from being successful. It appeared that his thought process changed from, "How can I do better?" to "How can I bring him down."

Soon he was libeling me across the internet, writing lie after lie about me. He attacked everything about me – my education, my training, my writing, my family, my name, and my success. If there was something negative he could say about me, he did so. He even went as far as to start personally emailing people who supported me and asking them to stop supporting me. This is actually how I found out what was going on.

He became obsessed with me. Failing to control his negative thoughts allowed them to totally take over his mind, his words, and his actions. He irrationally started to think that if he could somehow destroy my reputation and my success, that he could step into my shoes and be successful.

This is the kind of irrational thinking that will start to expand if you are not careful to take control of your mind when you have those negative thoughts. What you concentrate on expands in your life. The more he concentrated on those negative thoughts, the more envious and angry he became. Eventually, his anger manifested in words and actions and his negative thoughts became something tangible.

Uncontrolled thoughts can quickly and easily spin out of control and start to disrupt your life. In this guy's case, his irrational thinking harmed him in ways that he could have never imagined. He lost many of the readers that he did have; his true character was revealed to the public and his reputation was forever tarnished. What little popularity he had with the few people who did read his books, was diminished and people lost almost all interest in his work. He drew unwanted attention to himself and it was found that he had some questionable things in his background. Others, who had the same type of experience with this guy, came out of the woodwork and their anger with him was renewed. And all of his problems originated from his uncontrolled thoughts that he allowed to take root in his mind. They started to control his mind, his words, and his actions, and his life suffered for it.

Your thoughts are much more powerful than you know. A negative thought, which you may think nothing about to begin with, could easily start a chain of thoughts and actions that you could never have imagined. This is why men of the code take control of their thoughts and their mind.

Think about it this way. Life is like being in a boat on a river. There is no such thing as staying stationary; you are moving in one direction or another. It takes effort to move up the river, against the current, but it takes no effort to simply sit in the boat and drift wherever the river current may take you. If you want to get to a specific location, you have to take control of your boat and force it to go in the direction that you want to go.

Your mind works in the same way. It is rarely completely still and silent. Thoughts are constantly flowing, just like the current of the river. Scientists have found that we have between 50,000-70,000 thoughts per day, this is between 35 and 48 thoughts per minute. As I stated, you can't stop random thoughts from appearing in your mind, but you can decide which ones you will allow to take up residence there.

In order for you to reach your goals, you must take control of your mind and direct it in the right direction. Otherwise, you are simply going to go wherever your thoughts take you. Someone has to be in charge, either you take control of which thoughts you entertain or your uncontrolled thoughts will stealthily take charge of you, without your conscious consent.

Science is finding that our thoughts are much more powerful than you may think. I am not going to get into all of the mind science associated with your thoughts, as that is a whole book in and of itself, but I will touch on just a few points.

First, science has proven that your thoughts are physical things. All physical reality is made up of vibrations of energy. Your thoughts are also vibrations of energy. This is not some theory or new age concept, but rather it is proven science in the field of quantum physics. Your thoughts are powerful and influence what happens to you. In short, your thoughts create your life. I know that this can be a hard concept to grasp, but it is beneficial for you to understand.

Your job is to take control over your thoughts and direct them in such as way that you produce the outcome that you desire. What you focus on, you attract. If you focus on success, you attract success; if you focus on fear and failure, you attract failure.

This seems very easy and simple at first, but it is much harder than you may think. Remember, you have somewhere between 50,000 and 70,000 thoughts per day. That is a lot of thoughts to keep under control! Does controlling your mind mean that you have to control every single thought? Of course not! That would be impossible, no matter who you are. Your job is to cultivate the garden of our mind and to keep it free of weeds. You can weed your garden, but you really can't ensure that weeds never pop up.

We can't control every single thought, but we can disallow certain negative thoughts and keep our thoughts positive and focused on the things that we want in life. A man cannot think two opposing thoughts at the same time. Try it. Try to think of a pink elephant and your hand at the exact same time. You can't do it. Likewise, you can't hold a negative thought and a positive thought in your mind at the same time. One or the other will be stronger and push the other out of your mind.

Humans are creatures of habit. What we must do is form the habit of strengthening our positive thoughts, while at the same time, disallowing our negative thoughts to take root in our mind. Remember, for things to truly be right on the outside, they must first be right on the inside. If you try to change your external circumstances, without first changing your internal condition, (your thoughts and beliefs), then any change you make will be temporary at best.

Once you comprehend this truth, the importance of the power of your thoughts becomes very clear. You must train your mind to focus on thoughts of success, health, prosperity, happiness, and all of the other traits that you want to cultivate in your life, while at the same time, weeding out negative thoughts of anger, hate, fear, envy, jealousy, cowardice, and the like.

This is a process, not an overnight, quick fix. It is a life-long process that is never finished, but is only strengthened or weakened according to the effort that we put into achieving control over our thoughts. As with everything in the warrior lifestyle, you never reach the point where you have achieved your goal and now you can sit back and rest on your laurels. This is a lifestyle; it is meant to be a way of living life for the rest of your life, not some fad.

You can only achieve mental strength by learning to control your mind. Men of the code must think for themselves, but they must also be sure that they are thinking correctly. If you are entertaining the wrong thoughts, your thinking will be skewed. Just because you think something or believe something, even if you have the strongest convictions about what you believe, it doesn't mean that what you believe is right.

Make sure that your convictions in your beliefs are well-placed. Remember, the terrorist believes his actions are right, but his belief doesn't make him right. The author, in my previous example thought that his dishonorable actions were the best thing for his career, but his thinking was clouded by his jealousy and anger. Be sure you are thinking rationally.

Your emotions don't control your thoughts; your thoughts control your emotions. Therefore, you have control over your emotions. You don't have to give in to fear, anger, hatred, jealousy, and the like. You don't have to be controlled by fearful thoughts. Fear will keep you from achieving your goals. Don't let it! Your motivation to be the man that you want to be must be much greater than any fears you have that may hold you back.

Stop focusing your thoughts on fear and failure, and start focusing on what you want to attract into your life. Refuse to remember your failures and negative emotions, and only remember the lessons that you learned from those experiences. You have to get rid of all that negative baggage that you carry around in the form of negative memories.

The only person that can change your negative thoughts, and turn them into positive thoughts, is you. Your thoughts are one of the few things that you have the ability to completely control. You have to think for yourself and take control of your life.

Be selective about your thoughts. Whenever you find that your thoughts are heading in a negative direction, stop them. Mentally say to yourself, "No, I will not allow those thoughts!" and replace them with thoughts that will help you achieve your objectives. You don't need anyone's permission to do this. You don't need anyone else's advice. Just do it. You have to have a mind of your own. Think for yourself!

Realize that you are going to be most vulnerable to negative thoughts when you are tired, angry, upset, hungry, and just overall mentally drained. Everyone needs some down time. Don't push yourself too hard. It is perfectly okay to veg out in front of the television from time to time and just relax. Remember what your ultimate objective is – to be a better man than you were yesterday. As long as you are moving forward, that is what counts. The rate at which you move will vary. Just keep striving for excellence.

Another vital point that I want to stress to you is that you must stop complaining about things. Complaining will quickly drag you into a negative mind set. When you complain, you are focusing your thoughts on everything negative in your life, and thus, attracting more negative things to you. Remember, you attract into your life what you focus on most. If you are spending a lot of time each week complaining, what you do you think that you will attract into your life?

One way to get out of the habit of complaining is to start practicing thankfulness and appreciation for what you have and how far you have come in your journey. When you do this, you will see that your thoughts will follow along. Never forget that it is what you focus your thoughts on *consistently* that you attract into your life. Nobody is going to be perfect, but you can be *consistently* better than you were the day before.

Start practicing being grateful for all of the blessings in your life and you will see that you have much more to be grateful for than you do to complain about. The problem is that people compare their lives with a very small minority of people who are doing better than them. It may seem like a lot of people from your vantage point, but when you see the big picture, you will understand how well off you truly are.

Spend some time researching how many people in third world countries live. This will be an eye-opening experience for you, especially if you are not already aware of the circumstances around the world. When you see how great your life really is, compared to the majority of people in the world, you will not have much to complain about.

Your thoughts have the power to truly change your world, but you must make the effort to control and use that power. The power of your mind is always working. The only question is whether or not you are going to take the time to make that awesome power work for you or allow it to work against you.

Harnessing Your Spiritual Strength

When the One Great Scorer comes to write against your name,
He marks, not that you won or lost, but how you played the game.
Grantland Rice

I am not going to get into the different religious and spiritual beliefs here, that subject is a deeply personal subject. But I do want to touch on a few points before I end this chapter on mental and spiritual strength. Most men have some type of spiritual beliefs, although it seems that not many take their beliefs very seriously in today's society.

The superior man will understand what his spiritual beliefs are and why he holds those beliefs. He doesn't accept anything blindly on the word of others, but instead, is willing to spend time doing his research to get a thorough understanding concerning the origins of his beliefs and whether or not he truly agrees with the different parts of his spiritual beliefs.

A man's spiritual beliefs are a very personal and private part of his life. His beliefs should have a basis in fact and should help him improve his life. If a man's spiritual beliefs do nothing to improve his life, then what good are they? If he doesn't live according to the teachings in which he claims to believe, are his spiritual beliefs truly important to him?

As with every part of a man's code, when it comes to his spiritual beliefs, whatever they may be, he should walk the walk, not just talk the talk. If you claim to believe that God wants you to live your life in a certain way, but you live your life in a totally different way, that is hypocritical. If you spiritual beliefs are truly important to you, then live them.

Be sincere about your spiritual beliefs. The superior man doesn't profess spiritual beliefs merely to please other people. That too, would be hypocritical. Superior men have the courage to live their life their way. They don't feel a need to pretend to be something that they are not in order to impress others or to placate those who want to influence their beliefs.

Real men take the time to look deeply into whatever belief system that they may be interested in, make their own decision about what they do or do not believe, and then integrate their beliefs into their life. They aren't swayed by the arguments of others because they have done their homework and know what they are talking about.

There are a lot of spiritual beliefs to explore, and you may find it very enlightening to explore several of them to get a thorough understanding concerning the origins and beliefs of each one. This is not as big of a job as it may first appear.

Every man will meet his Maker sooner or later, so it is important that he knows what he believes and why, and lives accordingly. Once you decide what spiritual traditions or beliefs are right for you, integrate them into your code and your lifestyle. Make them an integral part of your life.

You will find that the inner peace that you experience from your spiritual strength will only enhance your efforts to live by your code. Whether it is prayer, meditation, or studying the words of your scriptures, I believe that you will find your spiritual life both encouraging and insightful in your journey to be a man of the code.

Reflections for the Superior Man

We are what we think.
All that we are arises with our thoughts.
With our thoughts, we make our world.
Buddha

When we direct our thoughts properly,
we can control our emotions.
W. Clement Stone

Only in quiet waters do things mirror themselves undistorted.
Only in a quiet mind is adequate perception of the world.
Margolis

The things you think about determine the quality of your mind.
Your soul takes on the color of your thoughts.
Marcus Aurelius

Whatever you think, be sure it is what you think.
T. S. Eliot

Be careful of your thoughts;
they are the beginning of your acts.
Lao Tzu

Your thoughts create your reality because your thoughts
determine how you respond to situations in your daily life.
Wayne Dyer

Whatever the mind of man can conceive and believe,
the mind of man can achieve.
Napoleon Hill

Think like a man of action,
act like a man of thought.
Thomas Mann

God enters by a private door into every individual.
Ralph Waldo Emerson

All things share the same true nature.
Bodhidharma

Chapter 22

The Power of Your Words

Do not say a little in many words,
but a great deal in a few.
Pythagoras

Your Words are Powerful

If thought corrupts language,
language can also corrupt thought.
George Orwell

Superior men understand the power of their words. They understand that their word is their honor and that keeping their word is a vitally important part of truly being a man of honor. Our words hold much more power than you may think, but not many of us really stop to think before we speak.

The purpose of this chapter is to get you to stop and think about the power that your words hold. Your words have the power to motivate and inspire. They have the power to build people up or to tear them down. People will judge you by, not only what you say, but how you say it.

Words have destroyed some presidential candidates and have lifted others up to be the most powerful men of their times. Your words are truly charged with life-changing power, but they must be used correctly; if used incorrectly, they also have the power to destroy everything you have worked for in your life.

What you say, and what you don't say, can greatly impact your life, your reputation, and your career. But so many of us take our words for granted; we waste the power behind our words through careless, thoughtless banter, never considering that we have a great untapped power at our disposal. You do have this great power at your disposal, maybe it is time to take your words more seriously.

Not only do your words have the power to change your attitude, your thoughts, and ultimately, your life, but they also have the power to change other peoples' lives, for better or for worse. People listen to what you say and it does affect them, even if you never know it. The more people look up to you, the more your words affect them. Your words are especially powerful where your children and wife are concerned. Let your words be uplifting and useful, instead of destructive and hurtful. Even if you have to rebuke someone, do it without tearing them down.

Always think *before* you speak. This means that you actually have to slow down, really listen to what others are saying, and then actually think about how you will respond, *before* you talk. This is very hard for most people to do. Most people do not really listen to other people; they are too busy thinking about how they are going to respond, even before they have even heard what the other person has said. This is an unwise habit, much like answering the questions on a test before you have actually read them.

Men of the code take pains to make their words meaningful. Your words should be as good as gold. Say what you mean and mean what you say. Be known as a man of your word. Never say more than you mean and never say more than you meant to say.

People really do listen to what you say and they rarely forget, at least they rarely forget the meaningful things that you say, whether they are positive or negative. If what you say has had a big impact on their life, they will very likely remember your words for a lifetime. Take your words seriously and listen more than you talk. The more you practice thoughtful speech, the more powerful your words will be.

Speech and Silence

Much talking is the cause of danger.
Silence is the means of avoiding misfortune.
The talkative parrot is shut up in a cage.
Other birds, without speech, fly freely about.
Saskya Panita

In this world, the rarer a metal or gem is, the more it is worth. Scarcity adds value. If you want your words to mean more, and to be more powerful, don't talk too much. Think about it. Which man do you prefer to get advice from, the man who rambles on and on about everything or the man who only speaks when he really has something to say?

There is an old Chinese proverb that states, "Outside noisy, inside empty." Essentially, this means that the more someone talks, the less wisdom they truly have. Think about a five gallon bucket filled with water. The less water it contains, the more noise it will make if you hit it with a stick. A totally empty bucket will make much more noise than a bucket that is filled to the top with water. This is where the wisdom from "outside noisy, inside empty comes from.

Now think about how this analogy applies to men. The less wisdom he has, the more noise he makes; the more wisdom a man has, the less noise he will make. Those who know more, talk less. Wise men tend to be much more careful with their words because they understand how easy it is to say the wrong thing or to get themselves in trouble with their words. As I said before, to think before you speak means that you have to slow down your speech. When you slow down your speech, you are naturally going to talk less.

Those guys who talk too much are constantly putting their foot in their mouth. They give out too much information and they say things that shouldn't be said. Their love of their own voice exposes their ignorance over and over again. It is much better to be quiet and learn from those around you, than to be the one who is always giving out information, but never learning anything new from the conversation.

Private things should remain private. You always come out ahead by not saying what doesn't need to be said. Too many men love to argue and debate. They get into the habit of be opinionated and talking too much. And once you have developed that habit, silence in a conversation seems uncomfortable, so they just continue to babble. Inevitably, the more you talk, the more likely you are to disclose personal information or personal beliefs which may come back to harm you in some way.

Silence is almost always the safest bet. If you aren't sure about your facts or you don't know anything about the subject of the conversation, but want to be a part of the conversation, simply limit yourself to asking questions or simply listening. People love to talk, and they especially love to talk about themselves. The more interested you seem, and the more questions you ask, the more they like talking to you. But beware! Asking the wrong question can expose your ignorance just as fast as saying the wrong thing.

In taking this approach, you not only stand less of a chance of disclosing information that you don't really want to disclose, but you also have a much greater opportunity to learn more about the guy you are talking to. This allows you to size him up, to learn what kind of man he is, and to possibly learn useful information about him, or whatever subject you happen to be talking about. And, you will be thought of as a great conversationalist, without much effort on your part. You win all the way around.

Conversation is an art and one that is rarely taught to men today. We just take for granted that conversation is simply conversation, but there is much more to it than that. Being a good conversationalist is like any other skill, there are advantages to knowing what works and what doesn't. There are certain actions which make people want to chat with you, and are to your advantage, and there are traps and pitfalls which can turn the table on you. It is to your advantage to learn the art of conversation.

When you have something that needs to be said, say it, and say it in the right way. If you don't have anything that you need to say, then don't feel the need to constantly talk. Say what you need to say and leave it at that.

Plato taught that, "Wise men talk because they have something to say; fools because they have to say something." There is an enormous difference between those two, and a big difference between the wise man and the fool. The superior man is supposed to be a wise man, not a fool. Distinguish between really having something to say and simply wanting to say something. If you mainly talk when you have something important to add to the conversation, or something vital to say, you will find that your words not only have more power, but that others will value your words more.

It is much easier to preserve your honor and integrity in moments of silence. This is particularly true when you are feeling out of sorts. If you are upset or angry, it is much easier to allow your emotions to dictate your words. This is almost always unwise. When you are very emotional, for whatever reason, that should be a warning sign to you to be even more careful about what you say. Anger has a way of really bringing out the worst in people.

When you are angry, it is best to be silent, unless you absolutely have to speak at that time. If you have to say something when you are angry, be extremely careful with your words. Remember to never say more than you mean and never say more than you meant to say. Men have a habit of making empty threats or insulting comments when they are very angry. Resist the temptation to do this. I know that it is hard, but you will save yourself many apologies, much heartache, and better preserve your reputation by doing so. There is a time to speak and a time to remain silent. Become an expert at knowing which is which. When in doubt, remain silent!

I want to touch on one more point about distinguishing between when to be silent and when to speak up. Martin Luther King, Jr. stated, "There comes a time when silence is betrayal." Although staying silent is usually a pretty safe move, there are times when your silence is absolutely the wrong action to take. You can do wrong, not only by what you do, but by what you don't do. Being silent at the wrong time can absolutely be an act of betrayal or cowardice.

There is more than one way to betray someone. You can stab someone who considered you a friend, in the back. You can lie, cheat or steal from someone who trusted you. You can betray a trust by revealing information that someone confided in you in confidence. And, you can remain silent when you should have stood up and fought for your friend. While all of these are bad, and totally out of character for men of the code, remaining silent when your friend or family member really needs you to come to their defense, is totally an act of cowardice.

There truly is a time and situation when remaining silent is most certainly a betrayal. The Viking book of wisdom, *The Havamal*, teaches us that many, who expect support from their "friends" at a gathering, are shocked to find no support at all. Most people are cowards when it comes to making a decision between stepping out on a limb and doing what is right, or taking the safe, but cowardly path, and remaining silent when they should have spoken up for their friend.

If you make it your goal in life to do what is right, not what is easy, then you will never be caught betraying your friend through your silence. Always speak out for what you think is right; never allow your fears or personal ambitions to come before doing what is right. Take up for those who deserve your support. Speak up when you should and be silent when you should be silent.

Say the Right Thing and Say it Right

Tact is the knack of making a point without making an enemy.
Isaac Newton

There is always a right way and a wrong way to do or say something. Some people will argue with that statement and state that there is no right way or wrong way, there are just *different* ways of doing something or saying something. But that is not entirely true. Even if you do agree with that statement, you will have to concede that there is a best way to do what needs to be done or to say what needs to be said.

There are those guys who really pride themselves on being *brutally honest*. They go around and brag about how *brutally honest* they are, as if it is some kind of badge of honor. It isn't. Being brutally honest is simply being tactless. Hold on before you start writing me nasty emails. Have an open mind and continue to read this before you conclude that I am wrong.

You can almost always find a way to be completely honest and tactful, at the same time; you don't have to be brutal about it. People who go around telling you how brutally honest they are, many times are more brutal than they are honest. If they were completely honest, they would say that they actually get a bit of a rush from their *in-your-face* honesty. Why be brutally honest when you can just simply be honest and do it in the right way? Instead of being brutally honest, try being tactfully honest.

If you are one of these people who love to talk about how brutally honest you are, I urge you to look inside and double-check your intentions. What is your ultimate objective in being brutally honest? Is it really to help the other person see the truth? Or could it be that you kind of like putting people in their place?

The message may be the same in both of these objectives, but it is being delivered in a totally different way. One way originates from honorable intentions, while the latter originates from your ego.

Learn to use soft words and hard arguments. Don't allow your ego to get involved. By all means, be honest. But be tactful as well. Think about your ultimate objective in confronting the other person to begin with. What outcome do you really want from your efforts? When you confront someone with the truth, and you are intent on being brutally honest, do you think what you are saying is going to be well-received or cause the other person to become angry or to have contempt for you and what you have said?

In the vast majority of cases, the other person is going to be offended if you take the truth and try to shove it down his throat. That is not going to persuade him to accept what you are saying, and if he doesn't accept what you are trying to get across to him, you have failed in your objective. Why even bother if your actions are not going to accomplish something positive?

Wouldn't it be better to be honest, but use some tact at the same time, so your message is well-received and will possibly accomplish the objective that you had in mind when you decided to confront the other person? The great Japanese swordsman, Miyamoto Musashi, stated that you should do nothing that is not of some use. Always think about what your overall objective is *before* you decide on the right approach to use to accomplish your objective.

By all means, say what you have to say, but say it right. Always have your overall strategy in mind. Don't just shoot from the hip, but have a strategy and stick to it.

You should know something about the person before you decide to talk to him. Learn something about his personality, about his philosophy or the way he views the world. When you know the person, before you talk to them, you are better armed, and much more likely, to be successful in your goal.

The knowledge that you know about the other person will help you decide what approach to take to get your point across. With some people, you may have to actually be brutally honest; with others, being brutally honest does nothing more than make you one more enemy. You have to be discerning.

If you always keep your main objective in mind, know something about the person you are going to talk to, and have the right intentions, you will pretty much know how to deliver your message. Every person is different, so you have to customize your approach. A football coach plans his strategy for the team that he is going to play on the upcoming weekend; he does not simply have one strategy that he uses on every team. You should operate the same way. Consider your audience before you speak and tailor your strategy to the job at hand.

Speaking the truth with tact is not the same thing as being mealy-mouthed or cowardly. You can only be known as a man of your word if you are an honest man. No one respects a mealy-mouthed wimp who is afraid to get to the point. You should be straightforward and honest, just do it with style.

Communication Involves More than Words

Eloquence resides no less in a person's tone of voice,
expression, and general bearing than in his choice of words.
La Rochefoucauld

Professor Albert Mehrabian, currently a Professor Emeritus of Psychology at UCLA, conducted a study that concluded that only 7% of communication comes from the words that you use. His study found that 55% of communication is body language, 38% is the tone of voice, and 7% is the actual words spoken. This may explain why it is so easy to be misunderstood on social media comments or through email. We are literally communicating without 93% of our overall communication skills.

To further identify a person's meaning, it can be useful to use the 3-C's of Nonverbal Communication: context, clusters, and congruence. Context includes the type of environment the situation is taking place in, the relationship history between the people, as well as other background knowledge. We all know how taking a comment out of context can sound completely different than it was originally meant. We see this kind of dishonesty all of the time in our media.

Clusters refers to observing the nonverbal communication gestures in order to prevent us from allowing one single gesture to be used in determining a person's state of mind or emotion. Basically, you need to look at the whole picture, all of the person's body language.

Congruence refers to whether or not the words being spoken match the tone of the voice and the person's overall body language. For example, if a lady has had a really bad day and she tells you that she is fine, but her facial expression tells you that she is holding back tears, you can see that her facial expression and her words do not match.

Taken together, the 3-C's of nonverbal communication and Professor Mehrabian's 55/38/7 formula, give you a very good idea about what all goes into the process of good communication skills. There is much more to communicating than simply speaking the right words.

You should use this information to help you become a more effective communicator. Let's look at each part of the 55/38/7 formula a little closer to see just how you can put this to use in your life.

If 55% of your communication comes from your body language, how you move your hands, your facial expressions, etcetera, then you can see that this is of great importance. Don't try to communicate with a stone-cold poker face. If you do, you will be making the whole communication process much harder for the other person. He or she will not be as likely to understand what you are trying to communicate.

When you have an important message to get across someone, make sure you are a least a little bit animated. Make your body language congruent with your message. For example, if you are speaking to some guy who has just been extremely rude to your wife, you may want to get across to him that you are deadly serious about the fact that you will not tolerate such actions.

You would want to have a very serious expression on your face, with eyes that could burn through a sheet of ice. You may want to emphasize your message by shaking your finger in his face, etcetera. Let him know through your words, your tone, and your body language that what he did is totally unacceptable.

On the other hand, if you are talking to a 10 year old boy whose dad just died, you would want your body language to be completely different. Match your body language to your message.

I mentioned using the right tone in the example above. Professor Mehrabian's formula states that 38% of your communication comes across through your tone. Just as with your body language, you want to make sure that your tone fits your meaning as well. If you are joking around with someone, make sure that your tone doesn't sound like you are ready to wring his neck. If it does, the other person will be confused as to your true message and you will have failed in your communication objective.

Finally, we get to your words. I have discussed how powerful your words are, but when it comes to communicating with other people, your words account for only 7% of the communication process. Words are very important, but when it comes to getting your message across to someone else, you need to have the complete package – the correct words, the appropriate tone, and matching body language.

Together, the 3-C's of Nonverbal Communication and the 55/38/7 formula provide you with a good guide to effective communication. This is merely a very quick summary of the communication process. It may be helpful for you to take the time to do some further research on the subject, especially if you have noticed that you have some issues with people not completely understanding what you are trying to say to them.

Good communication is essential to your success anytime you are dealing with other people. I can't tell you how many problems develop from miscommunication or vague communication. Just remember that communication involves much more than words, but your words are vitally important, even though they only make up 7% of the communication process. That is a very important 7%!

Discipline Yourself Not to Use Profanity

The foolish and wicked practice of profane cursing and swearing is a vice so mean and low that every person of sense and character detests and despises it.
George Washington

I want to end this chapter by touching on the use of profanity. Profanity has become common place in today's society. You hear it everywhere from music and movies, to pretty much anywhere you go in public. The use of profanity is nothing more than a vulgar bad habit, and one that many people have embraced today.

I am not going to harp on this subject, but I do want to highly encourage you to not use profanity. At best, it serves very little purpose, other than to prove to others that you have a limited vocabulary. And at worst, it causes other people to lose some of the respect that they have for you. This may sound strange, but it is true.

If you have this common habit, work to break it, or at least to reduce it to the bare minimum. If you have been wise enough not to acquire this habit, don't start. Discipline yourself to find other ways to express yourself. You don't have to curse in order to make your point; superior men should be able to make their point in more dignified ways. Don't curse.

Reflections for the Superior Man

A slip of the foot you may soon recover,
but a slip of the tongue you may never get over.
Benjamin Franklin

Never forget what a man says to you when he is angry.
Henry Ward Beecher

When you have nothing to say, say nothing.
Charles Caleb Colton

Silence is one of the hardest arguments to refute.
Josh Billings

The real art of conversation is not only to say the right thing at the right
place, but to leave unsaid the wrong thing at the tempting moment.
Dorothy Nevill

Look wise, say nothing, and grunt.
Speech was given to conceal thought.
William Osler

Keep the golden mean between
saying too much and saying too little.
Publilius Syrus

Talk low, talk slow, and don't talk too much.
John Wayne

Think before you speak,
but do not speak all that you think.
Chinese Proverb

In dangerous times, wise men say nothing.
Aesop

Judge the nature of your listeners and speak accordingly.
Tiruvalluvar

Unless you are forced by necessity, be careful in your conversations never to
say anything which, if repeated, might displease others. For often, at times
and in ways you could never foresee, those words may do you great harm.
Francesco Guicciardini

Chapter 23

Learning from Your Mistakes

*A man must be big enough to admit his mistakes, smart enough
to profit from them, and strong enough to correct them.*
John C. Maxwell

Mistakes are Essential to Excellence

*Failure is instructive. The person who really thinks
learns as much from his failures as from his successes.*
John Dewey

Mistakes are just a part of being human. There has never been any human being, on the face of this planet, who has not made his share of mistakes. If you are afraid of making a mistake, you will never achieve excellence because you will never have the courage to go beyond your own comfort zone. Making a mistake is not the end of the world. It is simply a learning experience, and that is how you should look at it.

In order to reach for excellence in your life, you have to push yourself to newer and higher levels, you have to be willing to take some risks and do things, which at first, may be beyond your reach. You will make mistakes along the way. Mistakes are the steps in the ladder of success. Each time you make a mistake, you must learn from it and continue to climb that ladder.

There has never been a man who has achieved excellence without making his share of mistakes. The greater a man's achievement, the more mistakes he has made along the way. And, the more mistakes he has made along the way, the more knowledge he has gained.

Mistakes are to teach you how *not* to do something. Thomas Edison stated, "I have not failed. I've just found 10,000 ways that won't work." Think about that for a second. Edison had what most people would call "10,000 failures" before he was finally able to perfect the light bulb. But Edison did not look at those "mistakes" as failures. Instead, he looked at them as successfully discovering 10,000 ways not to make the light bulb.

He learned something from each of those mistakes, took the knowledge from what he learned, and used it to be successful. This should be how everyone views his mistakes. Mistakes are nothing more than learning tools.

You are supposed to learn a lesson from each mistake you make. If you don't, you are destined to repeat that mistake over and over again.

You will suffer the consequences of your mistakes, whether you learn the necessary lesson or not. Making a mistake without learning from it is like paying to get a tune-up on your car, but never getting the work done. You paid the price, but you still have to deal with the same problem. Why pay for something if you are not going to get a benefit from it?

Yet most people do this. They will make a mistake, deal with the consequences of the mistake, but never truly get the benefit of the experience by learning from their mistake. Wouldn't it be wiser to simply pay the price, learn the lesson, and move on?

Instead, many repeat this cycle of making the same mistake over and over again and never really learn the needed lesson. You cannot live a life of excellence if you don't learn from your mistakes.

Make a point of learning something from every mistake that you make. Refuse to pay the price without getting the benefit. View your so-called failures as nothing more than a learning experience. Failure is never permanent unless you allow it to be. Each failure should be another building block in your life. Failures should make you wiser and stronger, not weaker and depressed.

Think of it this way. If you are working on one of those maze puzzles where you start at one point and have to figure out how to get through the maze to the finish line, each dead end is a mistake. But, in making each one of those mistakes, you discover another part of the maze that doesn't work, bringing you that much closer to your ultimate objective.

Each time you find a dead end, you have narrowed your search and are that much closer to achieving your ultimate objective. Finding these wrong paths is merely a part of the process that you have to go through in order to figure out the puzzle and ultimately reach your goal.

Life works in much the same way. Mistakes are just part of life. Each time you make a mistake, you need to learn from it. Take the lesson that you have learned from that mistake and use it to ultimately win and be successful.

Too many men allow their mistakes to cause them to give up. They find a path that doesn't work, and instead of learning the lesson and using it to bring them closer to their ultimate success and excellence, they give up. Instead of learning their lesson, they declare defeat and lose out on any benefits that this lesson couldn't have provided for them.

In order to live a life of excellence, you cannot be a quitter. You cannot allow one mistake, or many mistakes, to cause you to question your self-worth or your abilities. You have to use your mistakes to your benefit, period. Anything else is just plain paying the price without getting what you paid for. Not smart! You have to be willing to make mistakes in order to achieve anything worthwhile in your life.

Let's look at another example. Say you are ready to settle down and find the perfect woman to spend the rest of your life with. Do you think that she is going to somehow magically appear on your door steps? Of course not! You have to make the effort to find her.

You are most likely going to have to go on many dates, with many different women, to finally find the right one. You will meet many women and many times you may think that you have met the right woman for you, only to find out later that she was not really a good match.

Now you can use those "mistakes" to your advantage by learning something about women and about about what you are, and are not, looking for, or you could simply not learn anything from your dates and think that you are just meant to be alone for the rest of your life. Which option do you think will bring you closer to your goal? Of course the latter will.

If you view each date, with each woman, which you thought might be a good match for you, as a learning experience, you would acquire an enormous amount of knowledge about women and about what you are looking for in a woman. This knowledge is vital in helping you find your perfect mate. Each date will bring you that much closer to your goal.

Each one is a learning experience in which you gain more knowledge. That is how you reach any goal. You have to work for it. You have to keep trying and not be afraid of making mistakes or failing to reach your goal. You have to turn every *mistake* into a lesson learned.

The most successful people are usually the people who have made the most mistakes on the path to their success. Babe Ruth broke the record for the most home runs in a season, and he also broke the record for the most strike outs in that very same season. In the NBA, some of the greatest players are also the very same players who have missed the most shots in NBA history, including the highest scorer in NBA history, Kareem Abdul-Jabbar and the second highest scorer, Karl Malone. Other excellent players who are on the top 10 list for missing the most shots in history, include Michael Jordan, Wilt Chamberlain, and Kobe Bryant, who has missed more shots than anyone in the history of the NBA. These are all very successful players, but how successful do you think they would have been if they were afraid of making a mistake, or if they had given up? You should never allow failure to influence your future in a negative way.

Never allow the fear of making a mistake stop you from trying to accomplish what you want to accomplish in life. Never! When you allow fear to dictate what you will and will not try to accomplish, you will accomplish very little.

Have the courage to at least try to accomplish your goals. If you are not willing to take the risk and put in the necessary effort, then you don't deserve to be successful. Success comes to those who are willing to take the risk, who are willing to fail, time and time again, but who are also willing to learn from their failures and mistakes.

You will have failures. Everyone who has every accomplished anything great in life has had to overcome failures. Failing does not mean you are a failure. Making a mistake doesn't mean you are dumb or incompetent. Failures and mistakes are nothing more than learning opportunities, but it is up to you whether or not you will seize the day and learn from them, or whether you will be defeated by them.

In the end, your success is up to you. You are the only one who can decide whether or not your will push past your mistakes and live a life of excellence. Choose to learn from your mistakes!

Refuse to Dwell on Your Regrets

Finish each day and be done with it. You have done what you could.
Some blunders and absurdities no doubt crept in; forget them as soon
as you can. Tomorrow is a new day; begin it well and serenely and
with too high a spirit to be encumbered with your old nonsense.
Ralph Waldo Emerson

We all have things in life that we regret. Like making mistakes, having regrets is simply a part of being human. What we don't want to do is allow our regrets about what we did in the past, or failed to do in the past, cause us issues today.

We all have regrets, even those people who claim that they have no regrets and would not have changed a thing. People who say that are basically referring to the fact that they are happy with their life now and they realize that if they would have changed something in their past, their present life would possibly be different than it is. Even so, I can guarantee you that there are some things in their past that they would have done differently, knowing what they know today.

Think about it. Even if you feel that you have made no mistakes whatsoever, don't you kind of wish that you would have invested in Apple computers back in the 1980's? There will always be things that you can find in your past that you would have liked to have done differently. That is just the way it is, and that is not a problem. The problem comes when you dwell on the things that you regret and allow them to depress you, make you feel guilt, or upset you in some other way.

The past is the past. Learn from your mistakes and move on. It is not only unhealthy to live in the past, but it will hold you back from being the best that you can be in the present. You can't change the past, but you can change your future.

Can you think of one positive thing that comes from sitting alone and meditating on the things that you regret from your past? I can't. If you must sit and think about things that happened, or didn't happen in the past, think of them in terms of what you learned from them, not how much you wish you could change them. Focus on the lessons so that you have fewer regrets when you look back at your life from today forward.

The past is over. You can't go back and relive it or change it. So focus on what you can do, which is live your life to the fullest now. Forget the past and focus on the present and the future. Start each day anew, move forward and don't look back.

To do this, it is important that you learn to forgive yourself. Not forgiving yourself for the mistakes that you have made in the past is one of the main reasons that people allow their regrets to continually creep back into their lives again and again. Once you learn to forgive yourself, you no longer feel the need to revisit your past mistakes and feel bad about them. You have dealt with the issue, learned your lesson from it, forgiven yourself, and moved on.

Forgive yourself! We all make mistakes and all of those mistakes are in the past. Quit beating yourself up over them! Think about how it is when you forgive your wife or children for a mistake that they have made. Once you have forgiven them, you don't remind of them of their mistake every time you see them, do you? Of course not; that would be ridiculous!

Once you have forgiven them, you put the whole thing behind you and move on. If you son has been told over and over not to throw his ball in the house and one day he throws his ball and knocks over your wife's glass of red wine on your light colored carpet, you deal with it at that time. You discuss what he did, discipline him, accept his apology and move on. You don't remind him of his mistake every time he walks back into the room where the mistake happened. Once you have dealt with the issue, you leave it behind and move on.

But we are much harder on ourselves. We have a tendency to beat ourselves up over and over again about the same mistake. This comes from not controlling our thoughts. A thought pops into your mind that you really wish you would have done this or that differently, then you start to dwell on it, and before long you are beating yourself up about it all over again. This pattern repeats itself over and over until you learn to forgive yourself.

It is time to take control of your mind. Stop allowing it to rule you and start ruling it. Take steps to forgive yourself once and for all. Deal with what you need to deal with and tie up your lose ends. Figure out what lesson you were supposed to learn from your mistake and then close the door on that incident for good.

Nothing constructive comes from continually beating yourself up over things that happened in the past. Learn the lesson from your mistakes and move on. And make sure you don't repeat the same mistake over again. The first time you do something, it is a mistake. You should have learned your lesson then. If you continue to do the same thing, time and time again, then it is a choice.

Making the same "mistake" over and over, and then apologizing each time, doesn't cut it. That is either being careless or insincere, both of which are not characteristics of the superior man. A sincere apology also carries with it the decision not to make that same mistake again.

Life is hard enough on its own; don't make it harder by adding to your load. Carrying around regrets is like put on a heavy pack and wearing it everywhere you go. Sooner or later that extra weight will wear you down. Get the monkey off your back and free yourself. Forgive yourself for all of your mistakes and bury them once and for all. And starting today, when you make a mistake, deal with it like a superior man.

Be man enough to deal with those mistakes when you make them. Apologize when you are in the wrong. Make amends when you can make amends. Be sincere in your apologies; don't be like a sleazy politician who only apologizes if he gets caught, and then, is about as sincere as a con artist on Bourbon Street.

Display your courage and your self-confidence when you make a mistake. People have high regard for a real man that is man enough to admit when he is wrong. But there is a right way and a wrong way to do so. I am sure that you have seen the insincere apologies of some of our politicians, where they hang their heads in shame, get teary-eyed, and can barely get the words out because they are so distraught about the fact that they have destroyed their career. That is not the apology of a superior man!

When you are wrong, admit your mistake and make a heartfelt, sincere apology. It is the right thing to do, and as a man of the code, you should always strive to do what is right in every circumstance. Deal with the mistake, do what has to be done, learn from it, and the put it behind you.

Don't hang your head in shame. Take responsibility for what you have done. If you are living as a man of the code, you won't be making disgraceful choices that are considered shameful, but rather mistakes in judgment or other careless mistakes. There is no reason to hang your head in shame.

Simply address whoever it may be that you need to apologize to and make a sincere apology, do it with confidence, class, and style, and then put it behind you.

This doesn't necessarily mean that the other party will forgive you or put it behind them, but that is their business, not yours. You have done your part, which is all that you can do. How they handle it from there is up to them. Your job is simply to make sure that your actions are honorable and right.

I want to end this chapter with one last thought. A precious stone, like a diamond, doesn't lose its value simply because it has been dropped in a gutter. If you dropped a very valuable diamond ring into a gutter, you would retrieve it, clean it up, and take better care of it from that point on. It would still be just as valuable after you cleaned it up as it was before you made the mistake and dropped it into the gutter.

The same thing applies to you. You may have done something really bad in your past, but that doesn't take away your current value as a man. Once you have made amends for your mistake, cleaned up your act, and are living as a superior man, your self-worth should be just as high as it ever was. Men make mistakes; mistakes do not make men.

Don't allow your past to somehow taint the rest of your life. Leave the past in the past and start from this very minute to be the best man that you can be. Everyone makes mistakes, some are bigger than others. We can't go back and undo what has been done. All we can do is start where we are, with what we have, and be the best man that we can be from this point forward. Make up your mind today to start living life as a superior man and leave the past in the past.

Reflections for the Superior Man

Waste not fresh tears over old griefs.
Euripides

Make it a rule of life never to regret and never to look back.
Katherine Mansfield

Great services are not cancelled by one act or by one single error.
Benjamin Disraeli

Look not mournfully into the past. It comes not back again. Wisely improve
the present. It is thine. Go forth to meet the shadowy future without fear.
Henry Wadsworth Longfellow

We must all suffer one of two things:
the pain of discipline or the pain of regret or disappointment.
Jim Rohn

You just keep pushing. You just keep pushing. I made
every mistake that could be made. But I just kept pushing.
Rene Descartes

First, forgive. Second, forget by choosing not to
dwell on that which is forgiven and in the past.
Dr. David Jeremiah

When one door closes another door opens; but we look so long and so
regretfully on the closed door, that we do not see the ones which open for us.
Alexander Graham Bell

Never regret. If it's good, it's wonderful. If it's bad, it's experience.
Victoria Holt

What the caterpillar calls the end of the world,
the master calls a butterfly.
Richard Bach

While one person hesitates because he feels inferior,
the other is busy making mistakes and becoming superior.
Henry C. Link

Mistakes are part of the dues one pays for a full life.
Sophia Loren

Chapter 24

Helping Others

Give a man a fish and you feed him for a day.
Teach a man to fish and you feed him for a lifetime.
Chinese Proverb

Compassion and Kindness

Take the trouble to stop and think of the other person's
feelings, his viewpoints, his desires and needs. Think more
of what the other fellow wants, and how he must feel.
Maxwell Maltz

Being a compassionate, kind man is a part of being a man of the code. You can be a rugged, tough guy and be kind and compassionate at the same time; the two are not in opposition of each other. In fact, the superior man should be compassionate and kind.

Many men think that they have to foster this tough guy image wherever they go. They are overly concerned with how others view them and are afraid to show their compassionate side because they feel that it would make them look weak. This is nothing more than their ego at work.

The real man isn't concerned with how others view him. He has confidence in who he is and what he is. He knows exactly how tough he is; he doesn't need to prove it to anyone else. If it comes time for someone else to find out about how tough he is, then things have escalated to a serious point. Make no mistake about it; real tough guys are compassionate, kind and giving.

Being compassionate is not a weakness, rather it is a strength. We should help as many people as we can during our lifetime. While I realize that not everyone has the money to make big contributions to help others, there are many other ways to help people besides giving money. You can be compassionate to other people in your everyday activities.

Compassion and kindness are very closely linked to courtesy and manners. Opening the door for others is being kind. Smiling at the store clerk, who has had a very trying day is an act of kindness. I could list thousands of small things that are nothing more than kindness in action, and they all take very little effort. Make it a point, as you go through your day, to be kind to those you meet.

Being kind to everyone you meet is an attitude which comes from compassion. If you have a compassionate heart towards other people, which I admit can be hard to do sometimes, especially in today's world where it seems that so many have become rude and crude, you will find that being kind is easy and almost automatic.

Try to find some way to compliment people. It takes very little effort to say to the store clerk, "You know, I just have to tell you, you have the nicest smile that I have seen in a long time." Find ways to make people feel good about themselves and you will start to see that you will reap many benefits yourself. People will start being nicer to you. People will start being more helpful and friendly. Of course, the perks that will come your way should not be your motivation for being kind, but they are a nice bonus.

If you are skeptical, this is very easy to prove to yourself. For a couple of days, go around scowling, being unfriendly and standoffish, and notice what kind of response you get from people. Now flip that and go around with a nice smile on your face, compliment people, make them feel good about themselves, and be helpful. See for yourself if you don't notice a huge difference in how people respond to you.

It takes very little effort to find something kind to say to those who cross your path. It cost you nothing, but pays big dividends. And you will be surprised at just how much power you have to improve people's lives by simply doing this one thing. One sincere compliment can make someone's whole week better and it only takes you two or three seconds to do it.

Too often, when we consider doing things for others, our minds go straight to, "What charity should I donate to?" I am here to tell you, you don't have to donate to charities to help people. Help those you meet everywhere you go! Be courteous, be kind, be compassionate, and you will find that there are opportunities to help other people all around you.

When I have taught this philosophy to others in the past, I inevitably get comments such as, "I tried that and people are ingrates!" or "I have helped people and they were still jerks to me." Yes, you will find many people that will be unappreciative, ungrateful, and just plain rude; be kind and compassionate anyway.

One of my favorite authors, Baltasar Gracian taught, "The man of principle never forgets what he is, because of what others are." Don't allow the actions of other people to cause you not be the kind of man that you want to be. Yes, some people will be ungrateful and rude. That is their business. Your business is being a man of the code. Do what is yours to do and don't worry about what other people do.

I am not saying that you need to make yourself a whipping boy; you don't. Men of the code don't tolerate abuse, rudeness, or the like. If you do something kind for someone, who then turns around and treats you rudely, respond as you need to and leave them to wallow in their own miserable life. But don't allow the rude behavior of some to cause you to not be kind to others.

If you are holding the door for a lady and she turns out to be one of these feminist Nazi type women and refuses to allow you to hold the door open for her, by all means turn your back to her and move on. Superior men do not bow down to anyone! But don't allow the actions of one obnoxious feminist to stop you from holding the door open for the next lady, who will most likely be very appreciative of your courtesy.

Handle each person individually and don't let the rudeness of one person cause you to have an attitude towards everyone else. Offer compassion and kindness to everyone you meet. You will find that the vast majority of people will be gracious and kind right back to you.

There are some people who just don't want help. These people are usually the people who badly need to turn their lives around, but who refuse to accept help. You just have to let these people do as they will with their life, as sad as it may be.

While you can offer to help, you can't force them accept your help. You can't change other people; they have to want to change, and then change themselves. You can offer to help them, but ultimately, they have to be willing to receive your help.

When someone continuously refuses your help, you have to move on and let the chips fall where they may. This can be very hard to do, especially if this person is your son or daughter, but sometimes doing what is right is a hard path to follow.

Support people the best that you can, but refuse to being taken advantage of. There comes a point in time where your kindness turns into enabling. If you are enabling a drug addict to continue to use his drugs, are you really being kind and helpful to him or putting him at an even greater risk? There is a big difference between enabling someone and being compassionate and helping that person. Enabling someone to continue their downward spiral is not truly being kind.

Offer your help, but make sure that what you are doing is actually helping that person to improve his life, not enabling him to continue to spiral out of control. There are those out there who will continue to take and take, as long as you are willing to give. They have no pride, no motivation, and no aspirations to ever change their lives; they are simply moochers.

Continuing to give these kinds of people money is equivalent to trying to help the wino on the street corner by giving him a $20 bill. That money is going to go straight to the liquor store and that is not really helping him, but is simply enabling him. They are con men who are highly skilled at tugging on people's heart strings and making others feel sorry for them. Don't buy into their scam! Helping such people is not real charity, but rather being conned.

It is up to you to be wise with your charity and your giving. If you are going to donate your time to community improvement, help the nice elderly lady clean up her yard or paint her house; don't paint the crack house on the corner. Be selective and help those who deserve your help. Yes, I know that this statement sounds a little judgmental and harsh, but it holds up nonetheless.

Time is precious and not everyone deserves your precious time. There are plenty of quality people in this world who need help; make sure your charity is given where it helps those who deserve it, not those who just want to use you. There are a lot of free-loaders and con artists in this world. When they take from good people who are trying to help those in need, then the people who truly need help, and who deserve to be helped, come up short. Be wise with your charity.

Be kind to everyone you meet. Be compassionate and have an open heart towards others, but be smart about it as well. You are responsible for making sure that you help the right people in the right way.

Giving Advice

You can lead a horse to water, but you can't make him drink.
John Heywood

I can't talk about compassion, kindness, and helping others without touching of the subject of giving advice to others. It seems that everyone wants to give you advice or tell you how to solve your challenges. While it is nice that you have people in your life that want to help you, most of the time their advice is worth what you paid for it. Some of their advice is based on what they want personally and other parts are based on their uninformed opinions, neither is truly going to help you with your problems.

Also, have you noticed that most advice is given to you without you actually asking for it? The majority of people feel some sense of satisfaction when it comes to giving other people advice; they just plain enjoy it. In fact, so many people give other people advice, that we even have a saying for it, "take it with a grain of salt." This means that most of the advice you get is just plain useless.

As a superior man, your advice should be sought after and valued, not considered something to be taken with a grain of salt. So how do you reach the point of having your advice be something that other people really take to heart? You make it a rule, for the most part, to not give advice to people unless they come to you and ask for it, and when they do ask for it, give the situation your full attention and advise them wisely, *after* giving their situation some thought.

As a rule, you should not give advice to others unless they ask for it. I hear so many people say, "If you want my advice..." and then they start rattling off clichés and unwanted advice that usually goes in one ear and out the other. Not only is their advice not valued, but most of the time, it is not thought out and is simply just their personal opinion given with no real knowledge about what they are talking about.

The same thing goes for you. You may even think that you know exactly what the other person should do, but if they don't come to you and ask you for your advice, it is best to keep it to yourself. This is not an uncaring attitude; it is just smart people skills.

Of course, there are exceptions to the rule. You have a totally different relationship with your wife and your children. It is part of your duty to watch out for them and protect them. With your immediate family, it is your duty to teach them the way to go, not to wait until they come to you. But, if you teach them well, and they can see the value of your wisdom, they will come to you for advice for the rest of their life.

Another point to remember is that it is perfectly okay to admit that you don't have all the answers. Saying, "I don't know what to tell you to do in this situation. My advice is to go and spend some alone time meditating on this and listening to your spirit," is much better than not knowing the answer and just throwing some random advice out there, hoping it hits the bull's-eye.

Nobody expects you to be able to fix every problem. When you know that you have some good, helpful advice to offer, advice that could really help the other person, offer it if they ask for it. If you don't have a clue about what he should do in his situation, either refer him to someone who may be able to help him or just plain tell him that you really don't know what he should do.

Informed advice is infinitely better than ill-conceived, emotional opinions passed off as advice.

Also, remember that you can give someone excellent advice, advice that would completely fix their problem, but you can't make them take it. Your job is to give them good advice if they ask for it, not to insist that they do what you tell them they should do. Give good advice, but never insist that they follow it.

Ultimately, it is their life and their decision; all you can do is offer your wisdom on the matter. There are some lessons which a person simply has to learn for himself. Do your part and then let it go.

Some people get very emotionally involved in other people's business. They get so involved, in fact, that they get offended if the other person does not take their advice. This is the wrong attitude. Their problem is not about you. Your advice should come from an open, giving heart. Your advice is a gift that you give them and once you have given it to them, it is theirs to do with it as they please. Getting offended when someone doesn't follow your advice is allowing your ego to get out of hand.

Timing is also very important when it comes to giving advice. You can give someone the best advice in the world, but if he is not ready to hear it and receive it, it is of no value. The right advice at the wrong time is worthless.

There is a right time and a wrong time for everything. There is a right time to give advice and a wrong time to give advice. That is one of the main reasons that you should wait until you are asked before you offer your advice. When someone comes to you for advice, you can be fairly sure that he is ready to hear what you have to say. If he doesn't come to you first, more than likely, he doesn't want your advice.

Moreover, be tactful and thoughtful when you give someone your advice. Don't be *brutally* honest; be tactfully honest. If they need to hear something that they are not going to want to hear, you stand a better chance of them listening if you present it to them without being harsh or putting them on the defensive. Keep in mind your reason for taking the time to give them your advice to start with.

They are not coming to you to be criticized, but for your wisdom. If, as part of your advice, you must criticize them for their actions, do so in a very tactful and thoughtful way. Be sensitive to their feelings. After all, this person obviously respects you or he wouldn't have come to you to start with. Be honest, but be nice. After you criticize his actions, find something else that you can praise him for, and then offer a solution. And for Pete's sake, make sure that you only criticize him in private, not in front of others. Always praise in public, but criticize in private.

Think of his feelings, but be truthful at the same time. Remember, that your ultimate goal is to help him. Give him the best advice that you can and then give him a good shot of self-esteem building motivation so that he walks away feeling confident and motivated to take your advice.

As a man of the code, you have developed knowledge and wisdom; don't hesitate to share it with others and help as many people as you can. Helping others is one of the most fulfilling things that you can do with your life. Be kind, be compassionate, and be giving. It is the way of the superior man. I want to end this chapter with a fitting quote from William J. H. Doetcker:

> *"You cannot strengthen the weak by weakening the strong.*
> *You cannot help small men by tearing down great men.*
> *You cannot help the poor by destroying the rich.*
> *You cannot lift the wage earner by pulling down the wage payer.*
> *You cannot keep out of trouble by spending more than your income.*
> *You cannot further the brotherhood of man by inciting class hatred.*
> *You cannot establish security on borrowed money.*
> *You cannot build character and courage by taking away a man's initiative and independence.*
> *You cannot help men permanently by doing for them what they could and should do for themselves."*

Reflections for the Superior Man

One kind word warms three winter months.
Japanese Proverb

Never lose a chance of saying a kind word.
William Makepeace Thackeray

If you have much to give, give of your wealth;
if you have little, give of your heart.
Arabian Proverb

Have benevolence towards all living things.
The Tattvartha Sutra

Compassion is the basis of morality.
Arnold Schopenhauer

You cannot do a kindness too soon,
for you never know how soon will be too late.
Ralph Waldo Emerson

In seeking to save another,
beware of drowning yourself.
Sir Francis Osborne

Do not let the ingratitude of many men
deter you from doing good to others.
To do good without ulterior motives is
a generous and almost divine thing in itself.
Francesco Guicciardini

Remember there's no such thing as a small kindness.
Every act creates a ripple with no logical end.
Scott Adams

Criticism, like rain, should be gentle enough to nourish
a man's growth without destroying his roots.
Frank A. Clark

Let men be wise by instinct if they can,
but when this fails, be wise by good advice.
Sophocles

Chapter 25

The Code and the Law

Where you find the laws most numerous,
there you will find also the greatest injustice.
Arcesilaus

Are Our Laws Really Sacred?

Any fool can make a rule
and any fool will mind it.
Henry David Thoreau

Many people look at the law as somehow being sacred, but have you ever stopped to think about where our laws come from? They are made by the very same politicians that most people seem to have very little respect for, but at the same time, they seem to somehow think that the laws that these people make are sacred and must be the final word on what is right and wrong.

Well, if you feel this way, I hate to burst your bubble, but the law of the land never has, and never will, be the final word when it comes to what is right and what is wrong. Most laws are not made to ensure justice; they are made as part of some underlying agenda that you are not privy to.

I worked as a page in a state House of Representatives one year and got to see firsthand the way our political system works and how laws are made. Most people would be absolutely shocked and appalled if they could see how laws are actually made, where they originate and what goes on behind the scenes. It is far from honorable, I assure you.

The people, who make laws for people like you and me to follow, exempt themselves from many of those same laws. If you lie to Congress, it is a federal offense; if a congressman lies to you, it is merely politics. This is only one example. There are many others.

Don't misunderstand me. I am not suggesting that you shouldn't obey the laws of the land; that would be unwise and go against the basic premise of self-defense. Self-defense covers everything, not just physical attacks. You have to be aware of what you have to do to keep yourself safe in every way; this means that you have to obey the law, at least for the most part.

What I mean by this is that you should obey the law in most instances, but that you should never put the law above doing what is right. The law is never the final word when it comes to doing what is right. Even Jesus spoke out against being legalistic.

There will be times in your life when you will have to make a decision between following the law and doing what is right. Always choose what is right over what is legal!

Remember, it was legal for the Nazi's to murder Jews, homosexuals, gypsies, and others. It was legal for the Catholic Church to torture individuals accused of being witches. It was legal for the Romans to torture people and use them as sport. It was legal for the U.S. Army to murder thousands of Native Americans. It was legal for people to buy and sell other people in the slave trade. This list could go on and on, but I think that you get the point.

Not only are our laws not the final word on what is right and what is wrong, many times they are not even close to being just or right. Most laws are made with purely political agendas, not based on justice or right and wrong. Other laws are made for financial gain and are nothing more than veiled taxes on the people. Speed limits are a great example of a law that is made merely for the financial gain of the state. Do you really think that the cop hiding in the bushes to pull over the soccer mom going five miles an hour over the posted speed limit is there to serve and protect you?

Our laws are not sacred. They are not the final word on justice or right and wrong. Laws are made for different reasons. They are made to control to populace. They are made to provide income for the country. They are made as part of political posturing. And they are made to try to restrain those who do not have the character to behave as they should. Laws can be described in many ways, but being sacred is not one of them.

Justice and Reason Should Guide Your Actions

*For there is but one essential justice which cements society, and
one law which establishes this justice. This law is right reason, which
is the true rule of all commandments and prohibitions. Whoever neglects
this law, whether written or unwritten, is necessarily unjust and wicked.*
Marcus Tullius Cicero

The superior man does what is right, whether it is legal or not. His conscious is his law and ultimately, he answers to a Higher Power than that of some politician. Does this mean that he is an anarchist? Absolutely not! It merely means that he does what is right, period. He needs no laws to keep him in line. Men of the code do not need laws to encourage them to do what is right; they do what is right simply because it is right.

Laws are made to keep those people in line who refuse to behave as they should. Just laws are laws that restrain one person or group from harming another person or group. Superior men harm no one unless it is in self-defense or the defense of his family, the weak, or the elderly. That is a core value in his code. He doesn't need some politician to tell him not to hurt other people or not to take advantage of others. He does not need the fear of punishment to restrain him from robbing banks or conning the elderly out of their money; his evolved spirit does that.

Justice and reason guide the superior man's actions, not the fear of punishment. He is a just man whose sense of right and wrong guides him. I can already hear some you arguing, "Yeah, but every criminal justifies his actions and believes he is right. You can't act on your personal opinion about what is right and what is wrong."

My answer to that is, maybe the average person can't be depended on to do what is right, but the highly evolved man can. Men of the code take the time to study the virtues and character traits of superior men. They study right and wrong, and integrate their knowledge into their everyday life. Superior men understand right from wrong because the live it daily and it is a part of their being. There are some issues which legitimately boil down to personal opinion, and then there are other issues which are universally right and wrong.

When it comes to issues that are legitimately personal issues, issues which harm no one else, there should be no laws either outlawing one's actions or allowing one's actions. It is an issue of personal judgment and how one elects to live one's life. An example of this would be what two adults do in the privacy of their own bedroom.

Did you know that there are laws on the books in almost every state concerning what is legal and illegal for you and your wife to do in the privacy of your own bedroom? This is a great example of something that is totally none of the state's business, but is rather a personal issue which harms no one else and should be decided by no one other than you and your wife. Yet, our ever enlightened politicians have taken upon themselves to make laws concerning this.

There are thousands of laws on the books that are written to address victimless "crimes." These are bogus laws designed solely for the purpose of controlling people because our lawmakers believe that most people aren't intelligent enough to make their own decisions. Superior men have little respect for such laws. Men of the code have great respect for freedom, and believe in a person's right to choose and their right to own the consequences of their choices.

Their life is governed by their personal code of honor. They do not need some political hack to watch over their every decision in order to keep them from harm. Superior men see both politicians, and the laws that they make, for exactly what they are and give them no more credence than they deserve.

Right Versus Legal

A unjust law, is no law at all.
Martin Luther

Justice should be the basis of every law. Laws should be based on serving and protecting the people, not infringing on people's rights or making money for the state. Knowing, as we do, that the vast majority of our laws are laws that have hidden agendas as their basis, instead of justice and protecting law-abiding citizens, the superior man gives them no more respect than is due. By this I mean that he obeys their laws as long as they don't interfere with his code of honor and his dedication to doing what is right.

Superior men always put what is right before what is legal. I have already given a couple of examples of this, but I will give you a couple more. Let's say that your wife has been stung by a bee and is having an allergic reaction to the bee sting. Do you do what is right and get her to the hospital as fast as you can, disregarding the speed limit laws, or do you obey the speed limit and get to the hospital as fast as you can within the confines of the law? I know what I would do!

Men of the code do what is right, whether it is allowed by the law or not. When it comes right down to it, their actions are guided by their code and what is right, not by what politicians, or their laws, permit them to do.

Again, please do not get me wrong here. I am not suggesting that you completely disregard the law. I am merely stating that you put what is right ahead of what is legal. If the two are in conflict with each other, always choose what is right over what is legal. But, if there is no conflict, and the law is not infringing on your personal rights in some way, by all means, live your life within the boundaries of the law. It is only when the law runs counter to what is right, that you have to make a choice.

Another example of an unjust law would be the blue laws, which we have in the United States, which dictate what activities you can and cannot do on Sundays. These laws are based on the religious views of the politicians that made those laws, but what if you don't practice their religion? Why should someone's personal opinion concerning what you should and should not do on Sunday be made into a law for everyone? It shouldn't! But we have them on the books nonetheless.

Our country is littered with laws that are based on nothing more than opinion, not justice, not what is right, and not rational thought. If you have a law which states that you cannot go shopping on Sunday because Sunday is a "holy day," that is someone's personal opinion based on their personal religious belief. Personal opinions should not be the basis for laws.

These kinds of laws are meaningless to the superior man. He sees them for exactly what they are. If there is no victim, there is no crime. Victimless laws are made either to fulfill an agenda or to provide income to the state via our legal system, which is little more than a money-making machine today.

Men of the code refuse to be tied down by such laws. They obey them when it is convenient or in their best interest to do so, but when they have a choice about whether to obey such laws or to do what is right, they always choose what is right.

Albert Einstein stated, "Never do anything against conscience even if the state demands it." This is exactly the superior man's attitude on the matter. He understands what is right and what is wrong, and chooses right, no matter what.

I was driving across the Colorado one day, in the middle of nowhere. I was going through the mountains; there were no towns or homes around, and very little traffic on the road that day. The guy in front of me hit a deer. He pulled over and was unconcerned about the deer at all, but was angry over the dent in his car. The deer hobbled off the side of the road and was lying there in agony.

I had my pistol with me, as I usually do, so I pulled over to do the right thing and put the poor animal out of its misery. I told the man that I would take care of it and took my pistol out to take care of what needed to be done. I walked about twenty feet off of the road and put the deer out of its misery and went on my way.

I had driven about 15 miles when two police cars came flying up behind me and pulled me over. You would have thought that I just robbed a bank or something. They pulled their firearms and approached me and yelled for me to get out of the car. My ten year old son was in a panic from seeing gun pointed at us. Apparently the guy that hit the deer was some anti-gun zealot and had called the cops because, God forbid, I had a pistol in my car.

After questioning me for close to 45 minutes, and lecturing me on how it is against the law to shoot that close to the highway, I finally got my Desert Eagle back and was allowed to go on my way, with a stern warning that "next time I would be arrested."

I did the right thing, but it was against the law. The law enforcement officers knew I did the right thing. They even admitted that they would have done the same thing. The man who hit the deer knew I did the right thing. (He just didn't have the intestinal fortitude to stomach what had to be done because of his lack of attention.) But somehow common sense eluded these people and they could not get past the fact that there is a law on the books that prohibits people from shooting that close to the road.

This law was meant to stop hunters from shooting from the road; it had nothing to do with my situation. But so many people have forgotten the purpose of the law and wrongly try to enforce the letter of the law instead. This is why we see so much injustice in our society today and so many ridiculous law suits. People care more about being legalistic than they do about what is right.

Always be willing to follow your conscience. Never be afraid of doing what is right because it is illegal. Which is more important, following the law or doing what is right? To the superior man, what is right will always trump what is legal.

Be Willing to Accept the Consequences

The superior man does what is right;
the inferior man does what is profitable.
Confucius

Many times doing the right thing does not get you praise or a pat on the back; it causes you hassles and unwanted consequences, as in my example about putting the deer out of its misery. Superior men do not do what is right in order to receive praise or profit from their actions; they do what is right simply because it is right.

When it comes to doing the right thing, when the right thing is in direct opposition to what is legal, you must be prepared to accept the consequences of your actions. Many men are willing to do what is right as long as it doesn't inconvenience them in some way, but the superior man is willing to do what is right no matter what. This is one of the things that set the superior man apart from the average citizen.

When you are committed to doing the right thing, even if it is going to cause you some personal problems, then you know that you have acquired the character of a superior man. Don't allow fear of the consequences to stop you from doing what's right.

You may be thinking that it is unwise to put yourself in a situation that would cause you problems, when it would be much easier to simply mind your own business. While it is true that it would be easier to simply not get involved, you have to ask yourself if that is the right thing to do. Doing the right thing is not always going to be the easiest thing to do. In fact, there will be many times when doing the right thing is not the easiest thing to do.

It is much easier to simply say that it is illegal to do that, so I can't and go your own way. It would have been much easier, and caused me much less hassles, if I would have merely ignored the guy hitting the deer, not stopped to see if he was alright, and not bothered to put the deer out of its misery. I would have arrived at my destination at least an hour earlier. I would not have had to deal with two irritated law enforcement officers. I would have not had to use my ammo. It would have been better off for me all the way around; but it wouldn't have been the right thing to do.

The superior man is always willing to accept the consequences for doing right. In addition, he is always able to rationally explain his actions, both to himself and to others. He fully understands why he does what he does, and the possible consequences connected to his actions.

This chapter is not meant to suggest that superior men are above the law or that we shouldn't obey the laws of the land. We should. It is simply meant to point out to you that there are times and situations where you must put what is right ahead of the law. Use common sense and think rationally. Use your code as a guideline to help you decide what is right in every situation.

In a perfect society, the law would be flexible enough to allow men of honor the flexibility to set the law aside when it is the right thing to do. But we do not live in a perfect society. We live in times where justice and common sense are no longer common. It is times like these that separate the real men from the inferior men, the men of the code from the sheep.

Make a firm decision today to always put what is right first and foremost in your life. Let what is right guide your every action. Don't get caught up in political correctness or sheepish attitudes toward what you can and cannot do. Be man enough to step up and do the right thing, regardless of what others do, and regardless of what others tell you that you can or can't do.

Reflections for the Superior Man

Ethical behavior is doing the right thing when no one else
is watching – even when doing the wrong thing is legal.
Aldo Leopold

Law applied to its extreme is the greatest injustice.
Marcus Tullius Cicero

There's no way to rule innocent men. The only power any government has
is the power to crack down on criminals. Well, when there aren't enough
criminals, one makes them. One declares so many things to be a crime
that it becomes impossible for men to live without breaking laws.
Ayn Rand

The true source of our sufferings has been our timidity.
John Adams

What is right is the ultimate law and trumps the law of the land.
Bohdi Sanders

There comes a time when one must take a position that
is neither safe, nor politic, nor popular, but he must
take it because conscience tells him it is right.
Martin Luther King, Jr.

Do what you think is right.
Don't let people make the decision of right or wrong for you.
Steve Maraboli

There are two sides to every issue: one side is right
and the other is wrong, but the middle is always evil.
Ayn Rand

A man dies when he refuses to stand up for that which is right.
Martin Luther King, Jr.

Be always sure you are right, then go ahead.
Davy Crockett

Oh, the fools, like a lot of good little schoolboys,
scared to death of anything they've been taught is wrong!
Emile Zola

Chapter 26

Raising Men Instead of Boys

Every son quotes his father, in words and in deeds.
Terri Guillemets

Real Men Raise Sons - They don't Babysit

Don't wait to make your son a great man;
make him a great boy.
Anonymous

Raising your son to become a great man should begin as soon as he is old enough to start teaching him. You can't wait until he is in his teens to start teaching him to become a real man; you have to start when he is very young and continue through his teen years. A father's duty is to do his best to turn his son into a superior man and this begins at a very early age.

It should be first and foremost on a father's mind, from the very beginning, that he should instruct his son and teach him to be a man of honor. So many fathers never really give this any thought. They think about all of the fun things that they will be able to do with their son; they think about being his pal and his buddy; but they seem to forget that it is their duty to first be a father. It is not your job to be your son's best friend, his buddy, his pal, or his playmate; it is your job to be his teacher, his guide, and his father.

Too many men in today's society have no clue how to be a real father. That could stem from the fact that the majority of men have no real concept of what it means to be men of honor to start with. They were not raised by real men, so how could they really know what it means to be a real man or to understand how to be a good father?

It is time to break that cycle, that never-ending, downward spiral. First learn how to be a real man yourself, and then teach your sons. Don't resign yourself to believing that you were never taught these things, so you really can't teach your son how to be a man. It is never too late to become a man of honor and you will never get a second chance to raise your sons to be men of honor. You get one shot at raising your sons, ONE! If you don't take it seriously, you are guilty of allowing the cycle to continue. It is time for men to stand up and return to the ways of raising great men, instead of overgrown boys.

In order to do this, you must see your duty as a father as meaning much more than providing food, shelter, clothes, and entertainment. You have been entrusted with the job of turning a boy into a man! You wouldn't even build a fence without a plan, but most men never sit down and think about how they are going to guide their son to be a superior man. In my opinion, this is a big mistake. Of course, you don't get to plan your son's whole life out for him; ultimately, he chooses his own path. But you should plan how you will do your part when it comes to raising him.

Start at the earliest age possible. Teach your son manners and respect. Teach him self-reliance and responsibility. Back in the days of the Vikings and the Celts, even children's games were designed to be both fun and impart essential skills to them at the same time. Boys were taught to use wooden swords and sparred with each other for fun. Although this was a fun activity for the boys, it also taught them useful skills. Training your sons to be men, doesn't have to be drudgery or bore them to death; be creative and make their time with you fun, exciting, and educational. This is where your planning comes in.

Take the time to sit down and really think about what you want to teach your son. Think about what kind of man you want him to grow up to be, and then work backwards from there. This will help you figure out what character traits you want to teach him, what skills you want him to acquire, what lessons you want him to learn, and how you will help him become self-reliant, independent, and self-confident.

Don't leave these things up to chance! It is your duty to impart these virtues, traits, skills, and lessons to him. It is your duty to make sure that he grows up with a healthy sense of self-worth, self-confidence, and self-esteem. You have been entrusted with one of the most important jobs that a man can have – raising your son to be a superior man. I assure you that if you fail to do your duty when it comes to raising your son, it will haunt you for the rest of your life. I cannot stress this point enough!

Think about how the kings of old raised their sons. They employed the best tutors available at the time; they didn't leave their son's education up to chance or to what was available to the average boy. They hired the best swordsman or martial artist to teach them how to fight and defend themselves. They made sure that their son was raised with wisdom, knowledge, the correct philosophy, and various skills that would prepare him for being both a superior man and a leader. Nothing was left to chance; nothing was taken for granted.

Yes, I realize that you are not a king. But, that fact doesn't excuse you from raising your son like a prince. Is your son not as important to you as the king's son was to him? Does your son not have just as much of a right to become a superior man as the king's son?

It is time for men to quit looking at their sons as kids and start looking at their boys as princes. Raise them as you would a prince. Give them the best that you possibly can, while at the same time, making sure they appreciate what they have and make the best of their opportunities.

You may be thinking that you don't know how a king would raise his son in today's world. Well, that is a good place to start. Think about how a king would raise his son in today's society and then do that to the best of your ability.

Would a king send his prince to some public school to associate with boys and girls of low character? Would he entrust his son's education to teachers who barely know their subject and have little to offer as far as character traits, honor or integrity? Would he send the prince to after-school programs that are little more than babysitting services? Would he allow the prince to listen to profanity-laden music or movies, or to be influenced by the minds of the people who put this garbage on the market?

Think about these and other questions about how a king would raise a prince, and you will get a good idea about how you should raise your son. I understand that you do not have unlimited financial resources like a king, but you can do your best to raise your son like a prince.

Teach your son, not just what to think, but how to think. One of your goals should be to make him self-reliant and self-confident in his ability to make the right choices. This doesn't happen automatically; it happens over time. A child's self-esteem can be a fragile thing. Guard it carefully. Keep a watch over what is happening in his life and make sure that you strengthen his self-esteem and bolster his self-confidence.

Make sure that you know who his friends are. Never allow your son to start hanging around with the wrong crowd. You must keep a close watch over what kind of people your son associates with. Don't be afraid to disallow him to associate with someone if you know that they are not a quality person.

The quality of your son's friends is more important than I can stress. The wrong friends can undo everything that you have worked for. Make sure that you stress to him the importance of only hanging around with boys and girls of honor and integrity. It is so easy for boys to fall into the wrong crowd, especially if you haven't really built up his self-esteem. Don't teach him to be a snob, but rather to be highly selective about whom he does and does not befriend. There is no nobility in thinking that you are better than others, but there is nobility in working to make yourself the best that you can be. That should be our goal in instructing our sons.

While we are on the topic of snobbery, I should make sure that you understand what I mean by raising your son like a prince. I don't mean that you should raise a spoiled brat. Spoiled brats rarely turn out to be superior men. You can raise your son like a prince without raising him to be spoiled. Spoiled refers to a deep-seated mental attitude about life.

Raising your son like a prince means that you raise him with a purpose. You purposely mold his character, his mind, and his skills to be a man of honor. It doesn't mean that you give him everything that he wants or pamper him like a rich brat, even if you do have the money to do so. This can take discipline on your part, as fathers do want to give their sons nice things, and you absolutely should give him what you can, up to a point.

Remember, your main objective as a father is to instruct your son to be a superior man, not to smother him in luxuries. You should teach him to earn what he wants in life, not that all he has to do is ask you for what he wants. Teach him the value of things. When fathers give too much, too freely, sons don't learn to value what they have because it comes too easily.

For example, if you give your son a new toy and he later throws a fit about something and smashes it on the ground, don't go buy him another one. He must learn that his actions have consequences. If you bail him out every time he does something, he will never learn that his actions can have unpleasant consequences. You must be man enough to allow your son to learn his lessons in life. By constantly interfering and stepping in to prevent him from experiencing the pain of his consequences, you also prevent him from learning the life lesson that comes along with that experience.

Teach your son to be man enough to accept responsibility for his actions; that is a major part of being a real man. Experience is the best teacher; don't rob him of the lessons that will stay with him throughout his life. Allow him the responsibility of making mistakes, owning them, and learning from them. Discipline yourself not to step in every time he gets in hot water. There are times when you should step in and times when you should allow him to learn his lesson. Be wise enough to know which is which.

This is just a very quick overview of raising boys to become men. There are entire books on this subject. In short, start instructing your son from an early age and continue that instruction up until he has transitioned into manhood. How do you know when he has become a man? That is what the rite of passage is for.

Rites of Passage

In times past, there were rituals of passage that conducted a boy
into manhood, where other men passed along the wisdom and
responsibilities that needed to be shared. But today we have no rituals.
We are not conducted into manhood; we simply find ourselves there.
Kent Nerburn

Many cultures used to have rites of passage where they were given training, wisdom, knowledge, and responsibilities that they needed to know before they were considered a man. In some cultures, the boy had to complete various tasks, many of which were actually dangerous, before he could be counted as a man.

Today, we have lost this vitally important part of transitioning from boyhood to manhood. There is no transition into manhood; boys are simply considered men when they reach the age of 18, with no fanfare, no initiation, no nothing. His eighteenth birthday comes and goes with little more fanfare than any other birthday. The day after his eighteenth birthday, the boy is still as much of a boy as he was the day before, only now the government sees him as an adult. Besides that, nothing else has changed.

Consider this, if a boy is arrested for something, like getting involved in drugs, one day before he turns eighteen, he is consider a minor, given some education and possibly some help. If he is arrested one day later, on his eighteenth birthday, he is considered an adult and may be sent to jail or prison for the exact same offense. That is a huge difference and the only thing that is different about the situation is that he is 24 hours older.

Now, I could write about the injustice of this fact, but that is a totally different subject. The point that I am trying to get across to you is that becoming a man does in fact come with much bigger responsibilities; shouldn't we as fathers and mentors make sure that our sons understand these responsibilities and are ready to handle the responsibilities that come along with becoming a man? If we as a society are going to up the ante at age 18, shouldn't we at least prepare our sons to be real men beforehand?

Maybe it is time that we get back to some kind of rite of passage for our sons. For far too long, men have shirked their duties when it comes to preparing their sons for manhood. There is much more to preparing a boy to become a man than simply making sure that he jumps through all of the right hoops in the public school system and helping him get into a college. It seems that most parents consider this their main responsibility. Parents want so badly to get their son into a good college, but neglect to make sure that their son is even ready for manhood.

Boys would be much better off if their parents would worry less about what our public school systems require and more about how to ensure that their son is fully prepared for manhood. Parents are overly concerned about pushing their son to get good grades so that he can get some kind of college scholarship, but they really don't understand that even straight A's won't guarantee him a scholarship. As a former teacher, I have seen many straight-A students receive only a small $500 scholarship, that's it.

Your sons would be much better served if you simply put school in the proper perspective and focused much more on preparing him to be a real man instead of preparing him to be another party animal in an over-priced college. While his education is certainly important, it is the not the be-all, end-all that it is made out to be. If parents would focus on raising men instead of boys, then the education piece would take care of itself.

Boys are not mature enough for college; college is for men and women, not boys and girls. This is such a huge mistake that has been made in this country. We want our sons to get the "college experience," but neglect the fact that college should be to prepare men for their careers; it is about much more than partying, football games, and fun.

We are raising a country full of boys and girls, not men and women. So many parents have bought into the idiocy of "everyone gets a trophy" and "there are no winners or losers." This is not raising men; this is raising boys with a skewed sense of reality and a warped sense of entitlement. Please show me any part of this politically correct philosophy that is preparing boys to become men! There isn't any.

These kinds of attitudes are teaching our sons that they do not have to compete, that everyone is a winner, no matter how poorly they perform. It is flat out lying to your sons and daughters! It is preparing them to feel entitled to everything in life, just for showing up, or in most cases, just for signing up. How is this teaching your sons that he should compete and push for excellence?

If he does his best and then sees Johnny, who has missed over half of the practices and who puts forth no effort on the field, get the same trophy as he got, what does that teach him? It teaches him that working hard is unnecessary and just plain doesn't matter. After all, I am going to get a reward no matter what I do. If he slacks off and doesn't put forth his best effort, what does this teach him? It teaches him that he can slide by, that is unwise to work hard when you can get the same reward as the others by putting in half the effort. It teaches him to feel entitled to a reward, not that he has to work hard and earn his rewards in life.

This is not teaching our sons the importance of working hard and doing their best. We should be teaching our sons that hard work produces it own reward. That there are benefits of hard work and that if you don't do your best, you don't get the reward. We need to teach our sons how to deal with loss, heartbreak, and disappointment. These are all important lessons which are missed by this politically correct, "we don't keep score" attitude.

Parenting is about raising children to be mature, well-adjusted adults, not spoiled, entitled brats. Parents need to get their heads straight. They need to quit thinking that parenting is all about making sure that their kids are pampered and constantly having fun, and start taking their duty as a parent more seriously. If you are a parent, your job is to prepare your children to be well-adjusted, mature, responsible, self-reliant adults, period.

As a father, your job is to raise men, not boys. You have a sacred duty to teach your son the ways of the superior man and to teach him about character, honor, and integrity. Teach him about the duties of a man and help him become mature. Allow him to make his own mistakes and then help him learn important lessons from his mistakes, lessons that he will always remember and that will save him much heartache down the road.

Teach him the responsibilities of manhood and help him to understand his duties as a superior man. Help him develop his own code of honor that will serve him for his entire life. Don't buy into this garbage about how boys need to be boys and that they have plenty of time to worry about responsibilities and duties when they are grown up. This attitude only creates spoiled, overgrown boys, not men.

Time and time again, I have seen the ridiculous actions of boys justified by irresponsible parents who simply write off their son's actions as, "Boys will be boys." Where has the discipline gone in our society? What happened to responsibility? Your job is not to make excuses for your son's behavior, but to mold his behavior. It is time for parents to grow up and be parents!

Although teaching our sons to grow into responsible men of honor is a lifelong process, there is something to be said for a rite of passage where a boy passes from boyhood into manhood. It can be likened to a boy taking his black belt test. He has worked on his techniques and katas, and studied the philosophy for years, and then comes the day when he is ready to prove that he has reached the point of becoming a black belt and living with all of the responsibilities that come with it. By successfully passing his test, he has successfully stepped up to a higher level and much more is expected of him.

The rite of passage works the same way. Hopefully you have taught your son well for many years. He has learned many lessons, some the hard way.

He has been guided and has put into practice what you have taught him about how to live his life. You have taught him about character, virtues, honor, courage, and integrity. He has applied himself in his studies, sports, hobbies, etcetera, and the time has come for him to prove his mettle using what he has learned and making the transition from a boy to a man. Once he has successfully completed the rite of passage, he has successfully made that transition and should now be thought of as a man.

After he has successfully passed his rite of passage, it is important that you now treat him as a man. In a way, the rite of passage is almost as much for you, as it is for him. It can be hard for a father, who has been used to seeing his son as a child and a boy for 16 or 17 years, to all of a sudden now see him as a man, but it is imperative. You can't tell him that he is now a man, but treat him as a boy, and expect him to see himself as a man. The rite of passage must be serious and it must be real, both to him and to you.

A rite of passage done correctly is not some sort of merit badge, but a huge step in the life of a boy, and it must be taken seriously. It is meant to be a life-changing achievement. If you want your son to take it seriously, you must take it seriously as well.

The Native Americans called their rite of passage for young men, a vision quest. The vision quest was meant to be a way that young men could find both spiritual guidance and his purpose in life. The boy was sent off to a secluded place in nature for a certain number of days to survive on his own and to try to uncover a deep understanding about his purpose in life.

His secluded time alone was meant to allow him to discover his self-identity, among other things. It was during the vision quest that the boy was supposed to receive insight into both himself and the world, as well as learn to be self-sufficient and increase his self-confidence. The insight that he was supposed to gain from his vision quest typically came in the form of a vision or a dream, and was meant to give him insight into his purpose and destiny in life.

Traditionally, the vision quest was used as a rite of passage marking the transition between boyhood and full acceptance as an adult in the tribe. This was truly a life-changing accomplishment for the boy. He was in the wilderness alone for days, providing for himself. It was real and it was dangerous. The vision quest was a very personal experience, and one that no one could take away from the young man.

He knew exactly what he went through and what he achieved. It was much more than some party that announced that he was now a man; it was a personal achievement where he sought guidance, purpose, and maturity.

After he returned home, he was both seen and treated as one of the adults in his tribal society. And he was expected to take on the responsibility of an adult, just as every other adult in the tribe.

There are different ways and ideas on how to come up with a rite of passage for your son in today's society. There are some companies that actually conduct vision quests or have organized rites of passage set up for young men. You may want to check these out or develop your own. But one thing should be constant no matter which rite of passage you choose for your son – you should take it seriously and make sure that your son takes it seriously as well.

After he has completed his rite of passage, you should treat him differently. Give him both more respect and more responsibility. Make it clear to him, and to everyone else, that he is now a man and that you expect him to now act like a man. How you act after the rite of passage is almost as important as the rite of passage itself.

As a father, you must always remember how much power your words and actions have, especially where you son is concerned. You must conduct yourself properly and be careful of both your words and your actions.

You have been given the responsibility and duty of raising your boy to be a man, a real man, but you also have the responsibility of knowing how to treat him as an adult at the appropriate time. Once your son has completed his rite of passage, you should no longer treat him as a boy, but as a man.

This means that you have to truly change how you see your son. You can't continue to see him as a boy that you *are raising*, but rather a man that you *have raised*. This can be a very hard transition for fathers to make. You should be making this transition, little by little, as you raise your son. Each year, his responsibilities should grow larger and larger, and you should give him a little more independence.

As he evolves into the man that you are raising him to be, your image of him should evolve as well, until one day you no longer see the child or the boy, but the man. When the boy has completely transitioned into the man, your primary job is finished, but your responsibility as a parent will continue for years. You should always be there to share your knowledge and wisdom as needed.

Being a good father is not a walk in the park; it takes a lot of work. It takes wisdom, knowledge, and discipline on your part. It takes years of commitment and focus on your ultimate objective – to raise a superior man, not an overgrown boy. It takes a real man.

If

If you can keep your head when all about you
Are losing theirs and blaming it on you;
If you can trust yourself when all men doubt you,
But make allowance for their doubting too;

If you can wait and not be tired by waiting,
Or, being lied about, don't deal in lies,
Or, being hated, don't give way to hating,
And yet don't look too good, nor talk too wise;

If you can dream - and not make dreams your master;
If you can think - and not make thoughts your aim;
If you can meet with triumph and disaster
And treat those two impostors just the same;

If you can bear to hear the truth you've spoken
Twisted by knaves to make a trap for fools,
Or watch the things you gave your life to broken,
And stoop and build 'em up with worn-out tools;

If you can make one heap of all your winnings
And risk it on one turn of pitch-and-toss,
And lose, and start again at your beginnings
And never breathe a word about your loss;

If you can force your heart and nerve and sinew
To serve your turn long after they are gone,
And so hold on when there is nothing in you
Except the Will which says to them: "Hold on!"

If you can talk with crowds and keep your virtue,
Or walk with kings - nor lose the common touch;
If neither foes nor loving friends can hurt you;
If all men count with you, but none too much;

If you can fill the unforgiving minute
With sixty seconds' worth of distance run -
Yours is the Earth and everything that's in it,
And - which is more - you'll be a Man, my son!

Rudyard Kipling

Dear Dad,

I am writing this to you, though you have been dead thirty years…

I feel I must say some things to you, things I didn't know when I was a boy in your house…

It's only now, after passing through the long hard school years, only now, when my own hair is gray, that I understand how you felt.

I must have been a…trial to you…I believed my own petty wisdom… Most of all, I want to confess my worst sin against you. It was the feeling I had that you "did not understand."

When I look back over it now, I know that you did understand. You understood me better than I did myself…

And how patient you were with me! How full of long-suffering, and kindness!

And how pathetic, it now comes home to me, were your efforts to get close to me…

What was it held me aloof? I don't know. But it is tragic – that wall that rises between a boy and his father…

I wish you were here now, across the table from me, just for an hour, so that I could tell you how there's no wall anymore; I understand you now, Dad, and, how I love you, and wish I could go back and be your boy again…

Well, it won't be long, Dad, till I am over there, and I believe you'll be the first one to take me by the hand and help me…

I know that among the richest, most priceless things on earth, and the thing least understood, is that mighty love and tenderness and craving to help, which a father feels toward his boy.

For I have a boy of my own…

Up there somewhere in the Silence, hear me, Dad, and believe me.

Dr. Frank Crane

Reflections for the Superior Man

He preaches well that lives well.
Cervantes

A noble spirit suffers when treated as a servant rather than a son.
Leon Battista Alberti

When you teach your son, you teach your son's son.
The Talmud

Fathers are to sons what blacksmiths are to swords.
It is the job of the blacksmith not only to make a sword, but also
to maintain its edge of sharpness. It is the job of the father to keep
his son sharp and save him from the dullness of foolishness.
Steve Farrar

Praise the young and they will blossom.
Irish Proverb

Nothing sinks a young man into low company, both of women
and men, so surely as timidity, and diffidence of himself.
Lord Chesterfield

Keep your son from those that make light of what is
commanded, for it is they that make him rebellious.
Ptah-Hotep

Diogenes struck the father when the son swore.
Robert Burton

When your son is young, discipline him.
Arabic Proverb

The child is father of the man.
William Wadsworth

Fathers must strive with their whole being, with all their diligence
and wisdom, to make their children honest and high-principled.
Leon Battista Alberti

Be careful to leave your sons well instructed rather than rich, for the
hopes of the instructed are better than the wealth of the ignorant.
Epictetus

Chapter 27

Facing Death like a Man

It is not death that a man should fear;
he should fear never beginning to live.
Marcus Aurelius

How to Neutralize the Fear of Death

So live your life that the fear of death can never enter your heart.
Tecumseh

The fear of dying is one of the most common fears known to man, coming in second only to the fear of loneliness. Yet, dying is something that we all have to experience; it is simply a part of being human. It is unavoidable, although we all try to put it off for as long as possible.

What everyone needs to realize is that by fearing death, we are actually wasting the time that we have to live. Anytime spent on worrying about something that we fear, is time wasted. Every minute that you allow fear or worry to control your mind, is a minute that you don't get to enjoy living.

There are three things that you can do to help to overcome your fear of death. First, come to grips with your spiritual beliefs. Study and be at ease with what you truly believe about death and about life after death. Most people believe that their spirit or soul lives on, even after the body dies. Some believe that their spirit will go to Heaven; some believe that they will be reincarnated. Some believe that they will be reunited with their ancestors. And still others believe that they simply go to sleep and cease to exist.

Whatever you believe, make sure that you truly believe it. If you believe that you will only get to Heaven through your religion, then start taking your religion seriously and act on what you believe. If you truly believe that when you die, you will immediately go to a place where there is no more sorrow, no more pain, and you will be reunited with all of your loved-ones, then why would death be something for you to fear? If this is what you believe, then start acting like it and banish the fear of death from your mind.

On the other hand, if you believe that when you die, you simply go to sleep, just like you go to sleep each night, and never wake up again, then what do you have to fear? You simply go to sleep.

The problem is that most people who profess a belief in a religion, or in what will happen when they die, are not completely convinced that their belief is true. They may have been taught what to believe concerning death, but they aren't 100% convinced that what they have been taught is the truth. Therefore, they have doubts about what happens when they die, and those doubts lead to fear.

If you hold certain spiritual beliefs concerning death, meditate on those beliefs until they become real to you. If you believe that you will be with God when you die, what do you have to worry about? If you have doubts about whether or not your spiritual beliefs are correct, then you should spend some time reflecting on your religion or your beliefs. If you don't truly have faith in your religion, why are you holding on to it? Is your "belief" based more on fear than belief? You must come to a place of peace concerning what you believe about death. Settle the question in your mind, once and for all.

Secondly, live as you should live – as a superior man with honor, courage, and integrity. Many people believe that what happens to them at the moment of death depends on how they have lived their life. Their fear of death comes from the knowledge that they have not lived a good life, a life of character, honor, and integrity, a life of love, respect, and being a good person. They are afraid that all of their actions will finally catch up with them at the time of death. Many religious people have these same fears.

The way to alleviate this fear is to live a good life. Make amends for any wrongs that you have done, start living as you should, and make every moment count. Like Tecumseh stated, live your life in such a way that you do not have any fear of death. This means that you take your actions seriously. Start living with honor and integrity. Love your fellow man and do what you can to help those in need.

If you have nothing to be ashamed of, then you have nothing to fear. Do you fear that you will be punished when you do a good deed? Of course not. Then why would you fear that you will be punished at death for living a good life? This fear only enters your mind if you know that you really haven't lived a good life.

Many religions teach that living a good life, in and of itself, is simply not enough; you have to have faith as well. If you believe that, then act on it. To profess to believe something, but not to live it, is being a hypocrite. If you believe in your religion, live it! If you believe that you must be a good person and live a good life to get to Heaven, then live as you should! The point is that you should be sincere in your beliefs, live as a man of the code, and quit worrying about it.

Live what you profess to believe. If you have doubts about your religion or your spiritual beliefs, then you should figure out why you have these doubts and come to grips with what you truly believe. Either way, you should live your life in such a way that you are not ashamed of your actions. Superior men always strive to do what is right. If you have the right intentions, and always do your best to do what is just and right, then no matter what you believe, you will not have to be concerned about your actions. You can die knowing that you lived the best life that you could.

The last thing that you can do to alleviate your fear of death is to make sure that all of your affairs are in order. Many men are afraid of dying because they are concerned about what would happen to their wife or children. They have not taken the time to get their affairs in order and they know it. They know that if they were to die today, they would leave a complete mess for their wife or their children to deal with. Maybe they have not taken the time to make a will or to ensure that their family is provided for in the event of their death. This is a common concern for men of honor.

The samurai knew that their lord, their daimyo, could demand their death at any time. In addition to that fact, they lived and died by the sword. They were warriors who could be called on to fight to the death at a moment's notice. The samurai's life was never guaranteed. Knowing this, the samurai made a point of keeping their affairs in order. They ensured that their parents were taken care of and that they had made arrangements for their family in case of their untimely death. Their preparations enabled the samurai to be at peace with the thought of their death.

Daidoji Yuza, a Tokugawa period samurai, stated, "One who is a samurai must, before all things, keep constantly in mind, the fact that he has to die. If he is always mindful of this, he will be able to live in accordance with the paths of loyalty and filial duty, will avoid myriads of evils and adversities, keep himself free of disease and calamity and moreover enjoy a long life. He will also be a fine personality with many admirable qualities. For existence is impermanent as the dew of evening, and the frost of morning, and particularly uncertain is the life of the warrior"

Like the samurai, your life is not guaranteed either. You may not find yourself in a life-or-death sword fight, but you could be in an unexpected car wreck or some other tragedy. No one is guaranteed tomorrow, so you should make today count.

If you find that your fear of death stems more from the fact that you are not prepared to die simply because your affairs are not in order, then put your affairs in order. Do it now; don't wait! Bump this up to the top of your to-do list and get it taken care of right away.

If your fear of death comes from the fact that your financial affairs or family life is in disorder, then the solution to that problem is obvious. Put your affairs in order and keep them in order. Maintain a good relationship with the members of your family. Don't hold on to unforgiveness or anger. When a problem arises, address it and move on. Life is too short to allow anger and unforgiveness to disrupt your family.

Get all of your financial business taken care of and nicely organized for your wife or your children. Maybe type up a complete check list for them, so they will know exactly where everything is, so they will have all of your account numbers, passwords, and information, if the time comes that they may need it. Make a will and let them know where it is located. Don't leave anything unsaid or undone.

You will be amazed at how much peace will come from knowing that you have your personal affairs in order and that your family will be taken care of should anything happen to you.

To summarize, you should come to grips with your religious or spiritual beliefs. Understand what you believe and why. Make sure that you truly believe what you think you do and be at peace with those beliefs. Live a life that you are proud of. Be a man of character, honor, and integrity. Live as if God is watching everything that you do, because He is. Be able to legitimately justify all of your actions and never do something for which you feel is wrong. And lastly, get your personal affairs in order and keep them in order. Maintain a good relationship with your family and make sure that they are taken care of in the event of your untimely death.

If you will take the time to address these three parts of your life, you will find that your fear of death will be greatly diminished, if not completely gone. Death is unavoidable. It comes for us all sooner or later. Your job is to live as you should while you are here.

How do You want to be Remembered

The most important legacy you will ever leave is your vision planted in the minds of your disciples and a passion as strong as a storm in their hearts.
Shannon L. Alder

What do you want your legacy to be? This is a question that very few men ever contemplate, but which all men should consider. Most men in today's society are too busy keeping up with work, the latest sports news, or other hobbies, to give this important question much thought. But men of the code are different; we take life a bit more seriously and think about the things that other men simply ignore.

You should think about how you want your family and friends to remember you. What kind of man do you want them to think of when they think of you? Your legacy is the life that you have lived and the things that you have accomplished in your life; make sure that it is what you want it to be. If it isn't, you need to make some changes and make them now.

Your life should be an example for your children, your grandchildren and your great grandchildren. Live the kind of life that sets an example for your children to aspire to and that your children can hold up as an example for their children, and their children's children.

What kind of life is that? It is the kind of life that men of the code live, a life filled with character, honor, integrity, and courage. It is a life filled with adventure, love and benevolence, a life where you help as many people as you can and provide for and protect your family. It is a fulfilling life where you have the courage to pursue your dreams and encourage those around you to do the same. It is a life of wisdom and knowledge. It is the life of the superior man.

Do you want your family to see you as the wise, kind and loving patriarch of your family? Then you must be the wise, kind and loving patriarch of your family. Do you want your sons to see you as the stern, but gentle father who passed down his wisdom, character and honor to his sons? Then you must be the stern, but gentle father who shared his wisdom, his character, and his honor with his sons.

Don't expect to live one way, but be remembered in a different way after you die. It won't happen. If you want your family and friends to remember you fondly when you are gone, then you have to earn that memory now. You must be that which you wish to be remembered as when you are gone.

Even if you have fallen short in this area in the past, there is still time to remedy that. It is never too late to be the kind of man that you could have been.

And when it is your time to leave this world, take pains to do so with dignity. Remember this up until the moment of your death. Even in death, you can leave a legacy to those around you.

Let your loved-ones see a real man, a man who has the courage to face death with dignity and confidence in his beliefs. This is the ultimate test of your spiritual beliefs and your final legacy. Don't give in to your fears. Have faith in the beliefs that you have taught your loved-ones. To the best of your ability, leave this earth on your own terms, having lived life to the fullest and having left behind a legacy that will live on long after you are gone.

Some Things are Worth Dying For

Life is not worth living if there is
nothing in your life worth dying for.
Bohdi Sanders

For the superior man, there are things in this world worth dying for. Although no man truly wants to die, all real men are willing to lay their life on the line for their loved-ones or for those who are deserving of their help in emergency situations. To not help your loved-ones, when you have the ability and the opportunity, is the height of selfishness and cowardice.

Real men "man up" when the going gets tough. They know that there are people worth dying for and causes worth risking their life for; and they refuse to allow the fear of death to prevent them from doing the right thing.

Spend some time in meditation and think about what you are, and are not, willing to risk your life for. Who are the people in your life that you would be willing to die for? Would you be willing to risk your life to save a stranger in danger or to do the right thing? These are questions that men of the code need to know the answer to before they actually find themselves in that kind of situation.

Don't wait until you find yourself face-to-face with a life-or-death situation to decide what steps you are, and are not, willing to take. In my martial arts books, I teach that warriors should use visualization to walk themselves through many different scenarios. This practice allows you to see yourself in a dangerous situation and decide how you would handle that situation, should you ever find yourself in that position.

I highly recommend that you do this and explore how you will respond to certain situations. The practice of visualization helps prepare you for the actual event.

You should not only know how to defend yourself and your family, but you should also know how far you are willing to go in different situations. In what circumstances would you be willing to risk your life for someone else? How would you do it? How would you do it in order to give yourself the best chance of surviving? What skills do you need? What would you do in the case of a home invasion? How would you protect your family?

Thinking about these, and other such questions, ahead of time, allows you to not only mentally prepare yourself in case you ever find yourself in such situations, but it also gives you some insight into what you need to do to physically prepare for those kind of circumstances.

It is always better to be prepared for an emergency and not need your preparations, than to have an emergency situation and not be prepared for it. Hope for the best; prepare for the worst.

The bottom line is that every real man has certain people that he is willing to die for. He also has certain things that he is willing to risk his life for. When you are willing to risk your life, you must be sure that you realize that there is always a chance that you could die. Many men talk about risking their life for something, but never really stop to consider that "risking your life" means that is a very real chance that they could actually die. I know that this seems strange, but it is true.

Make sure that you spend the necessary time to really consider the consequences of your actions. Know the risks involved in your actions, consider every angle, and then do what you know is right. There are people worth dying for and there are situations in which the superior man must be willing to risk his life in order to do what is right. Make sure that you develop your courage *before* it is needed.

We all need to prepare ourselves for the inevitability that we must die. The question is not whether or not you will die, but rather, how you will die and whether you will die with the dignity of a real man. Never allow the fear of death to dictate your actions. Always do what is right, period.

If you feel that the right thing for you to do is to risk your life in a certain situation, then do it. Don't allow the fear of death to turn you into a coward. That is like living your whole life with honor, and then in the last month of your life, blowing your whole legacy by a dishonorable act which was based on fear. That is not the way that you want to be remembered.

Take the necessary steps to come to grips with your own death. Think about the kind of legacy that you want to leave behind for your family and friends, and then do what you need to do to make that happen. This can only be done by taking the time to meditate on these things and to mentally prepare yourself ahead of time.

Use the samurai as your role model when it comes to preparing for the realization of your death. The samurai put their honor, and the honor of their family, far above their own death. They understood that every man has to die at some point in time, and they made sure that they died with dignity and honor, and left a legacy that their family would be proud of for generations to come.

Reflections for the Superior Man

It is foolish to fear what you cannot avoid.
Publilius Syrus

It is better to die on your feet than to live on your knees.
Dolores Ibarruri

Men do not care how nobly they live, but only how long, although it is within
the reach of every man to live nobly, but within no man's power to live long.
Seneca

It matters not how a man dies, but how he lives.
Samuel Johnson

Old and young, we are all on our last cruise.
Robert Louis Stevenson

Everybody who lives dies.
But not everybody who dies has lived.
Dhaggi Ramanashi

Do not seek death. Death will find you.
But seek the road which makes death a fulfillment.
Dag Hammarskjold

Live as you will wish to have lived when you are dying.
Christian Furchtegott Gellert

We should live as though our life would be both long and short.
Bias

Do you not know that disease and death must overtake us, no matter what we
are doing? What do you wish to be doing when it overtakes you? If you have
anything better to be doing when you are so overtaken, go to work on that.
Epictetus

The fear of death follows from the fear of life.
A man who lives fully is prepared to die at any time.
Mark Twain

All we have to decide is what to do with the time that is given us.
J. R. R. Tolkien

Chapter 28

Conclusion

The unexamined life is not worth living.
Socrates

Men of the code have to take the time to examine their life and make a conscious decision concerning how they will live. Making your own code of honor will help guide your decisions and keep you on the right path. Hopefully, you now understand that there is a major difference between simply growing older and maturing into a real man.

The process of being a superior man is an ongoing process; it never ends. You have to constantly examine your life, your actions, your words, and your intentions in order to make sure that you are maintaining your code and living up to your expectations of yourself. Nobody is going to make you live a life of excellence; you have to require it of yourself. You have to be responsible for every word that comes out of your mouth, every action you take, and for the intentions behind your words and actions.

Only you, truly know if your intentions are right, thus making your words and actions righteous. Taking the time to write your own code, and then referring back to your code often, is one of the best ways to keep yourself on track.

The first thing every morning, take some time to be grateful for what you have in your life and think about your code and how you will live up to it throughout the day. And, the last thing before you go to sleep at night, review your day and see how you have done. You won't always have performed perfectly. You will have good days and bad days. But you can always make a point to review how you did and make a decision to be a better man the next day.

If you constantly examine your life and keep yourself on track, you will find that you improve every day, if only in small ways. Remember, you are not competing with anyone else; your goal is simply to be a better man today than you were yesterday. If you will make this your goal, before long, you will be able to look back at your life and see that you have come a very long way in living the life of a superior man.

Don't let mistakes or bad days sidetrack you. We all have bad days where we don't live up to our code, but that doesn't mean that we give up and say that living as a man of the code is too hard or not obtainable. When you have a bad day and don't live up to your code, learn from it, put it behind you, and vow to be a better man tomorrow. Refuse to allow anything to cause you to quit! Stay the course and push forward!

You write a book one word at a time, and word by word, page by page, a complete prose appears. It takes time, thought, and patience. Becoming a superior man is much the same as writing a good book. Becoming a superior man is a process; it does not magically happen overnight. You build the life of a superior man, day by day, month by month, and year by year, until one day you notice that you are not the same man that you used to be; you have become a superior man, a man of the code.

Only those who continually re-examine
themselves and correct their faults will grow.
The Hagakure

Even the samurai, who dedicated their lives to their code of honor and their way of life, had to constantly re-examine their life in order to make sure that they were staying true to the man that they were dedicated to being. Being a superior man is not a goal that you reach and then you can sit back and relax; as I said, it is a constant, never-ending process.

Think of it this way. If you are into bodybuilding and you reach a very high level of defined muscle mass, are you set for life for having reached that goal? Can you then simply sit back, do nothing, eat whatever you want, and still maintain that same level of excellence, because you have achieved the highest level that your body could achieve? Of course not!

No matter what level you reach in bodybuilding, if you quit lifting weights, quit eating properly, quit exercising, and simply let yourself go, you will not only regress back to where you first started, but you could possibly even find yourself totally out of shape and obese. You have to constantly strive to maintain your physique and your health.

It is the same way with maintaining your code. You have to continually re-examine yourself, correct whatever faults you may find, and continue to grow throughout your life. Living the warrior lifestyle, as men of the code do, is a lifelong journey. It takes a lot of discipline and effort to stay on the right path, but very little to destroy what you have struggled for.

Constantly re-examining your intentions, your words, and your actions, helps you not only stay on your path, but enables you to fine tune your life. You will make mistakes. You will have days that you lose your temper or you allow your emotions to temporarily take control and you say something that you shouldn't; that is just life. Being a man of the code doesn't mean that you are perfect and that you never make a mistake; it means that you recognize your mistakes and your shortcomings, and you consistently work to correct them and become a better man.

Today is victory over yourself of yesterday;
tomorrow is your victory over lesser men.
Miyamoto Musashi

Your goal as a man of the code should be to be a better man tomorrow than you are today. Do this every day and little by little, you will find that you have become a completely new man. The change will be so gradual that you may not even notice, but when you stop to examine your life, you will be amazed at what a different man you have become.

You will notice a big difference between the way that you view the world and the way that other men view the world. You will notice that you no longer think like most of the men around you and those around you will notice this change as well. You will start to gain a reputation as being an honorable man, trustworthy and true.

Many men will look up to you. Other men will envy you or hate you because they can see something in you that they wish they had, but that they are not willing to discipline themselves to acquire. You may notice that your friends have changed and you now have a whole new group of men that you associate with, men of honor and integrity. You will no longer desire to be buddies with those men who live the life of inferior men.

Your attitude towards different things will change as you start to see the world through the eyes of a superior man. Your interests may change and you will start to see the world with more clarity than you had before, seeing behind the veil that most never even know is there.

All of your actions will be based on your code, your ideal of what is right and what is wrong. Some things, which other men consider perfectly fine to do, will no longer interest you because they just do not feel right to you. Other things which others may feel are not right, or that are not even legal, you may now see in a different light. You will start to see the world through the eyes of a man of the code, and many things will start to change in your life.

You will no longer seek the approval of others for your actions. The opinions of others will no longer be your guide for what is right and what is wrong. Your code will guide you and you will begin to see things differently. The more you search for the truth, the more you will see that you have been sold a bill of goods concerning many things in your life. You will start to see past the deceptions, you will start to go to the root of everything and find the hidden truth. You will no longer be satisfied simply turning a blind eye to injustice or the lies meant for sheep, for you will no longer be a sheep, but the sheepdog, who looks out for those around him.

Right will guide your every decision, and you will realize that there is never a wrong time to do the right thing, and there is never a right time to do the wrong thing. Men of honor travel the path of integrity without worrying about what others think about it. Their main concern is with what is right, period.

If you know in your heart that your actions are right, forge ahead without any fear of the consequences. Never allow fear to stop you from doing what is right. Examine all of your actions and make sure that your intentions are honorable and just.

Men of the code walk the path of integrity and honor. They chose right, even when everyone around them says they are wrong. Listen to your heart, not the opinions of others. Always let what is right be your guide and you won't go wrong. Travel the path of integrity without looking back.

I hope that *Men of the Code* has been a source of motivation and wisdom for you, and that it has inspired you to live the life of the superior man. May it be a constant source of inspiration and motivation for you on your journey as a man of the code.

Right is right, even if nobody does it.
Wrong is wrong, even if everybody is wrong about it.
G. K. Chesterton

Index

3

3-C's of Nonverbal Communication, 187, 189

5

55/38/7 formula, 188, 189

A

A Man, 38
A Real Man, 40
actions, v, xii, xiv, xvii, 2, 3, 4, 13, 17, 23, 24, 25, 26, 27, 28, 29, 30, 34, 37, 43, 44, 45, 46, 48, 50, 51, 52, 53, 54, 55, 56, 58, 59, 60, 61, 64, 66, 67, 73, 77, 78, 79, 80, 81, 82, 83, 84, 85, 86, 87, 88, 90, 92, 93, 100, 101, 107, 109, 110, 111, 112, 118, 123, 124, 125, 128, 133, 134, 149, 151, 156, 159, 161, 162, 166, 171, 172, 173, 174, 175, 177, 183, 186, 188, 197, 200, 201, 204, 209, 210, 212, 213, 218, 221, 223, 228, 229, 230, 233, 235, 236, 237, 238, 240, 242, 243, 246, 257
advice, ii, vi, viii, xiv, 5, 160, 177, 182, 202, 203, 204, 205, 206, 258, 259
Aeschylus, 108
Aesop, 112, 122, 190
Al Dacascos, i
Albert Einstein, 32, 58, 73, 93, 102, 137, 170, 211
Alexander Graham Bell, 165, 198
anger, 55
angry, 174, 177, 184, 186, 190, 211
Anne Byrhhe, 77
Aristophanes, 170
Aristotle, 33, 36, 42, 86, 114, 118, 170
assertive, 10, 152, 153
Ayn Rand, 62, 214

B

Baltasar Gracian, 8, 43, 45, 62, 102, 103, 122, 142, 158, 164, 200

Battista Alberti, 68
behavior, 77
Ben Johnson, 102
Benjamin Franklin, 108, 190, 246
Benjamin Franklin's Thirteen Virtues of Life, 246
Bias, 234
Bill Holman, vii
Billy Matheny, viii
Blaise Pascal, 114
blue laws, 210
Bodhidharma, 95, 180
Bohdi Sanders, 3, ii, iii, iv, v, vi, vii, xi, xiv, xvii, xviii, 81, 86, 87, 100, 127, 214, 232, 256, 261
Book of the Golden Precepts, 119
Booker T. Washington, 50
boys, ii, viii, xv, 9, 10, 11, 12, 13, 16, 18, 19, 34, 35, 89, 139, 215, 216, 217, 218, 219, 220, 221
Brad Pitt test, 156
brave, 53, 63, 64, 66
Bruce Lee, vii, 6, 8, 94, 153
brutally honest, 100, 156, 185, 186, 187, 204
Buddha, 69, 76, 77, 180
Bushido, 257
Bushido Code, 247

C

C. S. Lewis, 9, 20
Cervantes, 68, 77, 226
character, i, ii, iii, v, viii, xi, xii, xv, xvi, xvii, 1, 4, 6, 7, 9, 12, 14, 18, 19, 21, 22, 23, 24, 27, 28, 29, 30, 31, 34, 35, 36, 37, 42, 43, 44, 45, 46, 48, 49, 50, 53, 58, 71, 87, 88, 90, 91, 92, 94, 96, 99, 104, 113, 114, 116, 117, 118, 119, 133, 134, 135, 136, 147, 149, 151, 152, 153, 156, 157, 158, 162, 163, 175, 185, 189, 205, 208, 209, 213, 216, 217, 218, 221, 222, 228, 230, 231, 243, 244, 248, 257, 258, 259, 260
character traits, xvi, 22, 43, 45, 217
charity, 21, 200, 202
children, vi, xi, 3, 5, 9, 11, 17, 19, 40, 72, 128, 134, 135, 138, 139, 182, 195, 203, 216, 221, 226, 229, 230, 231

chivalry, xi, xv, xvii, 151, 153
Clark Gable, 8
code of honor, 55, 77
Code of the West, 247
communication, 187, 188, 189
compassion, 200, 201, 202
compromise, 23, 40, 44, 55, 58, 59, 60,
  61, 72, 84, 138
compromising, 45, 73
confidence, vii, xiii, 8, 15, 20, 36, 79, 99,
  110, 112, 114, 123, 124, 125, 126,
  133, 144, 151, 152, 153, 154, 160,
  185, 197, 199, 231
Confucius, 21, 22, 24, 26, 28, 30, 31, 32,
  33, 43, 59, 68, 86, 90, 106, 140, 142,
  159, 170, 212
conscience, 61
consequences, 61
conversation, 144, 160, 183, 184, 190,
  246
Conviction, x
Core Values of the U. S. Navy, 243
courage, iii, v, vii, xv, xvi, xvii, 1, 5, 14, 15,
  16, 31, 33, 37, 39, 53, 54, 55, 59, 60,
  61, 62, 63, 64, 65, 66, 67, 68, 69, 90,
  91, 94, 96, 101, 104, 105, 108, 112,
  124, 130, 133, 136, 138, 153, 162,
  179, 191, 194, 196, 205, 222, 228,
  231, 233, 243, 247
Courage, 64, 65, 67
courageous, 64, 66, 67
courteous, 87, 91, 92, 93, 148, 149, 150,
  151, 152, 200
courtesy, 4, 5, 21, 37, 87, 91, 92, 93, 94,
  149, 150, 151, 155, 164, 199, 201, 241
coward, 65, 67, 91, 156, 233
cowardice, 65, 66, 67, 68, 97, 99, 101,
  140, 176, 184, 185, 232

D

Dag Hammarskjold, 234
Dalai Lama, 8, 118, 126
Dan Tosh, v
Dana Gregory Abbott, vi
Davy Crockett, 214
Dear Dad, 225
death, 5, 8, 51, 68, 154, 167, 214, 216,
  227, 228, 229, 230, 231, 232, 233, 234
Death, x, 5, 227, 230, 234
dedication, 61, 115, 116, 117

defense, 105, 129, 130, 131, 140, 163,
  168, 185, 207, 209, 242
dependable, 152, 158
determination, 70
Dhaggi Ramanashi, 234
dignity, 4, 21, 28, 37, 94, 109, 110, 111,
  112, 113, 114, 231, 233, 243
discipline, xii, 4, 6, 22, 28, 29, 37, 48, 56,
  61, 75, 83, 89, 98, 110, 114, 115, 116,
  117, 118, 121, 173, 195, 198, 218,
  221, 223, 226, 236, 237
Discipline, 115, 117
dishonorable, 53
Dr. Frank Crane, 225
duty, 51
Dying, 232

E

Earnest Hemingway, 164
Emerson, 44, 91, 159
emotion, 63
emotions, xiii, 2, 26, 27, 55, 64, 66, 79,
  80, 105, 116, 117, 152, 153, 157, 172,
  173, 174, 177, 180, 184, 236
endurance, 37, 69, 71, 72, 74, 75, 76
Endurance, 69
enemies, 129, 142, 145, 147, 158, 161,
  162, 163, 164, 241
enemy, 128, 130, 145, 147, 158, 161, 162,
  163, 185, 187, 240, 241, 242
Epictetus, 42, 50, 118, 122, 226, 234
Epicurus, 122
Ernest Hemingway, 63
Euripides, 32, 164, 170, 198
excellence, xiii, 22, 23, 28, 30, 31, 46, 47,
  48, 49, 50, 61, 113, 115, 116, 118,
  177, 191, 192, 193, 194, 220, 235,
  236, 241, 243, 257, 258, 259
Excellence, 47, 48, 50, 257
experience, 115

F

failures, vi, 46, 70, 126, 167, 177, 191,
  192, 194
family, ii, 3, 5, 10, 11, 12, 29, 95, 111,
  112, 119, 120, 128, 129, 130, 131,
  135, 138, 139, 141, 154, 168, 174,

185, 203, 209, 229, 230, 231, 232, 233, 239

fear, vii, 5, 30, 40, 53, 55, 56, 62, 63, 64, 65, 66, 68, 99, 112, 125, 130, 176, 177, 194, 198, 209, 213, 227, 228, 229, 230, 232, 233, 234, 238, 240

fighting, 67

fortitude, 37, 67, 69, 70, 71, 72, 74, 75, 96, 110, 140, 212, 241

Francesco Guicciardini, 53, 66, 190, 206

Frank Dux, iii

Frederick Douglas, 134

friend, 20, 27, 127, 134, 135, 136, 137, 139, 158, 159, 160, 161, 163, 164, 174, 184, 185, 215

friends, 66, 111, 112, 224

friendship, 54, 136, 137, 142, 158, 159, 160, 161, 164

friendships, 158

G

G. K. Chesterton, 65, 150, 238

Galileo Galilei, 170

Gandhi, 32, 82, 94, 108

George Orwell, 181

George Washington, xv, 129, 143, 189

Gichin Funakoshi, 108

Goethe, 32, 94, 126, 147, 164, 259

H

habit, 36, 45, 48, 69, 92, 117, 160, 176, 178, 182, 183, 184, 189

harmony, 45

hatred, 90, 174, 177, 205

heart, 47, *224*

Henry David Thoreau, 50, 122, 126, 207

Henry Wadsworth Longfellow, 94, 198

Henry Ward Beecher, 42, 190

hero, 5, 12, 15, 16, 31, 55, 90, 128, 142, 154

Herodotus, 68

honest, v, xvi, 3, 16, 28, 59, 94, 98, ⁄ 101, 109, 145, 152, 156, 167, ⁊ 186, 187, 204, 226, 243

honor, i, iii, v, vi, vii, viii, ix, xi, ⁄ i, xvii, 1, 2, 3, 4, 6, 7, 8, 9, ⁊ , 16, 18, 20, 21, 24, 28, 29, ? 37, 44, 45, 46, 49, 51, 52 , 56,

60, 61, 66, 77, 78, 79, 80, 83, 87, 88, 90, 91, 96, 97, 99, 101, 106, 107, 109, 110, 111, 112, 113, 114, 119, 131, 133, 134, 135, 136, 137, 153, 157, 159, 162, 163, 181, 184, 185, 210, 213, 215, 217, 218, 221, 222, ⁊ 28, 229, 230, 231, 233, 235, 236, ⁊7, 238, 239, 241, 257, 258, 259, ⁊0

honorable, ii, xvi, 12, 25, 52, 53, ⁊, 55, 56, 101, 105, 111, 138, 144, ⁊ 5, 149, 156, 159, 186, 197, 207, 237 ⁊38

Horace, 42

hypocrite, 111, 113

I

If, 224

Immanuel Kant, 50, 94

independent, 119, 120, 121

inner peace, 179

integrity, i, iii, v, viii, xiii, xv, xvi, 1, 4, 6, 7, 9, 12, 21, 24, 25, 31, 36, 37, 45, 49, 57, 58, 59, 60, 61, 62, 7ʳ, 88, 90, 110, 112, 133, 134, 18⁴ 217, 221, 222, 228, 230, 231, 2⁊ ⁊, 238, 243, 257, 258, 259, 260

intentions, 2, 3, ⁊ ⁊, 28, 44, 52, 53, 54, 67, 79, 80, 84, ⁊1, 104, 186, 187, 229, 235, 236 ⁊8

Isaac New⁊ , 185

Isocrate⁊ ⁊02

J

⁊ . R. Tolkien, 234

⁊nes Russell Lowell, 114

⁊ealousy, 132, 133, 161, 174, 176, 177, 239, 245

Jean Jacques Rousseau, 56

Jean-Jacques Rousseau, 62, 76

Jesus, 77

Jim Rohn, 115, 118, 198

Jimmy Buffett, 76

John Adams, 214

John C. Maxwell, 191

John Heywood, 202

John Stuart Mill, 142

John Wayne, xv, 6, 16, 20, 68, 153, 190

judgment, 63, 119

Justice, x, 103, 105, 106, 107, 108, 208, 209, 210, 246

K

Kaizen, 3
kindness, 29, 37, 40, 142, 199, 201, 202, 206, 225
knowledge, iv, 2, 5, 10, 37, 45, 47, 64, 74, 83, 98, 133, 135, 165, 166, 167, 168, 169, 186, 187, 191, 193, 203, 205, 209, 216, 219, 223, 228, 231, 259

L

La Rochefoucauld, 56, 114, 164, 187
LAKOTA CODE OF ETHICS, 239
Lao Tzu, 7, 68, 77, 101, 108, 115, 122, 180
Leon Battista Alberti, 226
life, *224*
Lord Chesterfield, 42, 226
Lord Tennyson, 164

M

man of character, 45
man of excellence, 48
man of honor, 111, 113
man of integrity, 58, 59, 61
manhood, 1, 8, 32, 35, 157, 218, 219, 220, 221
manners, vii, 87, 88, 92, 93, 94, 142, 147, 148, 149, 150, 153, 155, 199, 216
Marcus Aurelius, 20, 33, 36, 62, 108, 122, 180, 227
Marcus Tullius Cicero, 127, 208, 214
Margolis, 180
Mark Twain, 32, 56, 64, 68, 143, 234
marriage, 131, 132, 133, 156
martial arts, 48, 116
Martin Luther, 21, 184, 210, 214
Martin Luther King, Jr., 21, 184, 214
Matsuo Basho, 170
Maxims and Reflections, 53
meditate, 6, 228, 233, 248
meditating, 112
meditation, 5, 179, 232
men of integrity, 61

Men of the code, 4, 5, 52, 54, 55, 85, 89, 97, 99, 100, 103, 107, 109, 113, 123, 127, 128, 134, 136, 139, 144, 145, 148, 150, 152, 177, 182, 201, 209, 210, 211, 235, 238
Michael McGann, iv
mind, v, vi, 1, 2, 5, 16, 23, 25, 28, 30, 32, 33, 35, 37, 43, 45, 48, 52, 53, 58, 59, 60, 66, 80, 98, 109, 111, 112, 113, 115, 116, 117, 118, 120, 121, 125, 126, 138, 140, 143, 144, 145, 146, 147, 149, 153, 156, 160, 163, 166, 167, 170, 171, 172, 173, 174, 175, 176, 177, 178, 180, 185, 186, 187, 196, 197, 204, 207, 213, 215, 218, 227, 228, 229, 239, 240, 248
mistake, 5, 130, 148, 153, 160, 191, 192, 193, 194, 195, 196, 197, 198, 199, 216, 220, 237
mistakes, 5, 34, 46, 70, 85, 130, 165, 191, 192, 193, 194, 195, 196, 197, 198, 218, 221, 235, 236, 239
Miyamoto Musashi, 126, 170, 186, 237
Moliere, 86
Montaigne, 35, 142
moral absolutes, 6
moral principles, 57
morals, vi, xvi, 3, 7, 87, 123
Motley Crue, 68

N

Napoleon Hill, 26, 70, 71, 76, 118, 171, 180
no tolerance policy, 13
Norman Mailer, 8, 9, 19
Norman Vincent Peale, 27, 173
no-tolerance policy, 104

O

obligation, 261

P

panic, 74, 154, 168, 211
Parenting, 221
Patrick Henry, 32
Percy Bysshe Shelley, 118
Persistence, 71

personal integrity, 58, 59
Phaedrus, 164
Phil Torres, xiv
philosophy, 3, 13, 25, 31, 58, 77, 136,
    186, 200, 216, 220, 221
physical encounter, 66
Plato, 136, 184
Plutarch, 86
praise, 38, 40, 50, 144, 145, 160, 204,
    212, 257
prepare, 37, 116, 122, 129, 130, 131, 216,
    219, 220, 221, 232, 233
prepared, xvii, 5, 25, 32, 37, 116, 130,
    140, 167, 171, 212, 220, 229, 233,
    234, 242
pride, 51
principle, 45, 48, 59, 61, 64, 117, 120
principles, 57, 58, 59, 61, 73, 111, 112,
    120
priorities, 29, 82, 83
profanity, 189, 217
Professor Albert *Mehrabian*, 187
Ptah-Hotep, 77
Publilius Syrus, 56, 190, 234
Pythagoras, 86, 108, 181

R

raising men, ii, 220
Ralph Waldo Emerson, 8, 42, 68, 91, 94,
    126, 180, 194, 206
real man, xvi, 4, 8, 16, 19, 31, 33, 34, 35,
    36, 37, 43, 46, 55, 59, 63, 78, 79, 87,
    127, 129, 130, 131, 132, 137, 138,
    139, 141, 149, 151, 153, 154, 155,
    196, 199, 215, 218, 220, 223, 231,
    233, 235
real men, xv, xvi, 7, 11, 12, 15, 33, 35, 37,
    70, 128, 129, 131, 139, 141, 149, 150,
    151, 152, 213, 215, 219, 232
Reflections for the Superior Man, 8, 20,
    32, 42, 50, 56, 62, 68, 76, 86, 94, 102,
    108, 114, 118, 122, 126, 142, 164,
    170, 180, 190, 198, 206, 214, 226, 234
regret, 27, 115, 138, 194, 195, 198
regrets, 5, 7, 53, 116, 194, 195, 196
relationship, 11, 127, 132, 137, 143, 144,
    145, 147, 148, 150, 156, 158, 160,
    168, 187, 203, 230
religion, 6, 145, 211, 227, 228, 229, 243
Rene Descartes, 198

reputation, 43, 44, 48, 51, 52, 54, 56, 62,
    80, 81, 110, 145, 149, 153, 174, 175,
    181, 184, 237, 246
respect, xii, xv, 5, 30, 37, 41, 81, 87, 88,
    89, 90, 91, 92, 93, 94, 99, 100, 109,
    110, 111, 112, 113, 114, 117, 133,
    142, 144, 148, 149, 150, 151, 153,
    154, 155, 157, 159, 160, 189, 207,
    210, 216, 223, 228, 239, 243
responsibility, xv, 5, 10, 11, 37, 89, 128,
    134, 138, 151, 153, 155, 197, 216,
    218, 219, 221, 223, 243
responsible, xi, xiv, 11, 17, 19, 42, 79, 93,
    121, 122, 152, 155, 202, 221, 235,
    240, 242
Richard Hackworth, ii
right and wrong, v, 14, 51, 58, 59, 61,
    101, 107, 123, 124, 167, 207, 208, 209
Right Versus Legal, 210
rite of passage, 34, 218, 219, 221, 222,
    223
rites of passage, 219, 223
Rob Roy, 56
Robert E. Lee, 20
Robert Louis Stevenson, 68, 234
rude behavior, 149, 150, 151, 201
Rudyard Kipling, 86, 224

S

sages, 45
Sailor's Creed, 241
Samuel Coleridge, 51
Samuel Johnson, 102, 126, 234
samurai, xvii, 130, 229, 233, 236, 247
self-confidence, ii, 5, 33, 34, 37, 67, 89,
    93, 112, 113, 117, 123, 124, 125, 126,
    152, 153, 154, 172, 196, 216, 217, 222
self-discipline, 116, 117
self-esteem, ii, 89, 90, 109, 117, 126, 156,
    157, 160, 205, 216, 217
self-reliance, 120, 121
Self-reliance, 119
Self-Reliance, 119
self-reliant, 4, 18, 19, 119, 120, 121, 216,
    217, 221
Self-respect, 89, 110
self-sufficient, 121
Seneca, 20, 56, 234
Shakespeare, 56
sincere, 111, 112, 113

sincerity, 112
Sincerity, 109, 111, 113, 114, 246
Sir Francis Osborne, 206
situational ethics, 3, 4, 101
Situational ethics, 3
society, i, iii, vi, vii, xi, xii, xv, xvi, xvii, 9, 12, 15, 31, 34, 35, 77, 88, 103, 105, 113, 131, 134, 145, 178, 189, 208, 212, 213, 215, 217, 219, 221, 223, 230, 260
Socrates, 52, 114, 142, 235, 246
son, i, vii, 10, 17, 19, 50, 72, 173, 195, 201, 211, 215, 216, 217, 218, 219, 220, 221, 222, 223, 224, 226
speech, xii, 30, 40, 182, 183
spirit, 112, 115, 119, 120
spiritual beliefs, 178, 179, 227, 228, 229, 230, 231
standards, xiii, xv, xvi, xvii, 2, 4, 7, 8, 12, 21, 23, 26, 29, 36, 43, 44, 46, 51, 57, 59, 61, 67, 69, 72, 88, 89, 90, 92, 100, 103, 110, 113, 115, 137, 141, 145, 148, 149, 151, 152, 258
success, ii, xi, xii, xiii, 22, 30, 62, 70, 71, 84, 123, 124, 125, 126, 137, 165, 168, 169, 174, 176, 189, 191, 192, 193, 194
Sun Tzu, 128, 130, 161, 164, 259, 260
superior man, xvi, xvii, 18, 19, 21, 22, 23, 24, 25, 26, 27, 28, 29, 30, 31, 33, 35, 36, 37, 43, 44, 45, 46, 47, 48, 52, 58, 59, 61, 69, 74, 77, 80, 81, 82, 91, 96, 97, 99, 100, 101, 106, 107, 111, 115, 116, 117, 119, 120, 123, 127, 131, 133, 136, 140, 141, 144, 147, 148, 149, 150, 154, 159, 167, 171, 173, 179, 184, 196, 197, 199, 203, 205, 208, 209, 210, 211, 212, 213, 215, 216, 217, 218, 221, 223, 228, 231, 232, 233, 235, 236, 237, 238
superior men, vi, 19, 22, 30, 45, 51, 63, 87, 88, 128, 131, 136, 141, 142, 148, 149, 167, 189, 209, 213, 218
Superior men, 24, 25, 27, 29, 30, 44, 46, 75, 80, 88, 95, 97, 98, 99, 101, 106, 107, 140, 148, 179, 181, 201, 209, 210, 212, 229

T

T. S. Eliot, 180
Tecumseh, 227, 228

Ten Commandments of Chivalry, 240
Terence, 108
The Hagakure, 236
The Havamal, 164
The Manly Man, 39
The Rules of Courtly Love, 244
The SEAL Code, 243
The Talmud, 102, 226
Theodore Roosevelt, 20, 42, 86, 94, 108, · 124
Thomas Carlyle, 1, 126, 142
Thomas Fuller, 164
Thomas J. Mota, ix
Thomas Jefferson, xv, 126
Thomas Mann, 180
Thomas Paine, 8
thoughts, v, xii, 23, 24, 25, 26, 27, 28, 48, 49, 52, 54, 65, 70, 79, 80, 81, 82, 83, 99, 109, 110, 111, 114, 118, 121, 125, 146, 162, 172, 173, 174, 175, 176, 177, 178, 180, 181, 196, 224, 239
Tiruvalluvar, 56, 138, 190
Tiruvaluvar, 122
training, 48, 70, 116, 117
Trivium method, 168, 169
true friend, 136, 137, 159, 163
true warrior, 67
truth, xiii, 3, 4, 13, 20, 21, 28, 37, 39, 44, 59, 62, 93, 95, 96, 97, 98, 99, 100, 101, 102, 104, 107, 111, 121, 135, 156, 157, 169, 176, 186, 187, *224*, 228, 237

U

U.S. Army Ranger Creed, 241
understanding, 58, 61, 64
United States Armed Forces, 242

V

Virgil, 71
virtue, 59, 63, *224*
virtues, 115
Voltaire, 46, 135

W

W. Clement Stone, 62, 180
Walter Lippmann, 54

254

warrior, i, vii, 5, 9, 16, 48, 128, 129, 130,
131, 138, 176, 229, 236, 258, 260
warrior lifestyle, 44, 57, 58, 69, 112, 115,
117, 260
warriorship, 53
Wayne Dyer, 180
West Point Cadet Honor Code, 245
wife, 5, 10, 11, 16, 60, 128, 131, 132, 133,
134, 138, 139, 147, 156, 157, 158,
182, 188, 195, 203, 209, 210, 229, 230
William J. H. Doetcker, 205
William James, 171
William Makepeace Thackeray, 206
William Shakespeare, 114
William Wadsworth, 226
Winston Churchill, 8, 92
wisdom, iii, vii, viii, 5, 9, 37, 46, 47, 64,
77, 103, 121, 123, 135, 165, 166, 167,
168, 169, 170, 182, 183, 185, 203,
204, 205, 216, 219, 223, 225, 226,
231, 238, 240, 247, 258, 259, 260, 261
Wisdom, 257, 260, 261
Wisdom Warrior, 260, 261
wise man, 66
Wolfgang Amadeus Mozart, 50
woman, v, 14, 16, 38, 131, 132, 133, 134,
149, 151, 154, 155, 156, 157, 158,
193, 243, 244
women, xi, xvi, 10, 11, 12, 19, 133, 135,
143, 149, 150, 151, 152, 153, 154,
155, 156, 157, 159, 193, 201, 220,
226, 245
word, 224
words, 59, 121

Z

Zig Ziglar, 62

About the Author

Dr. Bohdi Sanders is a multi-award winning and bestselling author. His book, *Modern Bushido: Living a Life of Excellence*, hit #1 on Amazon and topped the top 10 for a total of 104 weeks. Six of his other books have also been best-sellers and were also ranked in the Top 10 on Amazon. Dr. Sanders has been a martial artist for over 31 years and has trained in Shotokan karate, Krav Maga, Ninjutsu, and Jujutsu. His work has won national book awards and has been recognized by several martial arts hall of fames.

Dr. Sanders also holds national certifications as a Personal Fitness Trainer and a Certified Specialist in Martial Arts Conditioning through the International Sports Science Association. His books have been endorsed by some of today's top martial artists as highly motivational and inspirational. He is the author of:

- *Modern Bushido: Living a Life of Excellence*
- *Warrior Wisdom: Ageless Wisdom for the Modern Warrior*
- *Warrior: The Way of Warriorhood*
- *The Warrior Lifestyle: Making Your Life Extraordinary*
- *Defensive Living: The Other Side of Self-Defense*
- *Wisdom of the Elders: The Ultimate Quote Book for Life*
- *Martial Arts Wisdom...and more.*

Dr. Sanders' books have received high praise and have won several national awards, including:

- #1 on Amazon.com's Best Seller List: *Modern Bushido* 2013
- The Indie Excellence Book Awards: 1ˢᵗ Place Winner 2013
- USA Book News Best Books of 2013:1ˢᵗ Place Winner 2013
- IIMAA Best Martial Arts Book of the Year 2011
- U. S. Martial Arts Hall of Fame: Author of the Year 2011
- U. S. Martial Artist Association: Inspiration of the Year 2011
- USA Martial Arts HOF: Literary Man of the Year 2011
- The Indie Excellence Book Awards:1ˢᵗ Place Winner 2010
- USA Book News Best Books of 2010: 1ˢᵗ Place Winner 2010

Other Titles by Kaizen Quest

Character! Honor! Integrity! Are these traits that guide your life and actions? *Warrior Wisdom: Ageless Wisdom for the Modern Warrior* focuses on how to live your life with character, honor and integrity. This book is highly acclaimed, has won multiple awards and is endorsed by some of the biggest names in martial arts. *Warrior Wisdom* is filled with wise quotes, useful information, and insightful commentaries for anyone who strives to live a life of excellence. This book will help you live your life to the fullest. *Warrior Wisdom* is the book that you will refer back to again and again as you walk your path in life.

WARRIOR: The Way of Warriorhood is the second book in the *Warrior Wisdom Series*. Wisdom, life-changing quotes, and entertaining, practical commentaries fill every page. This series has been recognized by four martial arts hall of fame organizations for its inspirational and motivational qualities. The ancient and modern wisdom in this book will definitely help you improve your life and bring meaning to each and every day. The warrior lifestyle is for anyone who wants to live a life of integrity and honor. *WARRIOR* has been called the best book in the *Warrior Wisdom Series*.

The Warrior Lifestyle is the last installment of the award winning *Warrior Wisdom Series*. This book has been dubbed as highly inspirational and motivational. If you want to live your life to the fullest, you need to read the *Warrior Wisdom Series*! Don't settle for an ordinary life, make your life extraordinary! Sage advice and sound wisdom shines through on every page of this book, making it a must read for everyone who strives to live an extraordinary life of character and honor! The warrior lifestyle is not what you may think; it is for everyone who wants to live an extraordinary life. Check it out today!

Other Titles by Kaizen Quest

Modern Bushido is a multiple award-winning, #1 bestseller which hit the top 10 on Amazon for a total of 104 weeks! **Modern Bushido** is all about living a life of excellence. This book covers 30 essential traits that will change your life. **Modern Bushido** expands on the standards and principles needed for a life of excellence, and applies them directly to life in today's world. Readers will be motivated and inspired by the straightforward wisdom in this enlightening book. If you want to live a life of excellence, this book is for you! This is a must read for every martial artist and anyone who seeks to live life as it is meant to be lived.

Defensive Living takes the reader deep into the minds of nine of the most revered masters of worldly wisdom. It reveals valuable insights concerning human nature from some of the greatest minds the world has ever known, such as Sun Tzu, Gracian, Goethe, and others. **Defensive Living** presents invaluable lessons for living and advice for avoiding the many pitfalls of human relationships. This is an invaluable and entertaining guidebook for living a successful and rewarding life! If you have ever wondered how other people really look at the world and how they think, then this book is for you!

Wisdom of the Elders is a unique, one-of-a-kind quote book. This award-winning book is filled with quotes that focus on living life to the fullest with honor, character, and integrity. Honored by the USA Book News with a 1st place award for Best Books of the Year in 2010, this book is a guide for life. **Wisdom of the Elders** contains over 4,800 quotes, all which lead the reader to a life of excellence. If you enjoy quotes, wisdom, and knowledge, you will love this book. This is truly the ultimate quote book for those searching for wisdom! There are no fillers in this one; it is just packed with rock-solid wisdom!

Other Titles by Kaizen Quest

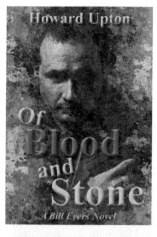

Of Blood and Stone is an unique mix of conspiracy theory, fantasy, and reality. Follow war veteran, Bill Evers, as he is recruited to track down a mystical artifact that has been stolen from a Mecixan museum. This cartouche, has been cursed and holds the power to completely destroy the world if it falls into the wrong hands. It could lead to the end of the world as we know it, as it holds a mysterious power over what could possibly be the most powerful army in the world. Martial arts action, mystery, intrigue, murder, magic, and mayhem await as you follow this high-paced, nonstop, action adventure.

Evil is alive and well, and is willing to leave millions dead in its wake. Bill Evers, a former soldier, mercenary, and martial artist is once again in action to try and stop the evil plan of the head of the leader of the Bilderberger organization. Things heat up fast in this one! The plot in *Occam's Razor* is not only evil, but it will shake you to your very core as you start to realize how easily this explosive novel could manifest in our current society. Real martial arts action, covert military missions, conspiracy theories, and non-stop action await you in this new action thriller. *Occam's Razor* is a non-stop thrill ride!

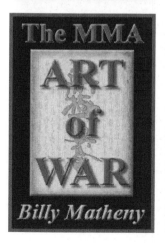

Sun Tzu's book, *The Art of War*, has been used for centuries to teach the time-tested strategies for being victorious against your opponent. MMA coach, Billy Matheny, has taken the wisdom of *The Art of War* to a place it has never been before – the MMA cage. He has integrated Sun Tzu's strategies with mixed martial arts. Matheny takes each of Sun Tzu's strategies and shows exactly how they can help ensure your victory in the MMA cage. If you thought that you were ready for the cage, think again! These strategies will take your fight game to a whole new level! This book will is a must read for the MMA fighter!

Looking for More Wisdom?

If you are interested in living the warrior lifestyle or simply in living a life of character, integrity and honor, you will enjoy The Wisdom Warrior website and newsletter. The Wisdom Warrior website contains dozens of articles, useful links, and news for those seeking to live the warrior lifestyle.

The newsletter is also a valuable resource. Each edition of The Wisdom Warrior Newsletter is packed with motivating quotes, articles, and information which everyone will find useful in their journey to perfect their character and live the life which they were meant to live.

The Wisdom Warrior Newsletter is a newsletter sent directly to your email account and is absolutely FREE! There is no cost or obligation to you whatsoever. You will also receive the current news updates and new articles by Dr. Bohdi Sanders as soon as they are available. Your email address is never shared with anyone else.

All you need to do to start receiving this valuable and informative newsletter is to go to the Wisdom Warrior website and simply sign up. It is that simple! You will find The Wisdom Warrior website at:

www.TheWisdomWarrior.com

Also, be sure to find posts by Dr. Sanders on Facebook. Dr. Sanders posts enlightening commentaries, photographs, and quotes throughout the week on his Facebook pages. You can find them at:

www.facebook.com/The.Warrior.Lifestyle

www.facebook.com/TheGentlemanWarrior

www.facebook.com/Bohdi.Sanders

Don't miss the opportunity to receive tons of FREE wisdom, enlightening posts, interesting articles, and intriguing photographs on The Wisdom Warrior website and on Dr. Sanders' Facebook pages.

Sign Up Today!